REVISITING THE SHADOWS

REVISITING THE SHADOWS

REVISITING THE SHADOWS

REVISITING THE SHADOWS

Memoirs from War-torn Poland
to the Statue of Liberty

BY IRENE SHAPIRO

DeForest Press
Elk River, Minnesota

Permission gratefully acknowledged for the following:
The poem "Handle with Care" is used by permission of One-by-One, Inc.
The maps on pages 67, 148, 197, 202, 249 and 262 from the U.S. Holocaust Memorial Museum's on-line Learning Center (www.ushmm.org/learningcenter), courtesy of the U.S. Holocaust Memorial Museum, Washington, DC.

Published by:
DeForest Press
P.O. Box 154
Elk River, MN 55330 USA
www.DeForestPress.com
Toll-free: 877-441-9733
Richard DeForest Erickson, Publisher
Shane Groth, Editor in Chief

Cover by Michael Dear
Photo on back cover, which first appeared in the *Scarsdale Inquirer*, by Ira N. Toff

ISBN 1-930374-06-2
Printed in the United States of America
08 07 06 05 04   5 4 3 2 1

Library of Congress Cataloging-in-Publication Data

Shapiro, Irene, 1925-
  Revisiting the shadows : memoirs from war-torn Poland to the statue of liberty / by Irene Shapiro.
      p. cm.
Includes bibliographical references.
  ISBN 1-930374-06-2
  1. Shapiro, Irene, 1925- 2. Jews—Poland—Biography. 3. Holocaust, Jewish (1939-1945)—Poland—Personal narratives. 4. Poland—Biography.
I. Title.
DS135.P63S429846 2004
940.53'18'092—dc22
                              2003015667

My years of teaching at the Bronx High School of Science have left me with a lasting pride and devotion to the students and the faculty of our extraordinary school. I wholeheartedly dedicate *Revisiting the Shadows* to the students and faculty members who will continue to maintain our excellent program of Holocaust Studies. May the accounts of their biology teacher's survival of unspeakable human atrocities remain meaningful for future generations of Bronx science students.

I first met Irene Shapiro when she was appointed as a biology teacher to the Bronx High School of Science, where she taught from 1964 to 1987. As Chairman of the Biology Department, I worked closely and directly with Irene, as well as during my tenure as Principal of the Bronx High School of Science (1977-1990).

Although new to the school, Irene soon became part of its unique culture. Irene adopted the biology department's teaching strategies which focus on inquiry and research.

Because she was open to new ideas, Irene achieved great success within a short time. Her intelligence and diligence made her a dynamic presence in the school community.

In addition, Irene shared her experience with students in the holocaust studies classes. This made her a valuable resource to the school's Holocaust Center.

Here was a woman who overcame tragedy to embrace youth and learning. Irene Shapiro's contributions will always be part of the Bronx High School of Science and the students she taught.

Milton Kopelman
Principal Emeritus
The Bronx High School of Science

CONTENTS

Part Five: Freedom Road to the Statue of Liberty

FOREWORD

In January, 1998, in search of songs for my then uncompleted book "The Undying Flame: Ballads and Songs of the Holocaust," I attended a concert in Teaneck, New Jersey, presented by One By One—an organization of descendants of the Holocaust and the Third Reich dedicated to bearing witness to the reality of the Holocaust, to speaking out against denial and revisionist history and to working for social justice wherever it is needed. On the program was singer-composer Rosalie Gerut, daughter of Holocaust survivors. She was accompanied by a guitarist listed on the program as Andy Shapiro.

After the concert I approached Rosalie to ask her if I could include her song "We Are Here" in my collection. She readily agreed, and then said, "You should speak to Andy. His mother may have some material that would interest you." Andy said that his mother was a survivor of the Bialystok Ghetto uprising and, indeed, knew a number of songs from that period that had never appeared in print before. Although, as it turned out we lived a few miles from each other in Westchester County, New York, his parents were spending the winter months in Palm Beach, Florida. Our initial contact was by telephone.

So I called Irene Shapiro in Palm Beach—a call that would result in a treasure of hitherto unknown (to me) songs and stories of that terrible winter of 1942-43 in Bialystok—and a valued friendship. As our conversation continued she asked, "Did you use to teach guitar when you were younger?" I replied, "Yes, and now that I'm older I'm still teaching it." Then came the kicker: "You were my teacher in the Bronx in 1956!" She went on to say that I let four-year-old Andy "strum" on the guitar during the lessons, and that I pronounced him a "natural." (As it turned out I was right about that.)

Irene sent me some marvelous songs in Yiddish, Polish and Russian—some of her own composition. But it was only after the snows had melted and she returned to New York that I came to appreciate fully the treasure that Irene herself represents. We met, we embraced, we schmoozed (forty-two years is a long time—a lot of snows had melted since last we saw each other.)

In the years immediately following the war most survivors refused to speak of the horrors they had endured. They wanted to spare their children the pain. They wanted to bury their own pain deep inside themselves. But as the years rolled on, and little by little time began thinning their ranks, the realization grew that bearing witness was the greatest gift that they could give—not only to their children, but to the entire world. Every survivor has a story to tell. Every story is different. Every story is the same. We are thankful for these stories…for these songs. We are thankful for Irene Shapiro's stories and songs.

Cut off in the ghetto, walled in from humanity,
And beaten by brute fascist might,
No matter if life now is dismal and frightful,
We trust that tomorrow will be bright.

"Song of the Bialystok Partisans" written by Irene Shapiro

Jerry Silverman

PUBLISHER'S PREFACE

It is with a sense of pride and privilege that we publish Irene Shapiro's *Revisiting the Shadows*. While there have been many books written about the Holocaust and by survivors, the voices of those lost to the violence should never be silenced to us. Young Golda Lipkies's admonition to Irene of "Do not forget!" immediately before Golda's execution echoes through the years and ages of suffered persecution...the individual cries of those who would also shout, "Do not forget me." Because genocidal intentions are still known in our world and still being made manifest, we must seek out the voices of those who may not be heard without the seeking. We can know enough to care...and care enough to know. We are able to learn from the words of those who expressed even their regrets in a time of history so filled with hatred and fear.

In an age of the power of the movie medium, I often wished in working on Irene's manuscript that we were able to put it into the full visual and auditory world of the cinema. It is difficult to portray the importance and presence of music in a printed book, especially for a family surrounded by the sounds of their father's violin and Irene's piano.

We wish to pay tribute to Irene and her husband, Marvin, and their family...a family that can enjoy the presence of this diligent and feisty lady. She was, indeed, one to be reckoned with. When I read and reread the personal account of the concentration camp swimming incident, I reflect that Irene is still, in New York, swimming laps.

Richard DeForest Erickson
DeForest Press

ACKNOWLEDGMENTS

I wish to thank One-by-One, Inc. for their contribution of the poem "Handle with Care," as well as my dear friends Mrs. Sonja Jelin-Wajsenberg and Mrs. Ursula Biszkowicz-Flicker of the Holocaust Center of Melbourne, Australia, for the contribution of their unpublished manuscript, *Holocaust: Bialystok, 1939-1945.* I used this as a resource for the historic background of the ghetto of Bialystok (see the Bibliography for the references used in their unpublished manuscript).

I also wish to thank the following people for their contribution towards the writing of this memoir: my husband Marvin Shapiro for his unrelenting help in matters concerning word usage and sentence structure; my dear friend Celia Keenholz for her professional help in dealing with word processing; my daughter Ellen Greenstein for her time-consuming task of editing the primary rough manuscript; my son-in-law Arnie Greenstein, for his splendidly succinct and lucid editing of the book's addenda (About the Author, etc.); my dear friend Dorothy Gross, for her professionalism and meticulousness in the final editing and proofreading of this memoir along with her persistent encouragement to see it published; and finally, all members of my family and the many friends who wholeheartedly supported and encouraged this project!

Part One

POLAND AROSE TO STAY ALIVE

"Czy umrzec nam przyjdzie na polu,
Czy w tajgach Sybiru nam gnic,
Z trudu naszego i bolu
Polska powstala by zyc!"*

(Whether we had to die in the battle
Or rot in the taigas of Siberia,
It was through our suffering and pain that
Poland arose to stay alive!)**

*A 1917-1918 Song of the Polish Legions (author unknown). Since the 18th century and until its rebirth in 1918, Poland was partitioned and occupied by Prussia, Austria and Russia. It remained free from 1918 to 1939 and was again liberated in 1945.

**English translation by author.

Rena Ela Hass

MY NAME WAS RENA HASS

My daughter-in-law remarked one day, "It must feel awkward to use the name Irene instead of Rena, your real name. Why did you change it?" I had no ready answer. Things just happened. Time went by and I became wife Irene, mom Irene, mother-in-law Irene, Grandma Irene, my American friends' Irene—I have been called Irene throughout my new life.

I became Irene during the dead time between my old and my new life and I said, "So be it." But it has been nice to be called Rena by my Polish friends here. And it made me feel all warm inside when I heard my sister call me Reniusia, the sweet diminutive form of my name of long ago (which she never used to call me in those days!). And at times, my American husband calls me Renia, awkwardly but so very softly. But I couldn't remember when and how I lost my old name, and I decided to revisit the young Rena to find the fragment of time that had swallowed it.

"Renusiu," says my mom, brushing a stray hair off my forehead, "only birds can fly, not little girls." Aching all over, I lie in my bed and feel sorry for myself. My pride has been bruised by my unsuccessful "pioneering flight" down the stairs to the basement of my house on Spichrzowa Street in Grudziadz, Poland. Through the window of the bedroom which I share with my parents, I see the ferryboat crossing the Vistula River on its way to the Left Bank, where one road leads to our river beach and the other to Gorna Grupa, my favorite country resort. In the living room, my bratty sister is crying again and Mama will go to nurse her. But I want Mamusia to stay with me, so I cry too, but my mom ignores my sulking and says, "Reniu, you brought your misery on yourself, now show us that you can be a big girl; don't cry...." Well, I guess Mom has to feed the brat so I let her go. I can hear the big puppy Rex bark and bark downstairs and I wonder if his mother needs to nurse him or if he is just barking to let us know that he is a biter.

Things get to be far better when Auntie Zosia Golemberska comes to visit. "So my tomboy Reniusiu," my auntie scolds me, "you want to fly and you want to pee like a boy! And when you were two years old, you ran away from home to march with the army and you got some spanking! And my hand hurts because I kept shielding your behind from your dad's spank-

Aunt Zosia Golemberska

ing! What will become of you!?" Now I decide to smile a little, especially since Aunt Zosia's beautiful daughter Wandzia will soon be home from school. Who knows, she may even come here and again sing for me the funny song (which I am not to tell about), the one about the crow that went bathing on the Left Bank and made Pan Capitan think that it was his wife bathing there (ha, ha). "Sir Captain," says the crow, "I am not your wife, sir, I am just a bird, a little crow!" Or the one about the woman who stuck the rake into another woman's...rim tzim tzim...mouth? Wanda will surely say, "Rena, remember that you promised to keep your mouth shut about the songs, right? We are pals, right?" I wish I had a sister like Wanda, a grownup sister like Wanda. I touch her arm. My aches feel much better.

Aunt Zosia is not my real aunt. My dad and her husband, Pan Golemberski, both play in the band at the Grudziadz Kawiarnia (cafe), and that is why Aunt Zosia and my mom became close friends. I love Ciocia Zosia as if she were my real aunt and I love Wanda. But her brother, Zdzisiek, teases me a lot, especially when he stoops down to dance with me and tells me that I dance like a cow. Much later on, when Zdzisiek leaves Grudziadz to study at the Polytechnic Institute in Warsaw, he will contract a serious parasitic infection and will suddenly die of that infection. Auntie Zosia will always wear black and cry a lot after Zdzisiek's death.

Nanny Mariasia, my beloved niania and I go walking after our lunch up the Castle Mount, the Gora Zamkowa. We walk up our Spichrzowa Street and then way up the pathway to the Klimek, the Castle Mount's watchtower. The tower used to be part of the Castle of the Teutonic Order which the Polish King Wladyslaw Jagiello conquered in the Battle at Grunwald, wherever and whenever that was. Now we have their watchtower, part of the walls of their castle, and most im-

portantly, their well. The well has a brick rim that is more than one meter high and it takes many many steps to go around the rim. There is an iron grating covering the rim of the well and you can lean against it and try to see the bottom, which, niania says, lies, at the bottom of the Gora Zamkowa. It is hard to imagine the depth of a well piercing this entire high mountain, a mountain that long ago bore a true castle of Poland's mortal enemy. Now you could throw pebbles into the well and, of course, spit into it. I do spit though Nanny always says

Nanny Mariasia Soltysiak

"Niusia, you are not a street urchin; young ladies do not spit. Come, let us make sand-cakes in the sand box." I don't like making sand-pies. I prefer sliding off the great big boulder that the Devil himself dropped onto the Gora Zamkowa. I am not sure why and when that happened, but here it is, nice and smooth. When it is time to pee in the bushes, we go together. I have to pull my panties down but Nanny does not have to do that because she does not wear panties. I often would like to see what her pee comes out of but she always admonishes me not to peek, with: "Rena, you naughty girl…"

Dad goes berserk one day and buys me a dollhouse with furniture, dishes and all. "*Du bist mishuge* (you are crazy)" I hear Mom say to him in Yiddish so that I wouldn't understand it. "Go return the toys." To me she says with a smile, "Tell Daddy that you make your own toys Reniusienka, my creative girl. Tell him how we pretend that you and I wash dishes together, clean the house together, and go to the market together." So, the dollhouse is returned and I continue playing creative "pretend" games, mostly by myself, sometimes with Mommy. When Dad's lady-student sits waiting in our living room to have her violin lesson, I like to stay with her and pretend to be my sister's mommy. But as soon as I attempt to take my little sister out of her bassinet, the lady-student starts calling for my mom. And Mom's scolding, "You are a very bad girl, Rena," is sure to be followed up by Dad's spanking (later during the day when Auntie Zosia is here to shield my behind). At least, this is the version of the story related to me by my dear Wandzia in the years to come.

It is during Passover that we go to my parents' hometown of Brzezany to visit their families. Mom is still fat and has to nurse my sister. My spinster-aunt Giza, who is my mother's youngest sister, tells me that indeed I was born in the very house where she and Grandma Sara live to this day and that I screeched all day long so that the neighbors called me a *kvetchke* (a whiner, in Yiddish). She also says, "Niusienko, you were the cutest, smartest little girl when you were a toddler. You held your nose and said in your Grudziadz-Mazurian clipped Polish, with a lisp, that the sewers in Grandma Sara's backyard smelled phew."

Grandma Sara recites poems for me and she treats me to the greatest pickles in the world. Grandma Sara and Aunt Giza have a pub in the Market Square of Brzezany. Ukrainian farmers tie up their horses and wagons at the posts in front of the pub and they come inside to drink beer and vodka with a pickle and pickled-herring chaser. When I am introduced to the big husky farmers with great big moustaches under their noses, they call me Irinka, but Grandma tells them that I am called Rinka. Later, Grandma Sara explains to me that my Hebrew name is Rachel or Rochel-Elke and that this name was given to me in memory of her sister, may she rest in peace. As to the Ukrainian Irinka, I am told that this is the diminutive version of the Ukrainian name of a Holy Lady, Saint Irina. Back in Grudziadz, Wanda derides the name Saint Irina and says that the Holy Lady's name was Saint Irena and that my parents had shortened that name to just Rena. Likewise, my middle name Ela was derived by shortening the name of another holy woman, Saint Elzbieta (Elizabeth). I wonder if I may have seen the pictures of both holy ladies at our cathedral, the Fara, since Nanny Mariasia had often taken me with her when she went to pray there.

We celebrate Passover at my father's family home in Brzezany. I love that house and I love all the fun happenings there. It surely is fun to drink from a barrel filled with well water. Grandpa Leon tells me that I ought to drink water very carefully so as not to swallow one of the well's frogs. Grandma Ida hugs and kisses me and says, "Niusienko, you know that your Grandpa Leon is kidding, don't you?" Do I really?

My Auntie Hela, Dad's sister, takes me to the outhouse and shows me how to squat on top of the toilet board and not fall into the multi-shaded brown stuff seen way down on the bottom. My dearest cousin Sylwinka teases me with, "Rena, how come you are all brown and smelly?"

I will always remember standing on a kitchen step-stool singing for the family, all of them clapping and *kvelling* over me (Yiddish for "drooling over me"), delighting me with their praises: "Our Renia has Dolo's musical talent," and such. And I will forever remember my dad (Dolo) taking out his cherished violin and playing gypsy songs that make you cry, with everyone in awe of his talent. Then, my father's younger brother Zygo with his guitar, and Dad with his mandolin, play the lively Ukrainian dances while Zygo's girlfriend Lusia keeps on dancing. She dances the lively Ukrainian *kolomyjka* all around the living room and onto the long, long balcony called a *ganek*. And as I lie down to sleep on the living room sofa, I hear the chiming of the clock on the tower in the painting of the square of St. Marks in Venice. Each hour on the hour it chimes the beautiful melody of Italian gondoliers, a melody that will haunt me for the rest of my life.

Our subsequent summer vacation trips to Brzezany involve two days of travel by steam trains that belch out clouds of smelly smoke. I feel nauseous most of the time and usually vomit by the time we reach Lwow. There is a short layover in Warsaw and a longer one in Lwow. The layover in Lwow is long enough to visit Dad's cousin, Zenka, and her family in the Jewish tenement area. Zenka and her brother Kuba often tease me because of my "choppy" Mazurian dialect, so one day I surprise my cousins and perform for them one of Lwow's street songs with singsong lyrics and a folksy *ta yoy*! I am rewarded for the song with a recording of Szczepcio i

Tonko, the popular comic singers of Radio Lwow. Thereafter, I consider myself somewhat a Lwowian girl and I show off my singsong speech before my friends in Grudziadz

On one occasion, Uncle Max, my mother's brother from Vienna, shows up at the train station in Lwow. He is on his way to Brzezany but we are, at this time, on our way to the sub-Carpathian oil town of Boryslaw to visit my mom's sister Rachela. *"Meine schoene Irenke...ja ja, du heist doch Renusia* (my pretty Irene, yes, yes, your name is Renusia)," says my uncle who speaks Viennese German to us. This is my first meeting with Uncle Max and this also is the first time that I see my mother burst out crying in public. Mom starts crying when Uncle Max tells her that Grandma Sara has died and that he is going to take care of Grandma Sara's pub and house in Brzezany. I wonder why no one wrote to us about Grandma Sara's death; perhaps my mom was shielded from the sudden bad news because of her heart condition.

I am always "our smart Renusia" to my Aunts Rachela and Giza who now live together in Boryslaw. Aunt Rachela is a dentist and a dental surgeon. Her dental technician, Eidikus, addresses me using the respectful form of "Panna Renia" as if I were a grownup. I don't know if that is because I am Dr. Rachela Schepper's niece or because, to Eidikus, the "Panna Renia" is a form of endearment. I love to watch Eidikus mold denture forms. But I hate it when Aunt Rachela says, "Rena, it is time to have your teeth checked, let's go into the office!" Aunt Rachela always wears a white coat because she socializes with us in the living quarters in between seeing her patients.

Aunt Giza one day takes me to see how the oil is pumped and how the heavy crude comes up and spills into pipes that take it into the refineries at nearby Drohobycz.

It is also fun to walk on the wooden sidewalks of Boryslaw. It is even more fun to be taken to the nearby resort of Truskawiec, although its mineral waters have a powerful odor of rotten eggs.

Uncle Munio and Aunt Pepka, my mom's younger brother and his wife, along with their stuck-up son Wolfus, live in the big city of Bialystok. Mom and I visit them, and Wolfus makes my life miserable. He constantly tells me that I don't know much of anything because I am just a dumb girl from a godforsaken little town somewhere in the Polish Corridor, which the Germans were only too happy to give up to the Poles. In order to be as smart as he is, says Wolfus, I would have had to attend the cosmopolitan schools of Bialystok or one of the other big cities of northeastern Poland, which the Russians surely hated to give up to the Poles. Oh, how I rejoice telling Wolfus that we have taxis, trolley cars, and elevators in the city of Grudziadz, while his provincial Bialystok has muddy streets, one-story Russian-style houses and horse-drawn carriages. And Grudziadz's PPG, the biggest rubber-product factory complex in Poland, is surely more important than all of Bialystok's textile factories taken together.

Wolfus gets even with me for my bragging and calls me Renela, a name that he concocts because he knows that I hate my middle name Ela. When Mom and I return to Grudziadz, I beg her to request that my middle name be removed from my school registration papers. She promises to do that and keeps her promise. While we are on the subject of names, Mom also tells me why some of our relatives call her Esterka and others Tyncia. It appears that the nickname Tyncia is an abbreviated form of her Polish name Ernestyna, while Esterka comes from her Jewish name Ester. Mom is called Tyncia by her in-laws and called Esterka by her own family who take pride in their Jewish ethnicity.

I like the fact that Uncle Munio goes to the movies a lot and reads a lot. He wears thick eyeglasses and is almost completely bald, things that attest to me of his wisdom. And wisdom is surely lacking in Wolfus, his hirsute son who has perfect vision!

The report card from my combined first and second grade classes at the private school I attended previously comes to my new school, the Tadeusza Kosciuszki Public School. It bears both my first and my middle name. But I become just Rena Hass in my new school and I will remain just Rena Hass throughout my school years. The teachers of the elementary grades call me Rena. In the junior division of the Gimnazjum (similar to junior high school that includes grades 7-10), my teachers (whom we address as "professors") call me Hassowna, a combination of my last name Hass and "owna," the modified Polish form of surnames ending in a consonant and used only for unmarried women. But my French teacher there, Madam Bochnigowa, calls me Renee. She tells me that Renee is a very pretty French name, and it is the first time in my life that I feel proud of my name. For once, Rena becomes a legitimate name and not just an abbreviated form of the Christian Irena!

In the senior division of the Gimnazjum (the *Lyceum,* grades 11-12), while we live in Bialystok under Soviet occupation, I become Rena Adolfovna, the middle name here denoting the patronymic term reserved for women. The Russians pronounce my first name "Reena," as in "Ireena." But then, all of our names, which are of course written in the Cyrillic alphabet, do acquire a new taste and texture when they are pronounced in the sonorous Russian language. To my family and friends I remain Renia, Reniusia or simply Rena, depending on whether it is uttered with a feeling of love or not.

I continue to search my memory in vain to pinpoint the event that made me lose my name, Rena. I open a folder that has my mementos from the Nazi occupation and find yellowed copies of official documents and notices dating back to 1945, the year of my liberation from Nazi concentration camps. I find a yellowed page of stationery titled UNRRA STUDENT HOSTELS-HEIDELBERG UNIVERSITY dated December 9, 1945, and it says I attended the University as Irene Hass. I next read a hand-written invitation to a British officers' dance on June 25, 1945, addressed to Irene Hass, three months after I was liberated from the camps. I recall that my Bialystok friends used to call me Irke in the camps, a common Yiddish nickname for Irene. Now I will have to search my earlier past and face the beginnings of my life in the camps...

It is August of 1943. After a shower in the wretched Saune, *I stand at the entrance to the infamous Majdanek Concentration Camp, shivering in a skimpy hand-me-down camp dress. I'm scared, oh, so terribly scared. Next to me stands my mom in an equally ragged dress, and Aunt Pepka, who looks surprisingly handsome in her short hand-me-down camp dress. A Polish inmate in striped prison garb registers us. I give her my age and name. She looks at me with disdain and says, "You Polish Jews, you have*

taken our Polish surnames—you should take our Polish first names as well!
Now, as to your name, there is no Saint Rena in Poland, we only have a
Saint Irena. As far as I am concerned, your name Rena is but a short form
of Irena, Saint Irena. So, we will call you here Irena Hass, and you better
like it!"

My mother says to me afterwards, "Stick to this name Irena, maybe
they will treat you better. Maybe later you can say that you are only half
Jewish? Maybe you can say that you were adopted by Jewish parents?
Who knows, maybe you could even claim that you are an illegitimate child
of your Niania Mariasia and of a Folksdeutch man? And who knows, maybe
they will transfer you to a better, special camp, and maybe even with your
mother? After all, you can always have a legal name of Irena and call
yourself Rena...."

I decide to keep my new name, Irene, throughout my new life, and it
begins to grow on me. Especially after I get to hear Woody Guthrie's "Irene,
Good Night..."

I COME FROM GRUDZIADZ

We were visiting my son and his family in Lexington, Massachusetts, and I was mulling over the proper opening to the story of the most significant portion of my childhood and my preteen years. While I busied myself with the raising of my three American children, I did not have the urge to revisit the shadows of my early youth. My feelings about it changed later, and that is why, in 1965, we went to visit Grudziadz. Now in Lexington, I glanced at my fifteen-year old grandson Eli and I recalled Eli's fifth grade assignment to interview an immigrant in his family. (I happened to be the only one who qualified for the subject of the assignment.) "Eli," I now asked, "do you recall that you interviewed me four years ago, and that you asked me where I came from?" Eli remembered. I confessed to Eli that I didn't have an easy answer to his question, but Eli reassured me that I had given him the name of the town of my birth, and that was the right answer. In fact, Eli remembered my telling him that when my mother was about to give birth to me, she decided to have me (her first baby) in her own mother's house in "this Bzheb...whatever." Then she took me right back with her to "that other Polish place...whatever its name was," which had become our hometown.

I asked Eli to tell me where he was from. He said, "I don't know, I guess from Boston, I guess because I was born in Boston...." I then asked Eli if he considered himself a "Bostonian" to which he answered that he did not. I asked if he considered himself an "Arlingtonian" since he used to live in Arlington as a baby, and again he said that he did not. He said that because he truly grew up in Lexington, he considered Lexington to be his hometown.

Now I could tell Eli about Grudziadz, "the other place...whatever its name was," my hometown in Poland. I told Eli that it was Grudziadz where I truly grew up.

I came from Grudziadz located in the delta-land of the Vistula River within Pomorze, the Polish Corridor between the German East and West Prussia. And I have traveled to Poland to revisit the shadows of my childhood in my hometown of Grudziadz.

Grudziadz

All know that Paris is
The fashion capital of the world.
Indura has its mudslides,
And Druskienniki its waters.
Venice has its gondolas,
Warsaw its famous pastries.
But there is a town that beats
the world's most beautiful cities...
It's Grudziadz on the blue Vistula!
It's Grudziadz where you can have fun!
Grudziadz, my dearest Grudziadz,
A stronghold of the young at heart!*

*Author's translation from Polish of an unpublished high school song.

I have not spoken Polish in some twenty years, but now I sing a Polish song. I sing the song of the city in which I grew up, Grudziadz, the city that I have not seen since 1938. I sing the song of the high school students of Grudziadz. It is now the summer of 1965, and this is my first visit to my native Poland, the first of many visits yet to come. With me are my American husband, my fifteen-year-old daughter, my thirteen-year-old son and my Polish brother-in-law. We are on our way to Grudziadz. We have left our nine-year-old son with my sister's family. This trip is intended to be my pilgrimage into the shadows of my childhood and into the shadows of the killing fields and gas chambers of Poland. We thought it prudent to exclude our youngest child from this grim visit.

Since early morning, we have driven from Slask (Silesia) to Poznan and then on to Torun, the capital of this Vistula land. Now we are nearing the left bank of the Vistula, the river that will forever remain my Polish Wisla. I sing my high school song and babble a mile a minute about my growing up in Grudziadz. To prepare my husband for Wisla's magnificence, I tell him, "Expect a river that is more beautiful and wider than New York's Hudson River." My brother-in-law suggests that we offer my husband a steep drink of good vodka because without a drink, neither the Wisla of my past nor the present day Vistula will measure up to the Hudson. But my husband magnanimously concedes to Vistula's grandeur anyway. My children, who all along have been sitting stone-faced in back of the car, suddenly start singing. When I hear "Oh say, can you see, by the dawn's early light, what so proudly we hailed…" I begin to feel that my American kids would like to remind me that even here, at the Polish Vistula, I am to remain their American mother!

As we drive over the bridge across the Vistula to its right bank, I modestly withdraw my claims for Vistula's dimensions. I notice that this is not the same bridge I used to cross in my childhood and I am told that, to thwart the occupation of Grudziadz by the German army, the old bridge was destroyed in 1939. While we are crossing the bridge, I scan the right bank searching for the Klimek, the magnificent Teutonic watchtower that used to crown the Castle Mount Gora Zamkowa. The watchtower was imprinted on all the picture-postcards, and later on, in my mind's eye.

The watchtower is no longer here. It was bombed out of existence by the invading German forces. A sandy hillock marks the spot where the tower used to stand, and I swallow my tears. Without the tower, this is not the familiar view of either Grudziadz or the Vistula of my childhood that used to greet me when I crossed the river on may way home from my summer vacations.

From the bridge, we travel along the trolley tracks to the centrally located town square (especially memorable on the 23rd of January many years ago) and then across the entire downtown area of Grudziadz. All these streets show so little change that I can hardly believe that I left them 27 years ago!

A view of Grudziadz over the Vistula River. Missing is the Klimek, a bastion-tower that used to be so characteristic of this view. The Klimek was destroyed by bombs during World War II.

We are staying with my Aunt Zosia's daughter Wanda, her son Andrzej and daughter Zdzisia in their apartment on Podgorna Street. Podgorna runs right under the Castle Mount, right under our old home on Spichrzowa Street, and is a block away from our later apartment on Kosciuszki Street. Wanda's other son, Rysiek, is attending an out-of-town technical school. Andrzej is a musician, a fine violinist like his Grandfather Golemberski. Wanda's husband died a few years ago and my dear Auntie Zosia died last year. She had waited for my visit to Poland but I came too late....We all sleep under eiderdown covers, which bring on my poor son's nasty attack of asthma. The next morning I have to take my son to the nunnery-clinic, which happens to be right next to our old apartment on Spichrzowa Street. A solicitous nun-physician gives him a shot of adrenalin and a prescription for oral antihistamine. The other nuns look on, curious to see their first American child.

Tomorrow and the two days after that we will be revisiting my old world. These will be the days when my children and my husband will discover the places of my childhood. We start right after the clinic and walk over to the landing of the stairs that lead down to the meadow-banks of the

Vistula River. At the landing, I point out a plaque commemorating the return from France of the remains of Slowacki, the beloved Polish poet and writer. I recall my mom telling me that the casket was returned by sea and then slowly barged up the Vistula for its burial in Warsaw. And it was in the Vistula's meadows that I used to play, while my nanny kept a watch over our freshly laundered linens, spread out in the grass to be bleached by the sun. Nanny would sit in the sun and sprinkle the linens, and I kept busy braiding the luscious dandelions of the meadow.

Next, we walk down Spichrzowa Street to look at the spichrze, the medieval brick granaries built there to store the grain barged down the Vistula from farmlands of the central and the upper reaches of the river. Then we go up Spichrzowa and pass by my family's first home in Grudziadz. I tell my children about my painful flight down the basement stairs, about my fear of the vicious dog Rex who used to be tied up in the orchard of our landlord, and about the time when I was no more than two years old and ran away from home. The sight of my first home reminds me, among other things, of the many mornings of painful shame in confronting my wet bed sheets. And it finally brings to mind the joys of moving into a brand new modern house on Kosciuszki Street, which we'll see when we are through visiting another treasured place of my childhood, the Castle Mount Gora Zamkowa.

A battery of my "kid-stuff" shenanigans lies in store for my children on the Castle Hill. Together, we slide down the Devil's Boulder, we spit into the Teutonic well, and we walk up and down the steps leading to the river. We revisit my haunts in the Castle Hill's "bush," but when nature calls my kids firmly refuse to pee in there the way I used to, so we settle for the restroom in the cafeteria of the park. Afterwards, we go down to the corner of Solna and Kosciuszki Streets.

Right around the corner stands the house with its long balconies and rounded niches, which I know so well. This was our second home at #4 Kosciuszki Street where we spent the later years of our stay in Grudziadz. I look up toward the bedroom window from which my mom used to throw me a five groszy coin (a nickel), to buy a chocolate marshmallow puff at the corner grocery store…and I see the store, it is still here! I remember that most of the grocery purchases were made there on credit, with the prices written down in an oblong notebook. I also recall that milk was bought in the dairy store down Solna Street, where they poured fresh milk from a milk can into our white enamel pitcher. And I can almost smell the wonderfully fresh rye bread, sweet smelling rolls and Danish szneki bought at the bakery next door.

I open the door that bears a glass lantern and is marked #4, the door of my childhood home. I guide my family toward the backyard in which I used to play. I look up towards the house-caretaker's attic apartment with the hope that I may see there his daughter Tula, my playmate, but there is

Looking up from the Vistula's meadow you see the tower of the Grudziadz cathedral "Fara" beyond the row of medieval granaries, some of which were turned into apartment houses. The Hass family lived in such a house, the one on the extreme left.

no one at the windows. (Wanda tells me that Tula still lives with her folks. I will later ring their bell but will find no one at home).

Inspired by the memory of Tula, I teach my kids to play ball the Polish girls' way—you paddle the ball against the wall, first with the right hand and then with the left hand. Then you toss the ball around yourself and let it bounce off the wall. You then let the ball go under your knee and again let it bounce against the wall till it drops. Lo and behold, my American daughter can do it, so I tell her next how we used to establish who goes first using a Grudziadz's version of the American "Eenie meenie miney mo." (Surprisingly, the ditty is in German and not in Polish!)

I let my son have his turn by doing some chinning on the carpet beating bar, hoping that the ancient wooden rod will hold him. We then enter the back door to the house and pass by a lobby apartment. How well I remember this apartment! In it lived a bona fide magician whose Jewish mistress was friendly with my family. He gave me a beautiful belt made of studded blue leather for my birthday. But I cannot remember the people who lived on the first floor, maybe because there were no children there.

We lived on the second floor, on the left side of the staircase. A family with two daughters lived on the right side. At times, I was sent to borrow a bit of this or that from them, and the older neighbor girl was sent to borrow a bit of this or that from us. But the older girl died of scarlet fever; we went to her funeral and that was a frightening experience for me. Would this family still live here? Timidly, I ring the bell and the door opens. I see a face that is much older than the one I used to know, but I recognize it nevertheless. "I am Renia, the older daughter of the Hasses who used to live across the way," I say. "I used to play with…" I am interrupted with a loud "Oh, Jesus Maria and All the Saints! The Hasses' Renia! Oh, what a kind neighbor your mamma was. You could always borrow some vinegar or sugar from her, any time of the day!" Now she pauses with a sign of recognition of the sad look in my eyes. Oh, yes, she remembers now who the Hasses were. So I tell her that my mom died in Bergen-Belsen and my dad in Majdanek. Oh yes, she knows why and how they died. "Those damn Germans," she starts and stops, casting her eyes to the upper floor. "The German landlady, Mertinowa, died some years ago, and her Polish daughter-in-law now lives in Mertinowa's apartment alone." How well I remember the notorious death of Mertinowa's son, killed while riding a motorcycle. He was nearly decapitated by a piano wire strung between two trees across a country road.

I ring the bell, our old bell at the door of our old apartment, my heart in my mouth. Yes, the current tenants of our apartment are in. Our former neighbor introduces us as "the American family who used to live in this apartment," and we are invited in. Along the entry hall I pass the bathroom door and I see myself wrapped in a bath towel, my father giving me a "piggy-back ride" from the bathroom to my bed in the children's room, there to be covered by my eiderdown pierzyna up to my nose. Next, down the hall on the left, comes the spacious kitchen with a door to our maid's room on the left wall. The rear balcony faces the yard and the tiled cooking stove is on the right. I don't see the wooden tool bench hand-made by my father or my blue embroidery handiwork that used to hang on the wall opposite the stove.

The door to the living room opens on the right wall of the hall. Where oh where is the wallpaper with its birds among the thorny rose branches that I always thought hurt the birds so terribly? The rounded niche has some potted plants in its tall windows, but they are not the cactus plants so lovingly cultivated by my father.

My piano used to stand at the wall between the living room and my parents' bedroom, just past their double door. Now I am back there in the living room of my childhood. I'm sitting at the piano practicing the scales, the Czerny exercises, the Schubert serenade, the Chopin waltzes, and of course, playing pop tunes whenever my father isn't at home. I play and sing the "Berceuse Slave" with the sad lyrics I have written for it. Father stands next to the piano and plays his violin while my sister gracefully dances beside him. (Could she be surreptitiously sticking her tongue out at me?) We have guests, and they are all seated around the great dining table of our living room. These must be my dad's German friends who are having their traditional afternoon coffee at our home.

My mom is serving coffee from her porcelain coffee pot. The pot is kept warm by a flowery flannel skirt, Fraulein Kalmukoff's gift for my Dad. Wanda tries to pull my leg by telling me the coffee pot warmer was made from Fraulein Kalmukoff's flannel gatki (long Johns, in Polish), which, of course, I don't buy. And there is Mom's babka cake, her cookies that are supposed to melt in your mouth but never do, and finally the torte. It is a very special layer cake filled with rich chocolate-butter and decorated with my dad's artistic vanilla-butter borders and flowerets. Oh, what a heavenly time my sister and I have licking out the leftovers of the torte fillings!

My reveries end and once again I guide my family through the maze of memories associated with the living room. The large credenza used to stand between the door leading to the balcony and the door leading to the spare bedroom. The small credenza used to stand at the wall between the living room and the hall. Do I dare tell my secret about the small credenza to my kids? I somehow discovered the hiding place for the key that locked the small credenza. Mom's cookies were locked in there because of my sweet tooth and my tendency to gain weight (or to become fat, according to my skinny sister). Now, with the key, I could help myself to the cookies whenever I wanted. One day, however, my sinfulness was discovered by my maternal cousin who came to visit us after his graduation from high school. Although my cousin did not tell on me, he did admonish me for being both dishonest and cowardly. Years later in New York, this same cousin, who in the interim became a professor of medicine, found it hard to own up to hurtfully chastising his little cousin (so contrary to today's beliefs of child psychology!) once upon a time.

As we come to the door leading to the spare bedroom I wonder, Should I tell my children the secrets of this spare bedroom? Perhaps some of them. OK then, let's go out onto the balcony, kids. The oleander tree, which was as old as I was, used to stand at one end of the balcony, a rocking chair at the other end. Geraniums and petunias were grown in the flower boxes along the ledge of the balcony and again, these plants were Dad's babies. None of these are here now. But the redbrick nursing home across the street is still here. And the window of the spare bedroom opening onto the balcony still bears lace curtains very much like ours. I tell my son why using the bathroom is much kinder to nature than peeing against a tree, whether you are a boy or a dog (or Rena the boy-pretender). Mr. Eichman, our handsome Hebrew teacher, used to sublet this spare bedroom. We soon discovered that our oleander tree was dying and that its soil smelled like a urinal. I could not remember the aftermath of our discovery or the fate of our ailing oleander tree. But I will forever remember tiptoeing to the door of Mr. Eichman's room when my folks were out for the evening and listening for the noises my keen child's ear could pick up behind that door.

The bedroom…it was here that I stayed in Mom and Dad's bed and memorized the multiplication tables. It was here my creative sister painted designs on her youth bed using the contents of her fallen diaper. It was here that I sat on the window sill with my legs dangling out, and cried that since there was no real homeland for us, there was no use to go on living—unless my folks would allow me to join the Hanoar Hatzioni (Zionist) Cub Scouts.

Finally, the new tenants invite us to have coffee with them in our former children's room, and I can no longer hold back my tears. The beautiful brown-tiled heating stove stands where it used to stand in the corner of the room. Although it is a warm summer day, I stand at the stove with my hands behind my back, just as I used to do on cold days when I came in from the outside. Then I look at the bed that stands where mine used to be, and I remember the many happy, and the many not so happy, daydreams there. The sweetest day-dreaming time would come during the dark fall and winter mornings before it was time to get up for school, when our maid used to come in with her bucket of coal and wood and make a fire in our stove, a fire whose flames would flicker and dance till the coals were set aglow and the metal door of the stove was locked. And I well remember when I came down with the usual childhood diseases and had to stay in bed.

Periodically, during the springtime, I would come down with tonsilli-tis. The pain wasn't too bad and the rewards were great: a week off from school, Mom's special care, ample servings of all the heretofore forbidden fattening foods, and my sister's offer to serve me with whatever I desired. And finally, I remember how my dad would let go of his music and come to me with "So how is my ailing Renusia, my talented accompanist-to-be?"

I often stayed in bed with my perpetually infected tonsils, but the ton-sillectomy itself wasn't bad at all. During my short stay at the hospital, I showed off with my unabashed eloquence before an approving audience of adult patients. I then went to stay in bed at home with—oh, paradise!—all the ice cream I wanted to eat. But the intestinal impaction (twist) was scary and I had truly a bad time with it. The doctors at the hospital couldn't diagnose the cause for my excruciating abdominal pain since, unfortunate-ly for provincial medics, appendicitis had to be ruled out because my appendix had been removed by then. I was sent home. There I lay in bed waiting for the pains to either subside or to worsen, in which case explor-atory surgery would be undertaken. I was scared. My mom hovered over me, ashen-faced; Dad banged his forehead against the wall repeatedly crying in Yiddish, "*Oy vey is mir* (woe is me)." Since I never saw Dad so distressed, I thought I was going to die. But I got better. (Not until years later, when similar symptoms appeared again, was I diagnosed as having an oversized colon that was prone to fecal impactions and twisting (volvulus).

I cast my eye on the wall opposite where my bed stood and where my sister used to sleep after she graduated from my parents' bedroom. I cast a glance at my daughter and her brother as I recall the times when I bribed my sister with all sorts of favors to do my chores. I feel ashamed of having done that. Unlike my daughter, was I a rotten sister? Probably.

We leave "our" home, grateful to its kind current inhabitants for letting us see it. We walk down Kosciuszki Street until its end and turn left, up the hill of Forteczna Street. Throughout my public school years, six days a week, I walked that route on my way to the Tadeusza Kosciuszki Public School. And now we are there, in the yard of my old elementary school. The same grey cement building, the same wooden gym annex, but the walnut trees around them are gone. I walk into the school building and I recall having to walk one flight higher each year for my next grade classes. I remember my fourth grade teacher, Pani Baranowska, and I remember her brother who taught the fifth grade. But most of all, I remember the music teacher, Mr. Szymanowski. It was in his chorus classes that I learned the many Polish folk songs, including the one I later translated into English: "*Tell me little pine tree, who took care of you? 'Twas the wind and 'twas the sun and 'twas the morning dew.*" Oh, how great did Felix Dzwonkowski's fine soprano sound when he sang that song with the accompaniment of our choral group. And how proud I was to sing with that choral group at the memorial held in Grudziadz after the death of Marshal Pilsudski!

As we leave my school, I look up toward the rafters and I am amazed to see that a brick is still missing up there! That particular brick had fallen on the head of one of our boys, and the principal had to come the next day to each and every class and reassure us that the boy would recover and would soon come back to school.

Before we leave the schoolyard, I look toward the area where the third-graders used to plant radishes, carrots, and other vegetables—but our garden plot isn't there anymore. It was apparently paved over. We walk out of the schoolyard and go down Forteczna Street towards Wybickiego Street where there are buildings that bring back to mind so many pleasant memories. Here stands the library from which so many of my favorite children's books came and further down, near the military barracks behind the corner of Prowiantowa Street, I used to go ice-skating at a huge outdoor ice-skating rink. In fact, all along Wybickiego Street there still stand the many red brick military barracks of Grudziadz's garrison. It was in one of these barracks that my father was stationed after his discharge from the army in the early 1920s. Later on, Dad's wartime friend Major Slupczynski's family stayed at the garrison. I played with his daughter in those days and it was at her home that I heard my first radio program, the delightful Polish Radio Children's Hour. And all through my early childhood our maid took me to buy the dark pumpernickel bread (*komysniak*), sold at the barracks' gates.

The Grudziadz's trolley is no longer yellow, it is now red. It takes us along Wybickiego Street and we pass the old Cinema Orzel (the Eagle) right after our first stop. My father conducted the cinema's orchestra in the days of the silent movies and I remember sitting in the orchestra pit, stretching my little neck to watch some awesome silent Hollywood movie. As the trolley slowly continues along the Wybickiego and the other main streets of Grudziadz, I look out the window and relish my childhood memories of these streets. These streets that I once thought to be long and wide now prove to be small and narrow medieval lanes. And what happened to our great big theater? Is this it…that little building behind the trees? Ye gad. It was here that my parents took me to hear my first opera, "The Pearl Fishers." And my first real concert here had a performance by a juvenile violin-prodigy whose splendid play convinced me that I had better give up the violin and try the piano instead.

There are two more days in Grudziadz; during each of these days at noon we listen to the trumpeter play Grudziadz's hejnal (taps) atop the Town Hall Tower. The haunting melody of taps was composed by Major Szpulecki, a fellow musician during Dad's army days. Wanda knows how fond Major Szpulecki was of my dad, so she calls to tell him about us. Szpulecki is heart-broken to learn of Dad's death. Apparently, Szpulecki had heard on the radio a violinist named Hass and thought that it was my dad. "They don't make musicians like Hass anymore," Szpulecki tells Wanda, and sends us his heart-felt wishes.

On one of our last days in Grudziadz we take a walk in the alleys of the Town Park where my family used to relax on Sunday afternoons, and then we walk over to the nearby German Gimnazjum where my father taught music until 1938. We also drive to the village of Rudnik where my family spent many a summer Sunday. We used to have our picnics here in the pine grove near the hilly sandy dunes, and we went to swim in what was once a vast lake (when I swam in it as a child) but is now no more than an overgrown little pond. As nature would have it, ecological succession has, in due time, swallowed the sand dunes and replaced them with young pine woods. But the wild strawberries still grow in the clearings amidst the pines and they still are as big and as sweet as they used to be.

We finally visit my junior Gimnazjum (junior high school), whose senior division in Poland was referred to as the Lyceum. Our Gimnazjum was an all-girl school and it was named after the mother of Poland's first Marshal, Maria Bilewicz-Pilsudska. We enter the school and I take a seat at my old desk at the front of the now empty classroom. My kids giggle when I raise my hand and stand up to recite the dates of Polish history. We later visit some of my former teachers and my children are impressed that they still remember me. My French teacher, Madame Bochnigowa, remembers that I used to bring French songs to class and that I spoke French with but a slight Polish accent. Madame is surely pleased that I became a teacher, but why of biology and not of French? Panna Minkiewiczowna, who was my homeroom and gym teacher, remembers that I used to play a fairly decent game of volleyball. She also remembers that my dad was a teacher, but she does not remember that I was the only Jewish girl in our homeroom. Yes, she recalls that I was on the freshman ice-skating team and that during a skating competition the boys yelled when I passed by them, "There goes the fat one." She does not recall that her father, the town's tailor, made my regulation navy-blue winter coat, nor the fact that I spent a summer in a girls' camp headed by her sister.

I look for our school auditorium but it isn't here anymore; it was apparently bombed by the Germans. My children learn from me that our school dances were held on Saturday afternoons in that auditorium. They find it a bit funny that boys were never invited to these dances and that our girls were made to dance with one another. The truth is, we weren't even allowed to socialize with boys in the streets of Grudziadz either. I remember the case of Jasia, the beautiful blonde who became a subject of merciless gossip when she was found walking hand-in-hand with a young cadet.

We stay with Wanda and hear about the days of the German occupation of Grudziadz. "There was only a handful of Jewish men in the city when it fell to the Germans," she begins. "These men remained there because they had to close up the PPG rubber factory. The father and brother of Lilka—your best friend, Rena—were among them. The Germans interned the Jews along with a few prominent Polish officials and clergymen in a camp outside town. Since I was acquainted with Lilka's family I went there to bring them food. Lilka's father was in distress; the Germans had broken his eyeglasses and had severely beaten him. The poor man complained that he couldn't see at all without his eyeglasses, so I offered to have them fixed. When I came back with the repaired eyeglasses, the Germans would not allow me to deliver them to my Jewish friend unless I remained in camp with him. I was so scared I just ran home. Lilka's brother must have led his father everywhere...even when they marched off to be executed in the woods of Dolna Grupa (a suburb)."

Now at last comes the time to head for the most meaningful area of Grudziadz to me, the place where our little synagogue and the Jewish Community Center once stood. I review in my mind what I remember about the Center's layout. I remember that on its first floor the Community Center housed a Hebrew school and in later years a small kindergarten for Jewish preschool children as well. The centrist-Zionist Hanoar Hatzioni, had a small room on the second floor of the Center; the right-wing, revisionist-Zionist Beitar, held their meetings in a shack behind the Center. Beitar's marches and other militaristic activities were conducted in the backyard, not far from a little lean-to where our shoikhet (ritual butcher) slaughtered geese, ducks, and chickens for his Jewish customers.

I remain in the formerly Jewish area of Grudziadz alone and ask my family to let me revisit the shadows there by myself. The now abandoned and rubbish-cluttered area evokes echoes of lively activities, pictures of young faces and sounds of young voices. But I know well that there is hardly anyone left alive of those whose activities, faces and voices I now yearn for...

Next day, we drive out of Grudziadz and after we cross the Vistula River we stop to see the place of execution and the common grave of the Jewish men who remained in Grudziadz in that fateful September of 1939.

I am not able to remain open about my Jewish identity when I go back to Grudziadz after my first visit there in 1965. My sister disavows her Jewish roots and requests that I shield her secret by "passing for a Gentile" when visiting Poland. So I walk the streets of Grudziadz accompanied by her Christian friends. I revisit the Castle Mount, the meadows of the Vistula, and the Park, but I am not able to openly revisit my Jewish places with them. But, when we pass by the spot where once stood our little synagogue, I swallow my tears and slow down a bit to say in my soul the Kaddish *(a Jewish prayer for the dead) for the extinct Jewish community of Grudziadz from which I came...*

I AM NOT ONE OF THEM

During my stay in Germany some eight months after my liberation from the concentration camps, I met a girl who had once attended the Grudziadz Gimnazjum with me. We met at the UNRRA Student Hostel where we were both housed, along with the other displaced persons who were studying with us at Heidelberg University. Miss Prager, the hostel supervisor, asked me one day to come to her office and meet the new Polish girl who had just come to our hostel. The new girl's face looked familiar but I couldn't place it at first. Miss Prager introduced me to the girl, saying that since both of us spoke Polish, she would like me to show the girl around. It took no time to find out that the girl had formerly been a member of Armja Krajowa, the armed forces of the right wing Polish underground, and that she came from Grudziadz. Although both of us had been on the same grade level of the junior Gimnazjum, we had had different homeroom teachers and different subject classes. She had attended classes whose students took German as their foreign language whereas I had attended classes whose students had taken French. Nevertheless, we spent a few pleasant hours together and we spoke of getting together again, but we never did. In the hostel, the girl was a pal with students who didn't show much interest in me, so I kept to myself. In the UNRRA cafeteria, I shared a table with all the other Jewish students while the new girl sat with the Polish students. She made no attempt to either invite me to their table or to join me at my table. We never got together outside the cafeteria either. She was, after all, one of them (Polish students) and I was one of us (Jewish students), and *our common Grudziadz bond did not matter.* Was I ever one of them in Grudziadz? *I must dwell on it a bit.*

     My childhood world of Grudziadz makes it hard for me to forget that I am somewhat different from my classmates. My classmates and I are friendly enough at school, but I am seldom invited to their homes. Perhaps it is because I am Jewish and don't celebrate the Christian holidays with them. Most troubling for me is Christmas time, although its special activities never cease to excite me. Each year I eagerly await the Christmas carolers who come to our doors with their elaborate crèches, and I get to know their lovely Christmas carols by the time I enter grammar school. On my way home I often enviously peek into the ground floor apartment windows and covet the Christmas trees there; I keep pleading with my mom to let me have a tree, and she finally gives in. A Christmas tree with my own adornments now stands in our room at the window during the day, and away from the window when it is lit up in the evening. Now I eagerly invite my classmates to see my Christmas tree and one day, though I am forbidden to do that, I light the candles when the tree is still at the window. As my mom has feared, the curtain catches on fire! My friends console me after this curtain disaster and reassure me that my parents are bound to soon forgive my misdeeds. But a Christmas tree never again appears in our home. My Christian friends and I do grow a bit closer and I soon begin to feel that perhaps I am "one of them" after all…perhaps?

     But religion persists being an obstacle for feeling like "one of them." I have to stand up with my head down while my classmates say their prayer, and it doesn't feel good at all. The after-school religion classes are also to be contended with. I sheepishly sit in back of the classroom and peek bashfully at the handsome priest until he eventually recognizes the look of concern on my face and hands me the text of the New Testament to look at. But as I continue to abstain from participating in his question and answer routines, the priest eventually becomes suspicious about the reasons for my self-consciousness. He undoubtedly checks my school record one day because he comes over and quietly says to me, "It is all right to just have a look at some of the pages of the New Testament." But despite his kindness I get an F in religion and angrily wonder why. The answer comes very soon—I attended the wrong classes of religion. The classes to which I had been assigned are taught by the bearded and very stout Rabbi Bromberg. These classes are taught at the Wydzialowa School, which is quite a distance away from the Kosciuszki Public School.

So, starting in fourth grade, I attend the afternoon classes of Jewish religion at the Wydzialowa School—where the Jewish pupils look at me suspiciously as if I did not belong. Rabbi Bromberg introduces himself to me as Dr. Bromberg (a doctor?) and I don't like him at all. He is fat, he waddles when he walks, he yells at the boys when they make jokes, and worst of all, people in the street look at him in a funny way when he passes by, surely noticing that he is different. And I wonder if I belong with these stuck-up Jewish kids who give me a cold shoulder because I missed a year of Jewish religion. Maybe I am not one of them either...

There finally appears a Christian girl in my class whom I soon befriend. This girl's name, Dondon, sounds foreign, and she looks different compared to the other girls in our school. She is dark-skinned and has dark hair and thick lips. When I ask about it, she tells me that her father is Hungarian, that he has a dark complexion and dark hair, and that her mother divorced him and married a Polish officer. I marvel at the looks of her mom and her kid-brother, both of whom are blond and blue-eyed!

Dondon's home is around the corner from us. We begin to pal around quite a bit, and although we do not do our homework together, we often meet afterwards and go walking along the high cliffs of Vistula's right bank. On one such occasion I become aware that some boys are following us, and they look familiar. I soon recognize them as Beniek, Kuba, and Adek, the three Jewish boys who attend the Jewish religion classes with me. As girls usually do in such situations, we begin to giggle; the boys respond by laughing, as if one of them told a joke. Are they poking fun at us? Feigning indifference, we pass them by and go home. The boys later tell me that they attend tutoring sessions with a teacher who lives near the right bank heights and that they sometimes go walking there after their lessons. Now we know that we can see these boys again if we continue our walks. Indeed, we do meet them several more times during that school year. The way that we synchronize our walks with theirs is that we first spot the boys after they leave their tutor's home, and then we dash out ahead of them toward the high bank of the Vistula. Our flirtatious rapport with the boys continues at a safe distance so that no one will see us together. I profess to be "falling in love" with Kuba and write appropriately amorous lyrics to the then popular song, "Remember Capri." In my song, the scenery of Vistula Heights replaces the vistas of Capri, and I title mine "Remember Kuba" instead of "Remember Capri." I swear Dondon to secrecy about my crush on Kuba and I feel that I can trust her for all times to come. Dondon and I are pals, and I finally experience comradeship with a Christian girl.

Alas, things change when we return to school after summer vacation. My heart sinks when I notice that Dondon ceases to respond to my warm greetings, walks away from me and gaily talks with the other girls instead. I am heartbroken but I manage to preserve my dignity by avoiding her altogether. Back at home, I confide in my mom about my hurt feelings. She says, "You are not one of them Renia, you never will be—they will never accept you as their own." But I would prefer to believe that there are other reasons for Dondon's behavior. I wonder if perhaps she stupidly told her mother about our walks with the boys, and maybe even told her that I enticed her to socialize with Jewish boys. But then, maybe my mom is right and they, the Christian Polish people, will simply never accept us Polish Jews as their own. I decide to pay more attention to the behavior of the Christian girls toward me to see if there is some truth to what my mom says. And the future gives me ample opportunity to watch and see.

Prior to my first year at the junior Gimnazjum (junior high school), my parents enroll me in a summer camp for freshmen girls. I end up having a very enjoyable summer, replete with nature hikes, swimming, campfire powwows and other camp activities. The camp life makes me feel like I belong, but the feeling does not last. When my mom and my sister come to see me during the season's last Parents Visitation Weekend, my sister is so taken by what she sees in our camp that my mom is prompted to ask the camp leader if she could stay with us. Unfortunately, toward the end of the visit, my sister pulls one of her "tricks" and chases a chicken onto the brim of an open well. I doubt that the camp leader will grant permission after that. Apprehensively, I sit at the door of the room where the campers and the leader debate the merits of my mom's request, and my spirit sinks when I hear what they say. No, my camp-mates don't mind my sister's childish pranks because they know that she would soon learn from them how to behave if she were their "own kind." But she is not one of their kind and they don't want her. The camp already has "one of the others, and one of them is enough." The camp leader, who is a teacher herself, agrees: "She is not one of us, they aren't our kind."

During the first year of the junior Gimnazjum, I opt to sit at the front of the classroom so that teachers readily notice my raised hand, and my hand goes up quite often. I soon become one of the best students of our class and one of the girls, who happens to be the daughter of the mayor of Grudziadz, asks me one day if the reason that I know all the answers is that I cram a lot, or is it that I have better brains. I gather that the statement "better brains" most probably implies "cunning Jewish brains," but I ignore this implication and modestly answer that I diligently do my homework each day simply because I have nothing better to do. Lo and behold, I get an invitation to the mayor's mansion for an afternoon with the mayor's daughter! With the proper guidance from my anxious mother, I practice sitting at the table with my elbows tightly tucked at my sides just in case I have the afternoon coffee with the mayor himself. No such luck. We have our milk and cookies in the children's room in the company of the children's governess.

This time I don't let my hopes fly too high—I don't let myself think of becoming a pal of the mayor's daughter. But I do hope, just a little, that I will go to the mansion for another afternoon. No, another "first student," not I, gets to be invited there, and this time Mom does not have to say that she told me so. Anyway, my social contacts with other classmates seem to improve later in the year. I now walk to and from school with two friendly girls who also help me catch up with the class work that I miss during the Passover. But not much more. As before, my classmates exchange home visits with the other Christian girls but not with me. There is however one girl, Anka, who does occasionally invite me to visit her and to go to the park with her family.

Anka's dad wears a leather glove over his artificial right hand. When we go to the park he usually walks with his twin sons, while Anka and I walk with her mom. At times I wonder why Anka's mom asks me so many questions pertaining to my being Jewish. Why does she want to know how Passover is celebrated at our home? And what our synagogue looks like inside? And whether we ever eat in the *Sukkah*, or dress up for *Purim*? How does she know about it all? I look at her dark eyes and her curly dark hair and I wonder if she used to be Jewish. Will Anka's dad leave his wife, just as Dr. Grygier (who took out my appendix) left his Jewish wife, even though she converted to Christianity?

It is hard for me to feel at ease in the presence of my Gimnazjum "professors." My teacher of Polish literature seldom calls on me when I raise my hand. She will often say, "Let us have the other girls speak." When she does let me answer one of her questions, she tends to dispute my answers by saying, "Does the class agree with that answer?" When I mention during a class discussion of wartime literature that my father was Marshal Pilsudski's legionnaire and that he fought and defended Poland against the invading Bolsheviks, my teacher's face shows an utter disbelief. She just clears her throat and says nothing. Her daughter, who is in our class, brags about her brother, one of the leaders of the National Democratic (Endek) students at Warsaw University. In due time, I will find out that Endek students copy-cat *Hitler Jugend's* agendas, including the humiliation and beating up of Jews.

More and more I begin to perceive that most teachers treat me differently than they treat the Catholic students. In the second grade of the junior Gimnazjum (8th grade), my chemistry teacher passes my laboratory workstation without ever noticing that I usually finish my experiments before the other girls. No, he definitely does not like me. Later in biology, I once foolishly point to my own rear end instead of that of the bee on the chart to show where bees have their stingers, and my biology teacher becomes furious. When the class erupts in laughter, the teacher gives me an outraged look, which makes me doubt that I will get my deserved A in biology. Then at a parent-teacher conference, my mother is coldly told that "our teachers do not have to put up with students of that kind." I don't care for biology very much, but I feel hurt when my biology teacher no longer calls on me, even though I continue to complete each assignment as diligently as I always have. My Latin teacher, whose husband works with my dad at the German Gimnazjum, shows no friendliness toward me whatsoever. She lets me translate Latin passages without ever praising even my most perfect translations! Why doesn't she praise me? Why doesn't she smile at me like she does at another "first student" in Latin?

Geography is taught in third grade and the teacher calls on me to recite what I've learned while I stand at the big map in front of the class. He seems to just let me talk, as if he didn't care whether I knew geography or not. Could it be because his wife prepared me for the Gimnazjum entrance examination? Surely he didn't ignore me because I happen to be Jewish? I can't believe that this teacher is anti-Semitic...not he, not the idol of the entire school. As for my math teacher—well, I panic at the blackboard in my algebra and geometry classes so badly that I can't tell if it is my fumbling or me that she doesn't like.

At Christmas time of my last year in Grudziadz, someone breaks into our classroom savings for the poor. The teacher's desk is messed up, the piggy bank containing our nickels and dimes for the poor is cracked open, and all the coins are gone. The homeroom teacher holds a meeting with us and asks if anyone stayed in school after classes on the day of the break-in. One by one, my classmates say that they would never commit the un-Christian deed of stealing from the poor. What shall I say? I just say that I go home promptly after the school day is over and that I do not steal. Why are all eyes on me?

My mom is called to school by the principal and is asked if she recently saw me with large amounts of pocket money. My mom comes back home and tells me about the questioning. Then she hugs me and asks me to show her the two ten-groszy coins that I hold in my uniform pocket for tomorrow's carfare and school milk. "I told them that two ten-groszy coins have always been the daily large amounts of your allowance of pocket money, and that Jewish children are taught to give to the poor and not to steal from them. Now you see what world we must live in, my child. We will never be treated the way they treat their own kind."

I visit my Gimnazjum teachers in Grudziadz in 1965 and get the address of Irka G., a girl who used to sit near me in all three grades of my junior

Gimnazjum (grades 7-9). I write to her several times. My letters are loving and warm and I suggest we write to each other and perhaps even meet one day in Grudziadz. But there never is an answer from Irka, and some time later my friend Wanda lets me know that Irka was simply too busy to maintain correspondence with me. Is this more evidence of the sad fact that I have never been, and will never be, considered one of them?

I AM ONE OF MY OWN PEOPLE

There were a few hundred displaced persons (DPs) who enrolled at the Heidelberg University after the start of the 1945-1946 fall term, and I was one of them. These displaced persons generally hung around together and sat at the same tables in the cafeteria. I alone would occasionally sit in the cafeteria at the "Polish table," and I alone had a close friend, a Christian Pole who often sat at our "Jewish" table. My friend's name was Poldek (Leopold) and he was a medical student just as I was. Poldek and I used to spend much time together. We walked around Heidelberg and talked about ourselves and about our common concerns, and we even crammed together for our weekly quizzes in human anatomy. But in due time we grew socially apart. Poldek began to favor eating with the Christian Poles and I ate almost exclusively at the "Jewish" table. I also began to spend more of my free time with the other Jewish students. It was with these students that I could share the stories of the unhappy days of my past in the camps, and it was only with them that I shared my dreams about the possibility of a future life in Palestine or in America. Finally, Poldek and I drifted apart and were no longer warm friends.

Before my departure for the United States in May of 1946, Poldek asked me to go out with him and have a heart-to-heart talk. He told me that he found much in common with me and very much regretted our growing apart. But I had to tell him that I found less in common with him and his Christian Polish colleagues than I did with my Jewish colleagues. I had to tell Poldek that with my Jewish friends I felt a sense of belonging.

On parting, we decided to correspond with one another and to keep on reviewing our relationship, which we did. But my relationship with Poldek eventually came to naught and I think he understood in time why I needed to feel that I was "one of my own people." As I matured, I also understood that this need must have started during my childhood in Grudziadz...

Few Jewish families live in Grudziadz during my childhood. But little by little, more Jewish families come here, mostly from Central Poland's cities of Lodz, Warsaw, Katowice and Czestochowa. I finally get to meet Jewish kids of my age.

My first Jewish friend, Slawka Kaplan, comes from Baranowicze, an eastern Polish city. Unlike the Kaplan family, the Sempolinskis come to Grudziadz from Germany. They have two daughters: Ela, who is a few years younger than I am and Roza, who is a year or so older. The family lives in an impressive downtown apartment with parquet floors and central heating. More impressive than their arrival, however, is their departure to Brazil. We soon receive a photograph showing Roza and Ela in rich-looking summer dresses and Pan Sempolinski in a white suit and Panama hat. All three of them are standing amidst the palm trees of Brazil.

Rutka Bzura, the next to arrive in Grudziadz, introduces me to the joys of a record player and to wonderfully schmaltzy Polish pop songs. One of these has heart-rending words: "A mother's heart alone knows all your pains...and life becomes so much harder when that heart no longer beats for you!" Two other Jewish girls, Pola Gelade and Nusia Halberstadt, become my early childhood friends, and both of these, according to my mom, are from the so-called "better homes." Oh yes, I am allowed to pal around only with those Jewish girls whose family standing meets my parents' approval. But soon other social influences prevail and I develop other social contacts which I relish most of all.

These later social contacts start when I enter the Gimnazjum. I usually walk home after classes, and it feels good to have people notice my school uniform and its insignia. As mandated, I always wear a pleated navy blue skirt and a navy blue blouse with blue piping around the collar and cuffs, along with a blue shield on the sleeve marking my status as a junior Gimnazjum student. The route from school to our house passes by the Jewish area on Groblowa Street and I usually slow down here to do some planning. Should I stop at the *podworko* (the backyard of the Jewish Community Center)? I know that I will be late for dinner if I stop, but...Resolutely, I round the corner of Groblowa, go around our little synagogue, go through the long corridor of the Hebrew school and enter the backyard of the Jewish Community Center, the *podworko*, where the Jewish kids hang out.

The young people who gather here don't come from the so-called "better homes," and their parents don't choose "proper" companions for them, either. At the *podworko*, I meet with a group of young Jewish people who seem to have a lot of fun with kids of their own choosing. Enviously, I listen to their "cool" chatter and their "smart-guy" remarks peppered by a Yiddish word or two. I soon learn "*Oy, abrokh!* (Oh, shucks)," the *shlep* (drag) and the *tukhes* (rear end) words which are hard to translate into another language.

There are members of two youth organizations among the older boys and girls of the *podworko* group. The members of the Zabotynski's right-wing Beitarists, who call for the forming of a Jewish army and for the wresting of Palestine out of the British and Arab hands, hang out at the shack in the outer yard. The liberals who call for a peaceful coexistence with the Arabs, the Hanoar-Hatzioni people, stick to the inner yard. But all the boys play soccer together using the area of both backyards as their soccer field. I hang around the liberals, who mostly ignore me except for Kraina, one of the daughters of our *shames* (synagogue-keeper), Szklar. Kraina shows interest in me. I guess it is because she believes that I will eventually become an inductee into the cub scouts of the Hanoar Hatzioni. At least she hopes so. Kraina explains to me that with only 150 or so Jewish families in Grudziadz, every kid counts when you have to compete with the "fascist" Beitar. I am coaxed to put up a good fight at home to get the OK for my joining the Hanoar-Hatzioni. One day, Kraina concocts an argument for me to join their group, which goes like this: the musical daughter of "our professor of music" Hass (he is the pride of the Jewish community) ought to compose a song for the Hanoar Hatzioni, and ought to teach it to the cub scout *kvutza* (troop), which she surely ought to join. Inspired, I fly home as if my book bag acquired wings. And I start writing this song:

Over there upstairs, in the little room,
there is much tumult and noise!
It's the Hashomer boys and the Hashomer girls,
who are happily carrying on, etc…*

* Author's translation from Polish.

Yes, I do write these words, a lyric to the melody of a lively polka tune. Yes, I do present the song to Heniek, the handsome leader of the cub-scout *kvutza*. But no, I am not allowed to join the Hanoar, not even after I try a sit-down strike on the window sill. "You are not one of their kind," says Mom. "Your place is with children from better homes." Oh how I hate the kids from "better homes," all of them except Lilka, who shares my feelings. So, here and there, she and I sneak out into the *podworko* to hang around the periphery of the in-group. This "cool gang," however, shows little regard for the two bumpkins whose parents think themselves to be "pish-posh-aristocracy."

During the High Holidays, most of the kids escape into the backyard of the synagogue after the obligatory stay inside the synagogue. Here again, I hang out with the in-group, and although they behave as if I were not one of them, I don't give up because I have no other group to which I can belong.

It is in the *heder* (the Hebrew school) of our synagogue that I also come in contact with the Jewish youngsters of our town. Unlike other strictly Orthodox synagogues, here boys and girls study the Talmud (the book of rabbinical commentaries, also civil and rabbinical law), the Humash (the Bible), and modern Hebrew, together. Mr. Eichman, the new Hebrew teacher who came to us from Warsaw, introduces us to the modern Hebrew language, which is now in use in Palestine. We not only study the Holy Books, using this modern *Sefardi* version of Hebrew, but also learn to read, write, and speak the language. Unfortunately, I commit a faux pas in one of my earlier Hebrew classes from which I develop an aversion to Hebrew school. The awkward moment happens during the reading of the Bible when I raise my hand and ask what the word *bris* (circumcision) means. I haven't yet been exposed to the rites of circumcision in my family, and I am, therefore, naive as to the impropriety of asking about such things in front of preteen boys. As could be expected, the boys react with explosive laughter and a long-lasting aftermath of giggling.

After my goofiness, I find it difficult to attend the Hebrew school, but in time, all is forgotten and I once again enjoy a friendly acceptance among my classmates. In fact, during the last year of my Hebrew classes, my parents allow me to join the boys in an old-fashioned Polish *kulik* (sleigh-ride) in the wooded countryside, organized for us by the Jewish community. Even though the boys pull my braids and play other tricks on me during the exhilarating ride through the snow, I finally feel that I am accepted by the group.

Ever since my fallout with Dondon I have missed having a girlfriend, a best friend, which Dondon was for me. Yes, I do miss having a pal. And during my first year of the junior Gimnazjum (7th grade) my wish is fulfilled when Stela Dymentman and her brother Ignac come to Grudziadz from Warsaw. Stela enters my class and we soon become very close friends. Stela's father has a small hat factory, and the foreman of the factory gives us cute, small sample hats when we visit there. I am immensely impressed with Stela. In class, she is unafraid to speak out of turn, totally undeterred by the stern looks and chastising words of our teachers. In the *podworko* she flirts with boys who are much older than she is, and her cutting remarks stop these boys from lording it over her. She is also the mistress of her own doings at home. I love to visit her home because her parents show no parental dominance over their children. They do not establish taboos for them, nor do they classify their friends based on the social standing of their families. In Stela's family you can just be yourself and do as you please.

Stela was born and raised in Warsaw, but even though she is a big city girl, she never deprecates me for my provincialism. I feel more sure of myself in the company of others, even in the company of the gang of the *podworko*, when Stela is with me. I am so charmed by Stela that, one day, I finally let her talk me into playing hooky from school. We head for the meadows along the Vistula, we lie about our age and con an old watchman into letting us go rowing in one of his boats. Then we are swept downstream by the currents so quickly that the watchman has to row over and pull us back into the boat basin. I feel great! When a few young Jewish people show up at the boat basin, Stela asks them to pose for a photo with the two of us sitting on their shoulders. So here we are; two girls who allow themselves to be photographed sitting on the shoulders of grown men while playing hooky from the Gimnazjum of Maria Bilewicz Pilsudska, whose girls are forbidden to socialize with boys! Stela's brother, Ignac, writes the required parental notes for us explaining our absence. Sure enough, I am believed to be so reliable a student that no one suspects that I would ever play hooky from school, and my aura extends to cover my friend as well. As a result of that trust, our absence notes are accepted without scrutiny. And of course, we later brag about our "date" and show off with our photos to the gang at the *podworko*. We attempt to impress our peers by professing to believe in "free love" (whatever this new philosophy meant—we weren't sure—and whatever it was supposed to suggest from our risqué photo poses!)

Stela flunks her finals, she is left behind, and in my second year of Gimnazjum (8th grade) I am again the only Jewish girl in a class whose "in" crowd does not include me.

By the time I begin to attend my second grade of the junior Gimnazjum, my Jewish consciousness has been nurtured by the increasing display of anti-Semitism. No longer do I feel comfortable sharing my hopes for Palestine with my Polish classmates; especially not after my friend Lilka tells me that someone covered a page of her notebook with a large inscription that read: "Jews get out of our Poland and go to Palestine!" I now listen to my parents' accounts of a pogrom (organized persecution of an ethnic group) in Przytyk, of the mandating of "Jewish seats" at Polish universities, and of the attacks on Jews by the Endeks—the young hoodlums of the Polish right-wing National Democratic Party. Full of apprehension, I stare at the pickets in front of Jewish stores, pickets bearing signs saying: "Don't Buy From the Jews" or "Buy Our Own Merchandise from Our Own Merchants!" Now I feel at home only within the Jewish area of Grudziadz, the area encompassing the Jewish Community Center, the Hebrew school and the synagogue. The Jewish *podworko* has become my refuge and now I am allowed to go there more often than before. My parents themselves become much more involved with the Jewish community. My father donates his free time to the organizing of a mandolin orchestra of young Jewish adults, and I become the orchestra's accompanist. My mother joins the Synagogue Sisterhood and she eagerly participates in their various functions, luncheons, and celebrations. During some of these celebrations, my sister exhibits her talents as a prima-ballerina, dressed in dazzling costumes handcrafted by my mom.

In my third grade of the junior Gimnazjum (9th grade), I am allowed to attend Friday afternoon youth dances organized at the Jewish Community Center. Mom remodels her old brown georgette dress for me. Alas, not one of the boys ever asks me for a dance, so I dance with Stela and some of the other girls. Most of the boys of my age don't dance anyway, but I do dream of being asked to dance by the handsome big boys like Heniek, who is now the leader of the Hanoar Hatzioni, or Ilek, who is the leader of Beitar and the captain of the Jewish soccer team, or Hela's blond brother, Max. Well, the handsome guys whose attention I covet at least give me a friendly greeting when I appear at the dances, and that feels good! Big Max gives me a big smile that shows his dimples and his very even white teeth and says, "Hello Reniusia!" And I read in his smile: "You are one of us."

In 1965, I revisit the shadows at the former Jewish area of Grudziadz. I sadly cross the littered vacant lot where the Jewish Community Center, the Hebrew school and the podworko used to be. I walk along Groblowa Street to the spot where Schleifer used to have his grocery store in which we bought our Passover supplies. I walk to the lot where Kuba's father used to sell the coals to heat our homes. I pause at the clearing where our little synagogue used to stand, and I wonder if at least some young people, who hung out in its backyard, did survive the Holocaust. Only in 1984 will I be able to find that out...

In the spring of 1984, my husband and I participate in the Gathering of Holocaust Survivors in Washington, D.C., and I initiate a computer-search for survivors from Grudziadz. To my disbelief, the computer lists the address and telephone number of Hela!

Back at home, I telephone Hela and leave this message on her answering machine: "This is Rena Hass, please Hela, call me as soon as you can." Hela tells me later that she nearly fainted when she heard my voice. I learn from her that several of the other kids from our podworko did indeed survive, among them Hela's sister and her two brothers (including Max, who unfortunately died later on in England), Heniek, Kuba, Ilek, and lastly, my friend Lilka. Unbelievably, eight of the young people whom I came to regard as "my own people" survive the Holocaust! Most of us, through the years, remain close to one another. Hela teases me and says, "Your parents were the stuck-up kind, but you were one of us despite that." I very happily agree with her.

I do not find my Stela nor others from Grudziadz, however, among the survivors of the Holocaust...

"WHERE SHALL I GO? FOR I HAVE NO HOME…"

A letter from my grandmother to my uncle in Palestine. Dolo is my father. (My translation from Polish.)

Brzezany, May 18, 1938

Our dearest Zyguniu !

Our greetings to you in the sunny Haifa of the land of Am Isroel (the Nation of Israel)! Yes, we are getting old, my arthritic hands are aching all the time and my diabetes is getting worse, but I don't complain…Oy, my heart hurts when I think of my poor son, Dolo.* The greatest musician that our Brzezany has ever produced, and now he has to be *afn tsures* (Yiddish, in a heap of trouble). Please, Zygunciu, do what you can to bring him to Palestine, maybe he can play there in Hubermans's Orchestra…he is now a full-fledged professor of music, but these German murderers are throwing him out…Your father has already pleaded with our Brzezany Rabbi, who knows an important rabbi in Amsterdam, to try and help our Dolo get out of Poland. But how does a poor Jewish musician get from Poland to Amsterdam? So please, Zygcio, it is up to you to help your older brother…
Your Mama

*Dolo is derived from the name Adolf.

Like the most valuable treasures, the worn letters of my parents and grandparents were safeguarded by my Israeli and American uncles and aunts. And when I have read these precious letters, my parents' and grandparents' cries for help dug deeply into my consciousness. They brought to mind a 1938 Yiddish song, a song I later heard in the camps. And with the memory of the song about a Jew in search of a home, the eyes of my pained soul saw the unshaven sorrowed face of my father as he mounted the steps of a moving van. It was the moving van that took the possessions of our Grudziadz home into the unfamiliar streets of Bialystok at the end of the memorable summer of 1938.

There is a sizable expatriate German community in Grudziadz and its environs, perhaps some 40,000 people in this town of 67,000 inhabitants. They are mostly Lutherans, the majority being either merchants or farmers. They do not mingle with the Polish people, and their children go to their own German schools. The complex of German Community buildings comprises the *Deutsche Buehne* (the German Theater), the elementary school, the Community Center and finally the imposing building of the junior and senior divisions of the German Gimnazjum, *Die Deutsche Hoch-Schule*. The German complex stands near the city park where we often go walking with my mom and dad. Most of the Germans live in either this area or in an area near Grudziadz's northern suburb of Tarpno. Ironically, an old iron gate stands near the many German homes in Tarpno whose inscription, in both Hebrew and German, identifies it as the gate of a Jewish ghetto! The gate must date back to the times when the Jews of Germany were forced to live in ghettos on the outskirts of towns. It is also possible that this Grudziadz Ghetto dates back to the Polish princes who governed these pre-Baltic lands of Pomorze, prior to the capture of these lands by Prussia in the 17th century. Perhaps the Folksdeutsch community here dates back to these distant times as well, since Pomorze has remained "the Corridor" between the West Prussian and East Prussian princedoms throughout its history.

My dad's German friends enter the scene of my childhood quite early.

Herr (Mister) Schumann, a retired teacher, gives me free German lessons because my dad doesn't charge him for the violin lessons of his daughters. I am having fun going up to Herr Schumann's fifth floor apartment because, unlike ours, his apartment house has an elevator! There isn't much fun, though, in copying old-fashioned "polite young lady's" phrases or proverbs, all written in the Old German script. But Herr Schumann does teach me German folk songs, and I do like these. One of the children's folk songs, *"Ein Maenlein schtaeht im Walde, gantz schtill und schtum, es hat von roten-Purpur ein Maentelein um…"* is about a little munchkin in a bright red coat who is left standing all alone in the woods. I especially like one of Goethe's poems set to the charming song: *"Sah ein Knab' ein Roeslein stehen, Roeslein auf der Heide…"* in which a finger-prick is meant to have the victim remember the prickly rose (or girl?) who did the pricking…

Thanks to Herr Schumann, I learn that the throaty German language can become soft and sonorous when it is spoken by a kind person. (I didn't know at that time that one day I would hear a different German language, a threatening language shouted out by men wearing threatening uniforms.) Yes, I truly get to like Herr Schumann, even more so when I overhear my parents say that Herr Schumann is a Social-Democrat who remains friendly to the Jewish people even when Nazism emerges among the Germans of Grudziadz.

Fraulein (Miss) Kalmukoff is my dad's pianist for the Operetta performances and his own solo performances staged at the German theater. Fraulein Mundt, who limps badly, is Miss Kalmukoff's friend, and the two become frequent guests at our home. Wanda tells me, in secret of course, that the two spinster-ladies have a crush on my dad. And well they should! Dad is a handsome and charming man who admonishes Fraulein Kalmukoff for her errors at the piano with a disarming gentleness. (Not, I notice, with the harshness with which he scolds me for my errors when I later become his pianist!)

I start my piano lessons with Fraulein Kalmukoff in fifth grade, soon after Dad finds it hopeless to teach me to play the violin. I run to Miss Kalmukoff's home for my weekly piano lessons, frequently late and without a handkerchief for my chronically running nose. The good Fraulein often lends me one of her own handkerchiefs and tells me that it must be returned nice and clean. I always play my scales first, Czerny's exercises next, then my "music piece," whatever it might be. My teacher can always tell when I haven't practiced for the lesson, but she seldom reproaches me for it. She approves of my school uniform but not of my shoes, which are usually in need of a shine. Fraulein Kalmukoff speaks with me in German but she occasionally asks me to teach her a few Polish words. She is delighted when I help her pronounce some Polish tongue-twisters. The Polish word for the beetle, *chrzaszcz*, is her favorite.

At a later time, Miss Kalmukoff lets me play the piano accompaniment music written for me by my father. In fact, she is the one who corrects my rendition of the *Berceuse Slave* and other semi-classical pieces that Dad and I prepare for our house parties. On one occasion, Fraulein Kalmukoff asks me to sing along with my piano accompaniment of the Yiddish song *Eli, Eli, Lamah Azaftani* (Oh God, oh God, why have Thou forsaken me?), a song about the centuries' long brutal humiliation, religious persecution, and murder perpetrated against the Jewish people. I can see that this German lady can understand some of the Yiddish lyrics and that she is at a loss for words. She finally whispers, "*Gott, wie traurig es ist* (God, how sad it is) ..."

"Yes," I add, "*Eli Eli* is a sad song because it describes the ageless suffering of the Jewish people."

But my music teacher's compassion for the Jewish people is short-lived. During later years, Fraulein Kalmukoff stops asking me to play my dad's accompaniment music for her and I begin to sense an estrangement between the two of us. I must finally own up to the fact that I am a Jewish student of a German teacher who does not relate to my growing Jewish consciousness. And both Fraulein Kalmukoff and the limping Fraulein Mundt eventually stop visiting our home.

Not only does my dad work as a musician for the German community, but also as the teacher of their children. Initially he teaches music only at the level of elementary grades, for which he qualifies by passing a primary level exam at his Alma Mater, the University of Lwow. My dad finds it difficult to study the various subjects of pedagogy for his exam, probably because he was never a good student. He used to brag that in his youth, one of his law professors at Lwow passed him when he heard him play his violin. Somehow, he does pass this primary level exam but Mom says the secondary and university level tests will be much harder. And both of my parents fear that the anti-Semitic professors who score these tests at Lwow may be prejudiced against Jewish candidates.

My mother's letter to her American relatives about Dad's job. (My translation from Polish.)

Grudziadz, June 7, 1936

My dear ones,

It has been some time since I have written to you. So much has happened in our lives that I found it hard to write. I may have mentioned to you that when they introduced the sound movies here, Dolo (Rena's father) could no longer find work as an orchestra conductor in the silent movies. He was granted a certificate to teach music on the elementary levels, but he still has to pass another pedagogy (exam) to get a teaching certificate for the secondary and higher levels, and that will be tough. Surely you know how they discriminate against Jews at the Polish Universities where these exams are given! In the meanwhile, Dolo went through a long search and many refusals (because he is a Jew) and finally found a job in the German Gimnazjum. We thought this would end our hardships and that our daily bread would be assured, but now with Hitler around, our livelihood has been threatened again. The director of the German Gimnazjum has been doing his utmost to keep Dolo at his school but the local Nazi Party has been undermining his efforts. We are now sure that Dolo's job will not last more than one or two years, and I don't dare to think of what awaits us later…
Your Esterka

Needless to say, Dad has to work very hard when he prepares for the advanced level exam, but at least he seems to have a bit of fun with the adolescent psychology part. With a cunning smile on his face, he tells me that now he understands why I have been so negative and stubborn and that he expects me to become even harder to deal with when I become a true adolescent.

For some reason, Mom feels that Dad has little faith in himself, that he doubts his ability to pass the exam and that he needs help. There perhaps is someone who could help Dad—a Jewish professor of philosophy at Lwow, Dr. Balaban. So, my sister and I are left in our maid's care while Mom goes to Lwow to talk to Professor Balaban. With Mom gone, Dad makes my life more difficult. He seldom lets me hang out with the gang in the *podworko,* and when I visit my Polish friend Dondon, he keeps asking if the two of us aren't perhaps seeing boys on the sly. We, of course, plead innocence but I sense Dad's suspicion that Dondon and I are up to something. (The truth of the matter is that we do meet with the three boys from the *podworko*— Adek, Kuba, and Beniek—high up along the Vistula.)

My father's letter to his American relatives. (My translation from Polish.)

Grudziadz, May 3, 1937

My dear ones,

Yes, thanks to my director, I will keep my job for another year, but what do I do later? As a Jew, I cannot get a teaching job in a Polish school… I would surely like to go to Palestine but that would take a lot of money, and where would we get that money? The few dollars that we have saved became devalued because of the depression here and anyway, how could I get our money out from a Swiss or German Bank now?
Your Dolo

Mom finally comes back from Lwow and assures Dad of her success with Dr. Balaban. My father indeed passes the advanced level exam in Pedagogy, perhaps really as a result of Mom's intervention. Subsequently, Dad also passes an exam in Music Education, which allows him to get a job at the German Gimnazjum. And that is precisely where my dad's troubles soon begin.

Plischke is a most promising student of my dad. He is the first violinist in Dad's orchestra at the Gimnazjum, and in the afternoons Dad gives him violin lessons at our home. My father meticulously searches out errors in

Plischke's violin technique and he corrects his playing with a soft: "Falsch! Falsch! (Wrong! Wrong!)" whenever he is even slightly off key. My dad seems to care for the boy and keeps talking about his talent and good character at our dinner table.

Left to right: Rena, Ernestina Schepper-Hass,
Izabela (Zula) Hass, Adolf (Dolo) Hass

At the Gimnazjum, however, troubles start brewing. Dad complains to us that some of his students refuse to march with the wind instruments band with which my dad ushers in the various sports events of the Gimnazjum. As for Dad's colleagues, he feels ill at ease with them because they often hush their talking when he enters the teachers' room. And some of the students now come to his class wearing the brown Nazi uniforms with swastikas on their sleeves. Most students no longer come to Dad for their violin lessons, but Plischke keeps coming until the end of Dad's final year at the German school.

(Is there a chance that Plischke will some day be among the German soldiers who will occupy Bialystok ? Will it be Plischke who will circumspectly inquire about Herr Hass at that time? Would Plischke want to visit with his Jewish professor? We will never find out…)

My parents' 12th wedding anniversary is the last one they celebrate with Dad's German friends. Viennese coffee and luscious tortes, liqueurs, and nuts are once again served at our big dining room table. My sister, bedecked in her ballerina outfit, dances to the tune of Dad's violin and my piano, and the guests graciously applaud the performance of the Hass family. But Mom later tells us that she could sense something untoward in the air at this last get-together, and Dad's German friends cease visiting us soon afterwards. In fact, none of our Polish gentile friends visit us during the late 1930s either—except of course for Aunt Zosia and Wanda.

My family now resorts to socializing with the parents of my Jewish friends Lilka, Julek Minc, and Fredek Hertz, whom Lilka and I affectionately call Ferdek (a little horse, a Yiddish-Polish hybrid). Fredek believes that it isn't Zionism, but rather Marxism that offers the answers to the problems of the Jews, who now face a rising Fascism. He lauds the heroism of the American Lincoln Brigade in Spain, and he believes that Polish Jews should fight Fascism in Spain, rather than fighting the British and Arabs in Palestine. Oddly enough, Fredek's mom is a flaming redhead (which is unpopular in the Poland of our day), whom Lilka and I mockingly refer to as "our red squirrel." (It will take the birth of my redheaded son to make me appreciate the beauty of Mrs. Hertz's hair!)

Around 1937, my family becomes involved in Grudziadz Jewish Community Center's affairs. There, Father organizes a young adults' mandolin orchestra and I become the orchestra's pianist. Mom joins the Synagogue Sisterhood, for whose luncheons and soirees she prepares all kinds of goodies. My sister prepares her best dance recitals for these affairs. Yet the mood at home is somber. One can tell that something is up, because Mom and Dad now often speak Yiddish to one another so that we and the maid can't understand what they are saying. Letters go to Brzezany and elsewhere, and many letters come from the United States and Palestine, Brzezany and Bialystok. I sense that something is about to change in our lives.

My father's letter to his relatives in America. (My translation from Polish.)

Grudziadz, April 12, 1938

My dear ones,

I am also begging—in the enclosed second letter here—for Srulek (another relative in New York) to send us a good affidavit (a pledge of support), one that would cover all of us: Esterka, the children and myself. I have previously asked my uncle in California for help but he claims that he can only send a single affidavit for me alone. He claims that he has already sent family affidavits to Vienna for his two sisters and their children there. And how could I go to America alone? Who would take care of Esterka and my children? The times are now so uncertain, we may soon be at war here in Poland and I would be cut off from my family, God knows for how long! Please, Bunio (my cousin in New York), do everything possible to get a family affidavit for us from anyone out there...and please hurry! I will lose my job in two months and then we simply must get out of here! Times are bad for the Jews in Poland now and American relatives have been helping out, so please don't you let us perish. We can always somehow manage in America. I can surely earn our daily bread with my violin, and we won't be a burden there to anyone. Send affidavits for all of us, get us out of this hell, please!

Your Dolo

Toward the end of the 1937-1938 school year, the principal of the German Gimnazjum asks Dad to see him after classes. At home, Mom is pacing the bedroom floor and keeps on anxiously looking out through the window for Dad, who is very late for dinner. Both my sister and I are desperately trying to concentrate on our homework, but we can't help peeking out the bedroom window to see if Dad is coming home. He finally shows up and somberly announces: "That is it." He and Mom disappear into the bedroom. They talk there and we periodically hear Mom's Yiddish "*Oy, vey is meer,*" which we know to mean "woe is me." Dinner is late and no one eats very much anyway, not even me, the chronic glutton.

Dad's eyes are inflamed and teary when he later shows us his letter of dismissal. He translates the letter into Polish. It is from Herr Hildebrandt, the principal, and says: "I very much regret to have to terminate the

Letter from Dolo Hass to the Kartins in New York pleading for affidavits for the family to get them out from "this hell."

employment of Herr Hass at the German Gimnazjum, where Herr Hass has rendered excellent service to his students as their teacher of music, as conductor of the school orchestra, and as conductor of musical performances of the German Community Center. I have been advised by Berlin authorities who finance Folksdeutsch education abroad, that, for purely racial reasons, the Jew Adolf Hass may not teach in German schools anywhere."

My vacations of the summer of 1938 are my last vacations in Brzezany, and I will never see my grandparents again. I come back to Grudziadz to help my parents pack for our exodus to the unfamiliar city of Bialystok and to say goodbye to my Grudziadz friends. During my last few days in Grudziadz I walk the streets that I know and love, and I try to memorize the many sights, the many corners, buildings, and stores that will forever remain in my memory. I say goodbye to my school, to the *podworko* and to the little synagogue; but most of all, I say goodbye to the home that I am about to lose forever.

On the day we leave, my dad hitches a ride in the moving van that will transport our possessions to Bialystok. My mom, my sister and I take the train. As the train takes off towards our new home in Bialystok, I look at the landscape—crowned by the watchtower high above the right shore of the Vistula—and I know that I will always miss my Grudziadz, my hometown. I close my eyes and I see my dad entering the cab of the moving van. I see his eyes and I read in those eyes the anxiety of homelessness that I also feel in myself.

Oh my dad, did your soul sing, in those sad moments, the song of the wandering Jew, "*Voahin Sol ikh Geyn? As Ikh Hob Nisht Kein Heim* (Where shall I go ? For I have no home) ..."

In the beginning, nothing in Bialystok feels like home. The crowded streets of the Jewish areas, a lack of town squares with surrounding greenery, unattractively cluttered stores—all of these appear alien to me. My dad does his best to provide us with a reasonably comfortable apartment and a reasonably comfortable living, but something is missing. Perhaps it is the sight of the blue Vistula—or perhaps it is the secure feeling we had in our home in Grudziadz. Bialystok does not look like a place where we can settle down for good. But then, where else shall we go?

Little do we know that soon we will lose our new home—and Bialystok will become a place of transit into hell.

I LONG TO SEE BRZEZANY AGAIN

I have quite often visited my cousin Martin and his family in Connecticut. Like most of my relatives, and myself, Martin was born and raised in Brzezany, a small town in the southeastern sub-Carpathian Podole, also known as Eastern Galicja. Since the late 17th century and until the 1918 treaty of Versailles, Poland's Galicja remained within the Austro-Hungarian Empire. Martin told me that thanks to the Austrian Emperor Franz Joseph, the families of Jews of Brzezany escaped the rape and murder committed by the invading hordes of the Jew-hating Ukrainian Cossacks. The good emperor allowed transports of Jewish families to find refuge in Budapest and in Vienna and to remain there until the end of the war, and even later. I finally understood my "Vienna connection" and the origin of my parents' fluent Viennese German.

Even though Martin's family emigrated to America, Martin still visited his grandparents in Brzezany, and I remember meeting him during one of my early vacations there. In fact, he and I used to go walking, holding hands, in Brzezany's Market Square. He dazzled me with his fascinating stories about America.

During my recent visits to Connecticut, Martin showed me a hand-drawn town plan of Brzezany's shtetl, the old Jewish areas centered around the Market Square. I felt a nostalgic squeeze around my heart and said that I would like to visit Brzezany again someday. "There is a Brzezaner Society in New York," Martin said. "They might be able to help you, but then, you are not from Brzezany, so why do you want to go there?" In his letter from

Mexico, my cousin Manio said the same thing: "You are not from Brzezany, Brzezany is now in the Ukraine. It is a dangerous place to go to. Why would you need to go there?" Even more discouraging was the Memorial Book of Brzezany that my cousin Nathan and other Brzezany immigrants assembled in Israel; I discovered that I didn't even appear in that book! And my relatives in Poland seconded the sentiments of the other cousins: Why would one want to go to the now Ukrainian Berezani where Polish and Jewish visitors have been repeatedly harassed by hooligans?

History has definitely wronged me by permitting Poland to cede its Brzezany to the Ukrainians. And now I who was born in a Polish Brzezany must consider a visit to an unfriendly Ukrainian Berezani...But regardless of all the inauspicious circumstances, I have wanted to go there. Oh, how I have longed to see the Brzezany of my preteen summers. And in my daydreams, I have revisited Brzezany many a time...

My sister wants to know how far Grudziadz is from Brzezany, so I take out a map of Poland and we can see that if you were to fly in a straight line,

Grudziadz was near the northwest corner of Poland, Brzezany near the southeast corner and Bialystok in northcentral Poland.

Brzezany would be some 400 miles from Grudziadz. It must be farther than that by train. Our little town of Brzezany lies between Lwow and Tarnopol, southeast of the old Polish capital of Krakow. Tarnopol itself lies near the Soviet border and Lwow is about 50 miles northwest of it.

I point out to my sister the eastern chain of the Carpathian mountains that stretch out directly south of Brzezany. "You could take the River Dniestr to the mountain town of Kolomyja, and from there you could climb the mountains to the resort towns of Jaremcze, Tatarow, and Worochta," I tell her. This impresses my sister because she knows that the mountain people, *Huculi*, who wear lively costumes and dance the *kolomyjka,* come from these eastern Carpathians. "Isn't that the Rumanian border there, straight down from Worochta?" she asks. "Yes it is." My sister now knows that I will travel far during this summer, really far away from her, nearly to the end of Poland!

An auspicious happening inaugurates my summer travel to Brzezany. Grandpa Leon introduces our family to the family of a train conductor who was transferred from Brzezany to Grudziadz. His family offers to take me along when they go back to Brzezany for their summer vacations. My dad remembers the loss of his wallet to the train pickpockets during one of the Warsaw train changes on the way to Brzezany, so he is surely glad he doesn't have to take me there. Henceforth, I will get to spend three consecutive summers of my junior Gimnazjum years in Brzezany, and this will be heaven!

Gone are the days of getting sick on the train, and now I enjoy the sights during the train ride and changing of the trains in Warsaw and Lwow. We have to travel for two days and one night, and I manage to snooze sitting up in the Warsaw-Lwow train crowded by tourists. Here and there passengers leave the train, and our friends' children and I can stretch out for a bit of sleep. A local train that stops at every town and village takes us from Lwow to Brzezany. Now I can see fields covered with wheat, heavy with ripe golden kernels, and dotted with red poppies and blue corn flowers. I see peasant huts topped by straw gables, huts with storks perched on their chimneys, backyards with geese and chickens, and children whose towheads are bleached white by the sun. At some stations, barefooted peasant women in white head kerchiefs (*babushkas*) sell blueberries and wild strawberries in taro leaves, hot corn, and squares of hot *bulbenik* (potato bread). At other stations, we deboard and drink cool well-water from a wooden ladle dipped in a pail.

When the train slows down and goes around the shores of a large pond, the *staw*, I know that we've come to Brzezany. Grandpa Leon is at the station with a big smile under his reddish-grey moustache, and he soon gives me a scratchy kiss and a warm Galicjan-Polish, "*Jak sie masz* (how are you), *Niusienka*?"

During my first summer vacation I stay at my grandparents' new home. They no longer live in the third floor apartment that I remember from my earlier childhood, the one with an outhouse at the end of a long *ganek* (wooden walkway). Now I will stay next door to the Ukrainian Community Center on the first floor of a house that has outside toilets flushed with water drawn from a barrel.

After my arrival, Grandpa and I follow Station Street to the Market Square and turn left into the street that leads to the suburb Adamowka. One block further and there, with her elbows perched on the window sill, is my smiling Grandma Ida who will soon take me into her arms. And I, Renusia, the Queen of the Day, can't stop babbling!

Grandma Ida and Granpa Leon Hass

There is always an awesome feast on the day of my arrival, a feast of Jewish-Ukrainian delicacies seldom produced by my mother. Potato *pirogen* (dumplings) and *knishes* (turnovers) alternate with *kasha varnichkes* (noodles with groats—crushed oats) and *bulbenik* (potato loaf). And, of course, there is the yellow corn-on-the cob, homemade pickles and home-baked rolls with fresh sweet butter; a preview of Grandma's meals that will soon fatten me beyond recognition. But because I am terribly forgetful in matters of Jewish religious dietary regulations, eating at Grandma's presents me with a daily challenge in using the dairy and meat utensils, which must never be mixed.

I sleep on the sofa in the living room where my beloved picture-clock plays its hourly gondolier chimes from the Venice Tower. In the morning, Grandma's Ukrainian maid wakes me up to a breakfast of fresh eggs with corn bread and milk, which she prepares for me on a charcoal stove. There will also be a take-along "second breakfast" of buttered bread, homemade sour pickles, and a dessert of local peaches and cherries, all of which I am to eat later at the *staw* (the pond). I usually stay at the *staw* until the early afternoon when it is time for dinner. (Alas, I will learn in the future, that this beautiful pond, created by the damming of the river Zlota Lipa, will be drained, and its bottom will be drilled for oil. How could Brzezany ever exist without its staw?)

Late afternoons in Brzezany are spent walking around the town's promenade, the *corso*. I usually go walking there until the evening, when it is time for supper. While I stay at Grandma's, my routines stay pretty much the same, unless we go visiting relatives or have picnics in the country.

Once or twice my grandpa takes me to visit his bedridden brother at the nursing home, and that visit is an awkward one. My great-uncle slurs his words so badly that I can't understand what he says, and I don't think he can quite understand what I say, or who I am. It surely is a relief to get out of the nursing home and go walking in the streets of Brzezany with Grandpa Leon. People greet him with respect and it seems that everyone knows my grandpa Leon. Maybe it's because he used to be the clerk at the County Court, or perhaps he has earned their respect because of his dignified demeanor, his well-pressed pants, polished shoes, and elegant walking stick. I feel proud to be walking alongside my grandpa Leon and to see people take their hats off to him and give his granddaughter a friendly smile.

I meet my cousin Manio soon after I arrive in Brzezany. He is my first cousin "once removed." That is, he is my dad's cousin who is much younger than my dad. Grandma Ida asks Manio to take me out for the *corso* walks in the late afternoons and early evenings. The *corso* of Brzezany is little more than the streets that border the market square. It is here that small groups of friends, mostly Jewish, exchange their gossip. It is also here that the girls cast flirtatious glances at the boys. But our Manio is a very special person along the *corso* because he plays a mean guitar and sings "cool" songs there. All that makes me feel and act very grown up, because I am privileged to be part of his gang of friends. I wear my best clothing and pin my braids around my head (the way my older cousin Sylwinka does), and I keep glancing around to see if I am noticed. What joy it is to be walking like that ! Unlike the nonexistent social contacts between girls and boys in Grudziadz, boys and girls here don't have to worry about openly socializing with one another.

I learn all of Manio's songs, songs that I remember forever. Manio's girlfriend comes from the nearby sugar-producing town of Chodorow, which is why she is nicknamed "Sugar Babe of Chodorow." I also like Manio's friend Mundek, who happens to be of short stature and is secretly nicknamed "the short-rear-ended Mundek."

Each *corso* walk incorporates a ritual of getting a scoop of ice cream and a cream-filled wafer at Vogel's candy store. Grandma continues to give me money for this treat during all my summers with her. Early on, Manio is sworn by Grandma to bring me home before supper—no matter what. My grandma is always waiting for us with her elbows on the window sill; and so my days in Brzezany go.

During my last summer in Brzezany I no longer spend much time walking with Manio and his gang. Both he and his friend Mundek are taking English lessons during the weekday afternoon hours. We often meet at the *corso* after their lessons and listen to their newly acquired English words and phrases. Manio, who is an orphan, tells me about Grandma Ida's brother, Uncle Barnie, who will soon bring Manio to California as his adopted son. As promised, Uncle Barnie does bring Manio to the United States. (I will not see my musical cousin again until 1968, when the two of us will meet at his home in Los Angeles.)

Swimming at the *staw* is a major attraction of my summer vacations in Brzezany. I walk to the *staw's* grassy beach called the glinka ("the clay" in Polish—perhaps the beach was originally a clay-landing which later became overgrown by grass.) There are always a lot of kids there, many of them of my age, who swim laps with me in the clear waters, and I soon develop the endurance of a strong swimmer.

My breakfast at Grandma's is so filling that I often fail to eat my "second breakfast," and I just leave the paper bag, with its contents untouched, in the grass of the *glinka*. But sure enough, one day my paper bag is brought back to Grandma, and I get to hear a sermon about poor Ukrainian children who go hungry while I waste food. I promise to change my ways but, as a rule, I don't eat the "second breakfast" now that my bulging tummy and breasts refuse to flatten under my woolen swimsuit. (On the other hand, it is because of these upper fatty protuberances that I can lie about my age, and thus get a bit of attention from older boys.)

On one occasion my grandma takes me to the baths. These, in reality, aren't quite baths, but rather a sauna. We sit on wooden benches, soap up with fibrous sponges, wash up in wooden troughs with hot water and then let the steam clean our bodies some more. Grandma and the other ladies whip their backs with bunches of twigs "to energize their circulation" (or so they believe!), and then pour cold water over their sweaty bodies. I shy away from the probing eyes of the older women who may be wondering if I am a budding woman, or still a kid who has a way to go. In turn, I am wondering if I will sag as they do when I am old? Will my hair thin out as theirs does? Will I have a belly that hangs down after having babies?

"Do the women in the sauna mind that it is a man who fills their water troughs?" I ask my grandma when we arrive home. "And is Brzezany's sauna its ritual *mikvah* (a pool which the ultra-Orthodox women use for the ritual monthly "dunking")?"

"To begin with," answers Grandma, "the attendant of the sauna does not have a habit of peering at naked women. And the sauna does have a *mikvah*, which is also used to dunk Christian women who have converted to Judaism. Perhaps my *goyishe* (assimilated) granddaughters from Grudziadz ought to also be dunked in the *mikvah*."

There are so many uncles and great uncles, aunts and great aunts, children and grandchildren in Brzezany that being introduced to them will not guarantee that I will remember their names in the future. Most of these relatives seem to be on my mother's side of the family, and Grandma Ida, who is my dad's mom, volunteers to take me around to meet them. I remember Great Aunt Royza, the sister of my dead Grandma Sara, because it was Royza's grandson Martin who came to visit Brzezany when I was small and who told me about America. And I remember Great Uncle Anschel, who is bound to "pull your leg," so you have to be careful what you say to him. We kids refer to Anschel's daughter Anna as "Anna, Anna *stara panna* (old maid, in Polish)." Of course, I will remember Great Aunt Baile because, on my way from the *staw*, I often stop at her candy store for a glass of seltzer. (Aunt Baile's daughter, Mincia, eventually emigrates to the United States and we will one day meet there and reminisce about the old times.)

My cousin and lifelong friend, Bela, and her brother Nathan are the grandchildren of another maternal great aunt of mine. In 1938, during my last summer in Brzezany, Bela and I become inseparable buddies. Bela is my age. Her brother Nathan is a few years older and does not bother us very much except when he meets me at the house of my older cousin Sylwinka, who is his good friend. It is only in Brzezany that I get to know my cousin Nathan, whom I find to be a charming and handsome boy. He incessantly talks about Zionism and Palestine, to which he will soon emigrate with his father. Although I will meet with Nathan in later years, both in the United States and in Israel, our friendship somehow never really develops.

I discover that Manio, who is Grandma Ida's nephew, has a sister, Linka, and a brother, Lusio. Lusio's wife is about to have a baby. I meet his big-bellied wife and wonder if the baby will come soon enough so that I can get to see it. The little Loncio does in fact come in time, and I get to know what *bris* (circumcision) is all about. I am invited to the *bris* reception, but they ask me to get out when the actual circumcision is performed. Waiting on the outside, I put my fingers into my ears, just in case.

Zula and Dusia, the daughters of Manio's sister Linka, are my favorite cousins. Although Zula is quite a bit younger than I am and Dusia is still a toddler, I do come to visit and play with my two little cousins.

During my second summer vacation in Brzezany I stay at the brand-new villa of my father's sister, Hela Finkelstein. Her husband Nysio is Brzezany's leading lawyer, and he often brings home eggs, chickens and other produce with which his Ukrainian farmland clients pay him for his services. The Finkelstein's villa has sinks, bathtubs, and flush toilets all with modern plumbing—luxuries heretofore unknown to most inhabitants of Brzezany. My stay in their villa starts with an unexpected bounty because, in the aftermath of the construction of the villa, the builders had to cut down a cherry tree, and now we can feast on the fruit.

I worship my beautiful older cousin Sylwinka and try to imitate her speech, her charm, and her wonderful rapport with grownups and peers alike. But I fail dismally at imitating Sylwinka, and she pokes fun at my attempts. Together with Aunt Hela, I go to the dressmaker where Sylwinka tries on dresses that are being made for her. envy the aura that surrounds the rituals of dressing my cousin in accord with the fashion dictates of the day. And, as we walk into town, people greet us and show as much respect to Aunt Hela and Sylwinka as they show to my grandfather. It seems to me that Aunt Hela speaks and behaves in an uppity-up manner, as if she were a Lady of the Court. I don't feel that I belong with this aunt and uncle who exude so much feeling of self importance, especially when my aunt says, "Your father could have finished his law studies if he didn't have this music- bug up his…. Well, now at least your father will be referred to as Pan Professor."

Sylwinka's little brother Tusio is a very serious boy. He is being groomed to become a pianist and Aunt Hela prods him all the time to practice his piano. For once I am thankful for my father's hands-off approach to my piano practicing, and I appreciate the fact that he is less rigid in his opinions and behavior than is his sister.

Sylwinka seldom goes walking with me in the *corso,* but when she does she does not look at the boys at all. She only stops to talk with the high-class young people with whom she acts in a lady-like manner. Only seldom do these high-class, rich young people seem to appear on the *corso,* and when they do, they congregate only with young people of their class. The girls of this exclusive group are often chaperoned by their mothers.

During my last summer in Brzezany, I again stay with my grandparents.

(Sylwinka has just graduated from the Gimnazjum and she and her family are spending the summer in the mountains.) Now I hang around with my cousin Bela and her friends. My grandma and I have now grown closer to one another, and I tell her about my *corso* successes and about the sorrows of leaving Grudziadz. My last day of summer vacation arrives, and it is a sad one indeed.

With a suntanned but worried face, I sit with my grandma in the living room, waiting to be taken to the railroad station. Apprehensively, I look at the packed valises at my feet and say, "I will always love you and miss you, Grandma. Can I sing my songs for you?

"You stayed with me all summer long," she says. "You now have only five minutes before you go away, and now you decide to sing for me? Shame on you! Well…go ahead, sing!"

My escort is late, so I sing Jewish songs, one after another. I sing my *Rebecca* song, my *Srulek* song, the *Shtetl Bendzin* song, and my *Der Rebbe in die Mikveh* song. I sing for my grandma for the first and last time during my last stay in Brzezany.…

What will become of my family and friends in Brzezany? During the Soviet occupation, Grandpa Leon dies of kidney failure in the spring of 1941. Uncle Nysio Finkelstein dies in the Ghetto of Brzezany before the Ghetto's annihilation in 1943. Bela and her mother survive the Holocaust, hidden on the farm of their Polish friends. Bela finishes dentistry in Germany and then comes to the United States.

The Ukrainian Black Guards carry out bloody pogroms of the Jews in the streets of Brzezany. During the final merciless slaughter, my grandma refuses to leave her home. The SS men beat her to death in her sickbed, and the Gentile neighbors hear, for a long time, the screams of my martyred grandmother. Those Jews of Brzezany who are not slaughtered on the spot are transported to Belzec, where they will be gassed to death. Aunt Hela and Sylwinka are among them. During the march to the transport train, my cousin Tusio attempts to escape and is gunned down.

Bela's friend, Hermina, survives and tells me about the murders perpetrated against the Jewish people of Brzezany. No other friends or relatives from Brzezany ever surface in the registers of the Holocaust survivors.

I will always long to see Brzezany one more time before I die, and I will, deep down, know why...

I BECOME AN ADOPTED BIALYSTOKER

Bialystoker Shtimme c/o
The Bialystoker Society
New York, NY

April 24, 1998

Gentlemen,

Mrs. Yetta E. suggested that I submit to you a song which I composed during the years of my confinement in the Bialystok Ghetto. The song is titled "Song of the Underground of the Bialystoker Ghetto"...I wish you to know that I am not a native of Bialystok but that I have become a proud adopted Bialystoker who shared the fate of my Bialystok brothers and sisters during the Holocaust. The people of Bialystok have become my people and I feel as if I belong with them and always will belong with them...
Yours truly,
Irene Shapiro

Yetta E. and I have been seeing each other for at least 40 years. We survived the Holocaust together and we've worked together at a high school in New York. Recently, the two of us attended a commemorative gathering of the Bialystok survivors of concentration camps. Yetta suggested I submit the song that I composed in Bialystok to the Bialystoker Shtime (The Voice of Bialystok), a weekly paper of the Bialystok Society in New York.

In addition to Yetta, I have been in contact with friends from Bialystok nearly from the day I arrived in the United States. In 1949 I worked as a Russian-English translator-typist for a firm that shipped parcels to the USSR. I discovered the whereabouts of my Bialystok classmate Ewa when a package was sent to her through our firm. From this point on, a network developed of schoolmates from my Bialystok High School. This network reconnected me with Sonia in Australia, Stela in Argentina, Fania in California, Hanka in Brazil, and finally Ewa who, in the late 1950s, emigrated from the USSR to Israel. Thus I reconnected with Bialystok.

After the loss of our home in Grudziadz, my family and I had a difficult time accepting Bialystok as our new home. But its kindhearted people readily adopted us, and we soon felt warmly about them as well. Our ties with the Jewish people of Bialystok became much stronger when we faced the adversities of the Soviet, and later of the German, occupation of the city. And in the concentration camps, my mom and I became "unsere Irke mit die Mame (our Irene and her mom, in Yiddish)" to the inmates from Bialystok.

Most of my friends in Bialystok were my schoolmates, and a few of these were destined to survive the Holocaust. The few who did survive became my adopted family and through the years we shared with each other the good and the bad in our lives. Through these connections, I cemented my allegiance to my adopted hometown of Bialystok.

We leave our home in Grudziadz and it takes us some time to believe that we belong in Bialystok. This city isn't lovable and it doesn't "grow on you" either. In fact, there is nothing really pretty about Bialystok. It is a typical textile factory town with small apartment houses along its main streets, Lipowa, Pilsudskiego, Sienkiewicza and Warszawska. There are Russian-style wooden cottages in its smaller streets and lanes. Off Warszawska Street there stands the Prince Branicki's mansion that became the residence of the Governors of the Province. The area around the mansion has landscaped greenery, unheard of in the rest of the city. Bialystok is a city of some 150,000 people. About 60,000 of them are Jewish; the rest are either Polish or Bielorussian Christians.

My parents and I live at the end of Lipowa Street near the distinctly modernistic Cathedral of St. Roch. Ours is the three-bedroom apartment on the mezzanine floor of a firehouse. The fire engines are housed in a garage next door and their wind instrument orchestra rehearses each evening in the hall above our heads. Staying with us in our smallest bedroom is a student who comes from a small town and who attends one of Bialystok's Jewish schools. The boarding fee supplements my folks' modest income, and so does my tutoring of a little girl who can't keep up with the demands of her grammar school.

My Grudziadz friend Stela visits us during the winter vacations, and we put her up in the boarder's room while he spends the school holidays with his folks. Stela teases me and says that I live in an ugly apartment in an ugly *Litvak* (Lithuanian-Jewish) town. But my friends soon manage to impress her because they are more cosmopolitan than are the guys of the Grudziadz's *podworko*. During my subsequent visit to Grudziadz I show off my big-city sophistication, but no one seems to be impressed with it. I guess my sophistication needs a little more practice.

After our arrival in Bialystok my folks befriend the Tartackis, a very kind and giving family. It was Mrs.Tartacka who found us our apartment and who kept bringing us food when we weren't yet set up for preparing our own meals. And now she continues to take care of a myriad of troublesome details. The Tartackis visit with us weekly and their friendship continues to grow as the months go by. Their daughter, Liska, becomes a most dependable singer in one of Dad's choral groups. I adore Mrs. Tartacka's sing-song Bialystoker Polish; it has an abundant admixture of the typical Litvak Yiddish sayings like, "*Nu, Ikh hob a Breire?* (Do I have a choice?)" or "*Shein, ogepatert, ogered* (All right, I had my say)."

During the late spring of 1938, we move to another apartment in Bialystok. Now we live in a fourth-floor walk-up, a three-bedroom apartment whose balcony overlooks the lower section of Pilsudskiego Street near the centrally located Kosciuszki Square. Like our earlier apartment, the new one doesn't compare favorably to the beautiful apartment we had in Grudziadz. You go through the kitchen in our new apartment to find the toilet; the bathtub is in the kitchen itself. But the front balcony is great fun to stand on, though a bit scary. You feel as if you are flying when you hang onto the balcony high up over the busy street. You can see people walk along the street all the way to Kosciuszki Square! Also great fun is the Macedonian store across the street where they sell *buza* and *kwas*, the two remarkable fermented Balkan drinks of mysterious origin. They also sell the greatest variety of halvah, nuts, and honey candies (some with poppy seeds and others with nuts, dates and raisins). Needless to say, my friends and I frequent that store almost daily after our classes.

There is a narrow lane called Wilcza near our building that leads into the Jewish district of Piaski. My school supplies are bought in Mr. Goodrich's store in Wilcza Lane, and the hot "bialys," bagels, and "plecels" eaten daily for breakfast are also bought in this lane. Farther down the lane stands the impressive building of the Great Synagogue of Bialystok.

My school, the Druskin's Gimnazjum, includes the grammar, junior (*male*) and senior (*Lyceum*) divisions of the Gimnazjum. (I entered the fourth grade of the junior Gimnazjum in Bialystok, which is equivalent to the sophomore year, or tenth grade, of American high schools.) Ours is a Grade A private Gimnazjum, the "A" implying that the Polish Ministry of Education has accredited the school for admitting its graduates to Polish universities. Druskin's students are Jewish but they are taught in Polish. Because its tuition is quite high, only the well-to-do parents can afford to send their sons and daughters to Druskin's Gimnazjum. The school, however, offers a few scholarships for the needy gifted students of each grade. My father teaches music at Druskin's and because of that, both my sister and I attend the school without having to pay tuition. Dad apparently cannot make a living by teaching only at Druskin's, so he also works at other Jewish private schools. (Bialystok has five private Jewish high schools, one of which teaches in Yiddish and one in Hebrew; the others teach their students in Polish.) There is one Polish State Gimnazjum but very few Jewish students attend there. My mother's brother Munio teaches history at the Hebrew Gimnazjum and my cousin Wolfus attends that school.

My Gimnazjum stands on the corner of Szlachecka and Polna Streets. I walk from my home on Pilsudskiego Street toward Szlachecka via the streets that are perpendicular to it. The elementary classes, the auditorium and the school offices are all in the lobby. The coatroom, bathrooms, and the *waibele's* ("little lady's" in Yiddish) candy stand are all in the basement, from which you also exit to the backyard. Part of the backyard is fenced off, and the school authorities flood that section during the winter to provide us with an ice-skating rink. The teachers' room and the humanities classes, including geography, are on the first floor. The sciences, math and language classes are on the second floor. There is a shop-shack in the back of the yard.

I follow the principal, Mr. Tilleman, into my first class of Polish language-arts. I face a distinguished looking Mr. Karczynski, a class full of inquisitive eyes and friendly faces of girls and boys (all Jewish, which I find hard to believe!). After introductions, the teacher resumes the class discussion and I am amazed at the vivaciousness and verbosity of my new classmates; one outdoes the other in arguing regarding the merit, or lack of it, of a Polish literary work under discussion. They talk, they argue with one another, and Mr. Karczynski seldom interjects a word. Where is the stiff Polish school decorum that I used to know—and depend upon? How am I going to compete with this gang of wiseguys? Bashfully, I push my braids into the back so that they don't become too obvious in this sea of trendy curly and straight hairdos, with not even a single set of braids! But I need not worry; the class is over and I become the object of a most friendly attention—invitations to sit near, to visit with and to walk to school with all kinds of kids! Maszka, Murka, Lilka—all of them covet my company, and the ruckus I cause goes on and on without end!

The next class is Latin, and I face the very distinguished looking Mr. Bergman. He lets me know that he is a friend of my family since he comes from—I can hardly believe it!—Brzezany, and that I better behave because he will tell on me. I end up sitting in the second row, surrounded by many of the girls who greeted me so warmly in the last class. My seat is right behind the two classroom "brains," Rachelka and Sara. Both are disadvantaged students who receive scholarships from the school. I later develop a great deal of empathy for these two girls because I identify with them. I wonder if they feel pangs of envy just as I do when they see the classy school uniform-dresses, the fine watches and fashionable white leather high boots of the other classmates, all of which they and I cannot afford?

The taller, and perhaps also older, girls sit farther back in our classes. So do most of the boys, who will always remain a bit aloof from the girls.

But I find it a novelty to see boys like the red-haired Rubin, curly-blond-haired Piorko, delicate-faced Lilek, and the handsomely robust Musio, right here in my class. And I find that at various times, I become captivated by a varying array of girls. First, I pal around with Hela and Nesia. Hela is my neighbor living around the corner from our first apartment in the firehouse. It is to Hela's house that I run away from home after my dad gives me a whack for being "fresh." And it is Hela's mom who gently persuades me to go back home and make peace with my father. Later on I am privy to Hela's confidential reports about her "dates" with her "steady boyfriend" Mejczyk, a boy-girl friendship that becomes both a novelty and a cause of envy for me.

I next become enthralled with Lilka, who is more mature than I am at that time and also very savvy in matters of sex-appeal and femininity. Soon, friendly female voices sound off a warning that I am about to be entrapped by someone who has long been the subject of unsavory gossip, so I sheepishly bow out of my relationship with Lilka.

Murka comes next. She is persuasive and provocative and is always surrounded by a few lieutenants. Murka knows everything about everybody who is anybody in our school. Maszka tags along with Murka, but I find her shy and rather withdrawn. I'm told this is because of the very ostentatious "nouveau riche" behavior of her mom, an object of gossip in our class. Maszka sits in our row of seats and it pains me to see her go to pieces when she is called on by the teachers.

I have nice "issue" talks with Tusia, Ewa and Sonia, and that will last for keeps: we will grow, mature, and still find in each other a sympathetic soul with whom it is always worthwhile to exchange ideas, or to just freely gab. Oh, how I like it here at Druskin's!

Most of the teachers here offer their students a challenge. Steckel is quite a physicist, Orlowski a demanding mathematician, Karlinska a so-so biologist, and Reifert a so-so geography teacher. Zawa Citron is an oh-la-la Francophile, and my dad soon gets to be known as a gifted music teacher. With me as his pianist, my dad brings to life a school orchestra and a chorus. Most of our choral songs are in Polish but we also sing lovely Yiddish and Hebrew songs, and of course the *Hatikvah* (Jewish national anthem) with which we open our assemblies. My dad works for hours arranging and teaching these and many other classical and folk songs in our school and in other schools, too. In addition to his schoolwork, Dad also gives violin lessons. I feel sorry for my overworked dad but I don't know how to tell him that, so I just do my bit as his pianist whenever he needs me. I continue with piano lessons but I don't practice enough to really master my playing. That, of course, upsets my pretty blond piano teacher but does not bother me at all. There is now more to my life than playing the piano.

Pretty soon, I catch up to the A-students of my class. I get to be known by many students of other classes, and finally the principal asks me to deliver a speech at one of our assemblies. My uncle, who teaches Polish at the Hebrew Gimnazjum, helps me write the speech. Thanks to him, the speech gets to be seeded with high-caliber words. I see the worry on Dad's face; he watches my lips to see if I will trip on some of these high-caliber words, but I do not. For my dad's sake, as well as for my own, I sail smoothly through the lengthy speech and then creep behind my classmates to calm my shaking, sweaty body. It appears that the speech made such an impression on the incumbent president of our Student Organization that, at the end of the current school year, she nominates me to run for the next year's presidency. I win the presidency but will never take office because Druskin's Gimnazjum will become a Soviet State School next year.

Druskin's is not only a school of serious academics, but also a fun school. We organize our own Saturday evening Student Shows for parents, students, and teachers. We stage tap-dance ensembles and sing humorous songs about our teachers (sometimes even sarcastic songs, as is the one about the high-heeled shoes of Mr. Druskin!) My own group, the "Singing Rewelersy Girls," belt out popular tunes while my dad sits in the audience and shakes his head with disapproval. What does he know about pop music!

But the greatest fun is to be had at our Friday dances after school, where I score a limited success with the boys. Not much—just a little success. Since our sophomore male classmates don't dance we just go on eyeballing the Juniors and the Seniors from within the safety of the Sophomore girls' group, and in desperation, we dance with one another. Finally, one day, I get to dance with two friendly Juniors, Izio and Yasha. I can see Hela's encouraging mime while I dance, because she and I just went through some of the latest "jazz steps." I guess Hela finds my debut satisfactory. Oh yes, I attend each and every Friday dance. Yet I don't score even one request for a date.

In fact, I don't know of any dating between my classmates and older boys (except for Hela!) either from our school or from the other schools. No wonder Hela is quite surprised when a handsome Senior, Oska, asks her to introduce him to me. To Rena? There had to be a catch, and there is one. We eventually learn that Oska wants me to join the Revisionist-Zionist Beitar of which he is the secretary.

Classroom gossip about my upcoming date with Oska lasts for days before the much anticipated rendezvous. Hela prepares me in the prescribed teen-formalities of the dating banter. Dressed up in all the refinements of my school uniform, I wait and wait for Oska. He does not show up and does not ever explain why. Somehow, with Hela's aid, I heal my deflated ego and go on living. This lack of success is to remain my secret forever after.

My classmates and I often spend afternoon hours in each other's homes, usually after our homework is (supposedly) done. We sometimes go for a walk down Sienkiewicza Street, in the direction of the Hebrew Gimnazjum, and at other times we go to the town park and sit there near the polluted river Bialka. On winter Saturdays we take a *dorozhka* (a horse-drawn cab) and go ice-skating at the Hebrew Gimnazjum or else go to the movies. And before we leave for our summer vacations, we often take the *dorozhkas* to go swimming and boating on Ogrodniczki's pond or on Dzikie's river. I often get sunburned and suffer in the aftermath of these outings, but they are fun anyway!

The summer of 1939 becomes a most memorable time in my life. Many unexpected happenings unfold during that summer. To begin with, it is then that I go to the rugged Maccabi Sport Camp in Jaremcze in the Eastern Carpathian Mountains, where the girls sleep in military huts and the boys in army tents. We wash up and brush our teeth in the ice-cold waters of a mountain stream that runs near camp. We eat simple meals, do aerobics and track, and play various ball games all through the day. Each camper gets an impressive "Certificate of a Coach-in-Training in Gymnastics and Sports" at the end of July, and that qualifies us to serve as Sports Counselors-in-Training at children's summer camps. I volunteer my services to the nearby Hanoar Hatzioni camp for scouts from the town of Stanislawow, and to my amazement, my folks allow me to stay on at the camp in Jaremcze. So I get to spend the entire summer of 1939 in the mountains.

The nearly two months spent at the Maccabi and Hanoar Hatzioni camps become the growing-up time for the immature girl that I surely am. I get to sing a lovely Hebrew song at the final Maccabi campfire; this time my voice isn't hoarse, and I look quite "teenish" in the blue camp-shorts and the white blouse on my sun-tanned body. After the performance, a senior camper approaches the group of my friends and invites me to go for a walk, and I consent. The two of us are obvious novices in the boy-girl dynamics, so we stroll about and talk about all kinds of inconsequential things, both of us aware of the stares in our direction. With the sound of the curfew taps, the boy tells me that he enjoyed my singing and that I am cute. I am glad that it is dark and he can't see the red marks from the freshly squeezed blackheads on my face.

"So how was it?" my bunkmates ask encouragingly. I respond with a vastly embellished account of the evening's walk!

Since the Hanoar Scout Camp will not arrive from Stanislawow for another few days, I arrange for a short stay with an in-session camp of Hashomer Hatzair *mahneim* (group leaders) from Pinsk. I am awed by the seriousness and high intellectual quality of the discussions taking place, fortunately in Polish. I learn that the Jewish Labor Movement hopes to establish Socialism in the future Jewish homeland in Palestine. This is the first time I hear Russian revolutionary songs, about Marx and Lenin, and about the establishment of a Jewish Homeland in the Soviet Birobidzhan. Later in life, my misinterpretation of the tenets I learn here will get me into trouble with my Communist principal, but at this time I feel totally committed to left-wing Zionism (despite the proletarian food and lodgings I must share with these *mahneim* of Hashomer Hatzair).

The accommodations and food in the Stanislawow Camp of Hashomer Hatzair are plush by comparison. I share a room with only one girl counselor, the food is fine, and I am pleased with the respect awarded to a sports counselor-in-training. My daily duties include conducting outdoor gymnastics, instructing swimming in the shallow depths of the Czeremosz River, and coaching volleyball and *pallant*. (The latter resembles softball but is played without either the pitcher or the catcher.)

I also assume the duty of patrolling the campers' bungalows in the evenings for one-hour intervals several times a week. It is during these patrols that I pleasantly "mature." I discover from a very handsome camp counselor, who shares the patrol with me, that not all kisses are alike. My kissing lessons fortunately start toward the end of the camping season so that I don't have to cope with an embarrassing eye-to-eye contact with my evening co-patroller for too long a time.

When the campers go home, I get to spend two days in Stanislawow. Because my vacation was extended, my return train ticket had to be changed. At this late time, I couldn't get a train to Bialystok from our train station at Jaremcze. I was only able to get a train to Bialystok from the hub station of Stanislawow. Furthermore, I now have to ride home via the eastern terrains of Poland instead of the customary central route via Warsaw. One of the campers invites me to stay in Stanislawow at their home, so I telegraph my parents about the details of my homecoming.

I buy two quarts of mountain raspberries from the mountain vendors and make juice for my parents from the raspberries during my stay in Stanislawow. When the juice is properly sugared, I pour it into a bottle and melt candle wax over its corked mouth. The bottle of this raspberry juice rides in my suitcase on the baggage shelf of the train to Bialystok. It will soon add a lot of excitement to my train ride.

It is the end of August of 1939, and because Poland expects a German invasion of its western and northwestern territories, a general mobilization is called for by the Polish military. The mobilized soldiers are transported to the threatened areas, including the county of Bialystok, and I enter a train packed with fully armed soldiers. Ill at ease, I sit wedged between the armed soldiers. When the soldiers ask me a question, I answer with obvious trepidation, as if I were being questioned by the police. And then all of a sudden, about half way to Bialystok, there is an explosion inside my valise. The soldiers jump up with their hands on their holsters and their eyes on me. All of us tensely expect something to happen and I can hardly breathe, until I suddenly recall my junior Gimnazjum chemistry lesson on Pasteur's fermentation of fruit. I loudly whisper, "It must be the sugared raspberry juice up in my valise." The soldiers cautiously take my valise from the shelf and slowly open it, revealing its raspberry-red, stained content. All is well again, and the laughing soldiers hand me the half-empty bottle of juice as they replace the valise on the upper shelf.

The Bialystok station is crowded with the mobilized soldiers and is, therefore, off limits to civilians. My mom and I meet outside the station, the raspberry juice bottle still in my hand. It seems to impress my mom. "Oh, how wonderful," she says after the many hugs and kisses. "It will be a real treat to have seltzer with raspberry juice, a real mountain raspberry juice at that! You're finally growing up, Rena." I walk very slowly and don't say a word about the rasberry-red contents of my suitcase.

When we arrive home and my dad comes downstairs to help with the suitcase, I get a second dose of praise. "Well, our daughter is finally getting there." Going upstairs, I desperately think how I can unobtrusively unload my valise into the laundry basket. But my parents insist on helping me with the unpacking and, thank goodness, all is well that ends well. My parents simply say that I meant well.

My friends are most impressed with my Maccabi Camp snapshots that were adroitly taken by my campmate, a daughter of a photographer. The girl was quite experienced in photography and knew how to make me look tall and attractive. I delight in looking so grown-up and I give away copies of some of the pictures to my best friends. (Little do I know that one of these photographs will, in the future, entice a Soviet Secret Service agent to come looking for me!)

The Germans invade Poland on September 1 of 1939, a day that will forever change our way of life. To begin with, we paste strips of tape across our windowpanes to prevent the glass from shattering in case of bombing. We are also instructed to weatherproof and carefully seal our windows and doors in case we need to use the room as a poison-gas shelter. We stand in line in front of stores to buy cereal grains, flower,

Fall of Poland
September 1, 1939

and canned goods that we'll stash away for the anticipated siege of the city. Clothing and shoe stores rapidly sell out their wares because people are anticipating shortages of goods. The Polish zloty, our main unit of currency, loses its value, and my parents let me have an overly generous allowance which I can put to good use, but for a short time only. Ice cream pops known as *penguins* show up on street pushcarts at this time, and my friends and I indulge ourselves with several of them at a time. Street peddlers are also selling heretofore unknown poppy seed and honey candy bars, and these become our second favorite type of sweets.

The schools are closed, so we stroll along the streets of Bialystok and listen to the marching songs of the boy scouts and cadets that boast of marching all the way to Berlin to beat the Germans. Here and there we see infantry soldiers firing their rifles at German planes, which obviously ignore this impotent defense. Occasionally, a small Polish tank drives through the town in either this or the opposite direction. Finally, one day, a bomb falls on a side street of Bialystok and damages a small house. We are no longer allowed to roam the streets, but we still have to stand in line for bread and occasionally milk.

We spend most of our time glued to the radio listening to the war news. Westerplatte, the military academy near Gdansk, fought the Germans to the last cadet there, and it now surrenders with honor. The Germans pour into Poland along the entire western and East-Prussian border. Polish armies continue to fight heroically, even though there are hardly any officers with them—the Polish Government, the Army Command, and most of the high-ranking officers have left for England. Warsaw is under siege and is bombarded day and night, relentlessly. Her citizens bravely put the fires out, rescue those who are trapped under the rubble of the collapsed buildings, and tend to the wounded as best they can. Warsaw Jews and Christian Poles erect street barricades and band together to defend their city from behind these barricades. And the valiant city of Warsaw holds out long after the German armies overrun the rest of Poland…

Rosh Hashana (the Jewish New Year) falls at the end of the second week of September this year and, one day before the eve of Rosh Hashana, a ghastly dawn greets the empty streets of Bialystok. There are no Polish soldiers, no Polish police anywhere. Not a soul, neither Jews nor Christians, venture out of doors. The noise of motorcycles, trucks, and tanks can be heard all over the city as the motorized German units slowly move along Pilsudskiego Street. Since we can't see much from our fourth floor windows,

Dad and I go to our first-floor neighbors and cautiously look out of their windows at the advancing German army. The neighbor's boy, a prodigy violinist, is plucking the strings of his violin while the rest of us just stand at the windows watching the Germans and waiting to see what will befall us...

I recognize the tune the young violinist is strumming and I can see Dad turn away from the window. His face is somber and I can tell he recognizes the tune as well. It is a marching song of the legionnaires, a song which my father so beautifully arranged for our school chorus. My dad's lips are moving as he mutters the moving Polish words of the song:

*"Czy umrzec nam przyjdzie na polu, czy w tajgach Sybiru nam gnic,
Z trudu naszego i bolu, Polska powstala by zyc..."*

(Whether we had to die in battle or rot in the taigas of Siberia,
It was through our suffering and pain that Poland rose to life!)*

*An excerpt from the 1918 Pilsudsky legionnaires' song. Author's translation from Polish.

They are here. The Germans are in Bialystok. In 1918, Poland rose to life, but now in September of 1939, Poland will be no more...

What will it be like now? What awaits the Jewish people of this occupied land?

Part Two

B CCCP
(IN THE USSR)
1939-1941

"Yesli zavtra voina, yesli zavtra v pokhod,
Boudz sievodnya k pokhodou gotov."*

(If the war comes tomorrow and you must go tomorrow,
Be ready for it today!)**

*A Red Army song popular during the 1939-1941 pre-war years.
**English translation by author.

V SOVYETSKOM BELOSTOKE
(IN SOVIET BIALYSTOK)

My husband and I had recently returned from a ten day tour of St. Petersburg, Moscow. We visited two very charming medieval towns of the Zolotoe Koltso (the Golden Ring), Yaroslavl and Suzdal. We had mixed feelings about visiting the Soviet Union when it so vehemently supported the Arab world, threatening the very survival of Israel. But now that our globe-trotting days were coming to an end and the Soviet Union was no more, we decided that it was time for us to go and at least see Russia itself. After all, I thought, I ought to see the land and the people whose armies protected eastern Poland's Jews for two years from the horrors of the Holocaust.

The tour and the guides were excellent; the country appeared to be almost on a par with Hungary, Poland and Czechia. I exploited my knowledge of the Russian language by talking with the Russian people whenever I could. Yet I felt somewhat disappointed with this trip. What was I missing? My husband hypothesized that I missed seeing a country that could no longer be revisited: the Soviet Union of my school years of 1939 to 1941...

The end of the second week of September in 1939 is Rosh Hashana, the Jewish New Year, and most of the Jews of Bialystok are praying at home. On the eve of Rosh Hashana, only the most pious attend the synagogue, and one can hear from behind the securely locked doors their subdued voices and muffled chanting. Yesterday, a German army unit entered Bialystok and the Germans have busied themselves with all sorts of installations ever since. Except for the occasional grinding noise of a German motorcycle, the empty streets are quiet this morning. Several German soldiers show up a bit later, some of them look into the almost empty store windows, others peek into doorways and try to start a conversation with whomever they might encounter. But there soon appear on Pilsudskiego Street a few Polish policemen whom the Germans march off toward Kosciuszki Square. Who knows why and where to—that is the first frightful sight of this day. Later that day a German tank and a few truckloads of soldiers cross the city and head for the outlying areas. But towards evening, there is another alarming sight: German soldiers are prodding several Jews who are wearing their traditional caftans and hats in the direction of Kosciuszki Square, the place they had earlier led the Polish policemen. Glued to our windows, we dare not say what we half expect will happen to the policemen and the Jews. All through the night, shots can be heard from the outskirts of town. I try to push these threatening sounds out of my consciousness.

The next day civilians begin to appear in the streets, and I too go downstairs. With my Aryan looks, I can safely blend with the Gentile women who have ventured out to find some food. Auspiciously, I find an open grocery store that sells flour, cereals and other basics. I go back home for money and a shopping bag, stand in line and eventually get a few food items. On my way home, I read the newly posted German wall placards. The Germans are demanding the surrender of all firearms and foreign money. They order members of the Polish military, police, and local government to register at the office of the German Wehrmacht. They further warn that all group assemblies, including those at places of worship, are henceforth strictly forbidden, that there will be an 8 PM to 7 AM curfew and that those who are found in the streets during the curfew time will be arrested. My parents don't act surprised at all when I go home and recapitulate the German orders.

A day later there appears the long-awaited notice about rationing bread, and we are told that local bakeries will provide bread for each district of Bialystok. I locate our district's bakery and begin my daily breadline routines. It seems that the Jews of Bialystok send their Aryan-looking representatives for bread because there are no typically Semitic faces, nor is there any Jew-baiting on bread lines, and somehow it feels as if it is the quiet before the storm.

Three days before Yom Kippur (Day of Atonement), while I am standing in the bread line, I overhear a conversation that makes me cower within myself. A dashing young German soldier begins to flirt with the Gentile girl standing next to me and I hear him say to her: "This Friday is the Jews' Day of Atonement and we intend to give the Jews their chance to atone on their Judgment Day. Now you Fraulein just peek out from any doorway near the Town Square and you will see how we will do that!" Afraid to call attention to myself, I stay in line and wait for my bread, and then I run home. Out of breath, I repeat what I have overheard. Mom tells the story to our next door neighbor and these two go to alert a few other neighbors. People start a search for hiding places in the basement, in the attic, in the crawl spaces under the roof, in the empty school supplies store on Wilcza, and wherever else anyone can find them.

We all have a sleepless night. I decide to go to the bread line in the morning anyway, perhaps for the last time. It is now two days before Yom Kippur and, while standing in line, I suddenly get an idea about an excellent hideout for my family: the storage room of the shop-shack in my school. Surely nobody would look for us behind the piles of plywood, the remnants of sheet-metal and other junk! Excited, I can hardly wait to get my bread and run home, when, suddenly, there is noise from a plane above, a plane dropping leaflets to the ground. There aren't any Germans here at this time so it is safe to pick up and read the fliers. Strangely enough, I also see no Germans on my way home as I run there with my bread and a bunch of poorly printed fliers in my hands. What these fliers say is absolutely amazing! They tell us in awkward Polish: "Keep calm citizens of Bialystok and do not provoke confrontation with the Germans. In the eastern outskirts of your town the heroic Red Army of the USSR is awaiting the withdrawal of the German troops. We are coming to liberate you! Long live free Western Belorussia!"

Belorussia? Why not Poland, I wonder as I run home. Then suddenly I get it. There is no Poland anymore…So on my way upstairs, I scream at the top of my lungs: "The Russians are coming!"

We stay at home for the rest of this day and the next day, discussing the meaning of the awkward Polish phrases on the leaflets and peering at the street from the lower floor windows. Radio Warszawa is off the air, the other European stations remain garbled up, we don't know what is happening, but we begin to see changes in the streets. The Germans seem to be packing! Their wiring is removed from our telegraph poles and their trucks, loaded with boxes and crates, are seen moving toward the Warsaw highway. Then, from earliest morning till dusk of the following day, trucks carrying the German troops, light artillery pieces, and piles of various weapons keep on heading out of town. At this time, however, not all of the Bialystok Jews remain in their homes. We see marchers carrying red flags and banners with Yiddish inscriptions; we see their raised fists and we hear them sing a moving song, a song that I have not heard before. The song's Yiddish lyrics command: "*Shteit oif, ir alle wer wee Shklafen, in Hunger arbet must un Noit* (Arise ye all who, as slaves, must labor in hunger and need)." My next door neighbor, a member of the left wing Hashomer Hatzair, tells me, with obvious disdain, that the marchers are members of the Communist-Yiddishist Bund, and that the song is none other than the *Internationale*, the anthem of Communists and their fellow travelers. What intrigues me more than the politics of the marchers is the fact that they are totally unafraid. They not only follow the Germans but also hurl nasty curse words and rotten tomatoes at them.

"Wow !" says my sister, and I wonder what these Germans will do to us if they ever come back here. In fact, a rumor is spreading that some of the paraders have heard the retreating Germans yell back at the offending Jews: "We will come back and you'll all be sorry!" (Yes, they will come back, but not tomorrow, not on the Yom Kippur Friday, the Friday when they planned to give us "a proper Day of Atonement." In two years, however, some of the Germans who are leaving Bialystok today will be commanding the troops that will come to reoccupy the city. They will come back thirsty for vengeance and murder.)

It is Friday, the day of Yom Kippur, and all is quiet. The Russians did not show up and the Germans aren't here either. Last evening I could see only a few Orthodox Jews brave the uncertain curfew and spend Yom Kippur eve praying in the synagogues. But today, on this holiest day, the Jews of Bialystok, including Mom and Dad, are pouring into the Great Synagogue and the smaller Beit Hamidrashim (prayer houses) to partake of community prayer. At our traditional, but awfully modest, fast-breaking evening meal, the family's talk centers around the strange happenings of the last week, and we wonder what could be holding the Russians up. Then, toward late evening, Mrs. Tartacka shows up, bearing news that the Russians are stuck in the eastern suburbs. They can't enter the city because their very heavy tanks might damage the water and waste water pipes under the streets. The armored tank divisions seem to be waiting for lighter trucks to transport their soldiers into the city itself. Some of the Russian officers have apparently stayed overnight in the suburban homes, hence the source of the news. I can see people congregate in the street below our balcony, and I guess that all of them are wondering how soon the Russians will come.

Everybody is on the lookout for the Russians again next morning, and finally in the afternoon, a bunch of kids come running from the direction of the eastern suburbs yelling joyfully, "They are coming!"

My dad stands next to me on the balcony as the Russians slowly ride in their trucks up Pilsudskiego Street directly below us, and I wonder why I see him in tears. My God! My Father is sobbing! Is he thinking of his years in the Russian P.O.W. camps? Or is he recalling the days when he was caught up in their Civil War in Siberia, liberated from prison by the Reds and then nearly executed by the Whites? (I will not get answers to these questions until Mom and I end up in Auschwitz, where she will finally tell me the whole story.) For now, I just enjoy seeing our liberators slowly ride in the trucks, greeted by so many, many Jewish men, women, and children. I enjoy seeing these smiling young soldiers wave to the folks in the streets, shake hands with bystanders, kiss the children and pin little red stars on them. My sister and I dash downstairs to get a better look at these soldiers who do not resemble the stiff military figures of our Polish past. These soldiers wear knickers and belted informal khaki shirts with few insignia. The enlisted men have non-decorated epaulets and the officers' epaulets bear small red stars.

Things begin to change, bit by bit, in the days to come. Signs written in the Cyrillic alphabet appear in the store windows, and the most ubiquitous of these signs looks like *nubo* and reads *peevo* (beer). Pretty soon, we pick up many typically Soviet expressions. In many cases, we don't even know an appropriate Polish translation for these sayings, so we just spice up our Polish conversations with them.

There are now long lines, not only for the local bread but also for the infrequently imported Soviet products. Their arrival is usually heralded by either our friendly Mrs.Tartacka or our enterprising neighbors. There is a mad rush for a spot in the lineups for vodka just as soon as it appears in the stores. Vodka is in great demand not because the people of Bialystok are heavy drinkers, but because vodka becomes an item of choice in the barter for farm produce.

Stores with prewar Polish-made goods remain open but their supplies soon dwindle, largely because of the heavy demand for these goods by the uniformed *tovarishchi* (comrades). Indeed, the Red Army is becoming a market for all kinds of manufactured goods, especially watches. It isn't unusual to be accosted in the street by a passing *krasnoarmeets* (a Red Army man) who says, "*Oo vas chasy est* (Do you have a watch for sale)?" In fact, a substantial portion of peoples' expenses are covered by the sale of possessions coveted by Soviet soldiers. Only very slowly does the import of goods manufactured in the Soviet Union begin, and the expropriated stores which sell these goods soon become the Univermags (the Government Department Stores). Almost without exception, the products of the Soviet manufacture are of poor quality. As Radio Moscow and the newspapers explain it, during the current Piatiletka (Five-Year Plan), the production of consumer goods must be given a low priority in favor of the production of machinery and arms. But the day will soon come, we hear, when the Soviet Union will surely compare favorably with the United States in producing consumer goods. "*Da* (yes)," predict the street-corner-soap-box uniformed Politruks (political counselors), "we must soon *dognat' i peregnat'* (catch-up with and overtake) the formidable productivity of the USA!"

Toward the end of September, our schools open and are promptly reorganized to become the Soviet *diesiatiletkas* (ten-year schools), and our 11th and 12th year classes (the senior division or *Lyceum* of the Polish Gimnazjum) become the 9th and 10th grades of the new Soviet school. Our principal, Mr. Tilleman, is not with us anymore. A Soviet military official is in charge of the reorganization of our curriculum and its language of instruction. A Parent Association meets with this Soviet official and the parents are coaxed to introduce Yiddish instead of Polish as the language of instruction, but our parents vehemently resist this change. "Why would you want to teach your children in the language of your oppressors?" asks the Soviet official. But the parents ask in turn, "And why should we want to have our children taught in the language of the uneducated Jewish masses? Will Yiddish make them eligible for your Russian Universities?" We hear via the grapevine that the Soviet official has chastised our parents for their derogatory attitudes toward the disenfranchised masses who, as he predicts, are about to become masters of their own fate. Finally, a compromise is reached: Russian will become our language of instruction while Yiddish and Belorussian will be taught along with the elective French or German.

The two-year Polish Lyceum (grades 11 and 12) offered choices in specialization: one in the humanities and classical studies, the other in sciences and mathematics. Those who enrolled in the division of humanities had to continue with their Latin and had to study classical Greek, in addition to a curriculum in European literature, social sciences, and modern languages. Those who chose the sciences and mathematics followed a curriculum replete with the sciences and mathematics you'd expect (including calculus), but without classical languages and with only a modest amount of social studies and literature. But the curriculum for the 9th and 10th years of the Soviet variant of our school, the *Vosmaya Sredniaya Shkola* (Secondary School #8), does not offer the former choice of major subjects. In fact, Western-European humanities and literature aren't taught at all, but are replaced by Russian literature, economic history of the Soviet Union, and the history of the Soviet Communist Party. In mathematics, all of us have to take advanced algebra, geometry and trigonometry, but not calculus; in the sciences we take chemistry, physics, and the evolutionary natural science. In addition, a military instructor gives us a course in first aid and CPR (cardiopulmonary resuscitation) in conjunction with the quasi-military training. Whereas the Polish school relied on oral examinations and essay tests, the Soviet 10-year schools mandate uniform short-answer mid-year tests in January and final tests in June.

Many of our old teachers are gone (Why?) and Soviet teachers are now teaching the Russian language, Russian literature, and various subjects that are meant to proselytize Soviet ideology. Several times a week, a *Politruk* (a Political Guidance Agent) shows up at our school and conducts class meetings and one-on-one interviews. We sense that he is here to imbue us with an appreciation of the Soviet way of life and with Marxist ideology. He is careful not to sound too dogmatic or rigid, but to most of us, he is just that. Now, however, we have a few new students and some of these are obviously familiar with Marxism, and are, therefore, more receptive to the *Politruk's* lectures. I remain unconvinced, though not hostile, but most of my old friends hate the Soviet propaganda. But I am always ready to join my friends in poking fun at the unsophisticated (by our Western standards) Soviet teachers and their ill-fitting and outmoded clothing.

Unlike the Soviet teachers, our new principal, Mr. Tykocinski, has our respect. He is a native of Bialystok, a Communist whom the Red Army liberated from Bereza Kartuska, a Polish concentration camp for Communists and other "politically incorrect" citizens of Poland. Mr. Tykocinski is an approachable young man who compares favorably with the "ogre" Tilleman, our previous principal. But Tykocinski is a die-hard Communist, and my naiveté about the inflexibility of his Communist thinking is about to get me into trouble later during this school year.

During the fall and the early winter of 1939, thousands of Jewish refugees flee from German occupied Poland into Bialystok. The Soviet border patrols mercifully look the other way as these refugees cross the border at Malkinia, the entry point near Bialystok. Eventually, when a few Nazi spies are discovered among the refugees, the border controls are tightened. In due time, identity papers are scrutinized more carefully, although the astuteness of the border guards leaves much to be desired, and gives rise to politically charged jokes. Many embellished versions of this border-crossing joke circulate in my school: At the Malkinia border crossing, Ivan Ivanovich Ivanov examines Moishe Pipik's papers. He can't make heads or tails of most of them, until he notices the copy of Moishe's urine test and reads in it the Polish words *"Cukru Niema* (no sugar)," the two words that often appear in our store windows. Grinning happily, Ivan waves Moishe in across the border, and says: *"Sakharu niet, znachit ty nie capitalist, davay v Sovietskiy Soyooz!* (Since you are not smuggling in sugar, you are not a capitalist, and we welcome you into the Soviet Union!)"

The largest numbers of refugees come from the two major centers of Polish-Jewish life, Warsaw and Lodz. The citizens of Bialystok offer temporary lodgings to the refugees and reportedly charge money even for sleeping accommodations limited to bedding laid out on chairs. In due time, the refugees trickle out into smaller towns; altruistic attitudes and permanent places to stay are easier to find there. In Bialystok itself, many refugees help themselves by selling whatever goods they managed to smuggle in. Jewish charity organizations and the local government do come forth with some aid as well.

Stela is the first one of my Jewish friends from Grudziadz who again appears in my life after we move to Bialystok. Stela comes in 1938, the others come later. Each time someone comes to us from Grudziadz it feels as if one of the relatives with whom I grew up came to visit. It feels as if not even the war and the downfall of Poland could annul the continuum of my belonging with these people.

Stela and I remain close friends even though we are separated. We write loving letters to one another and we plan to visit each other, both in Bialystok and in Grudziadz. But the war annuls our plans. While I stay in Soviet-occupied Bialystok, Stela's family ends up in German-occupied Warsaw. I worry about Stela's well being because we hear awful rumors about the fate of Warsaw Jews, improbable rumors like the Germans recruiting pretty Jewish girls for Warsaw's military brothels. Toward the winter of 1939, our acquaintance who carries goods across the German border smuggles my spare winter coat into Warsaw for Stela, and in its lining I hide a letter to my friend. I tell Stela that I will always think of her and ask her to think of me as well. But I also naively ask Stela to give up our old commitment to the idea of "free love," especially when such "free love" is solicited by the Germans who intend to use and denigrate Jewish women. Little did I know that far worse a fate awaited the Jews of Warsaw, including their women and children.

Nusia Halbersztat and her dad are the first Grudziadz acquaintances who pass through Bialystok during its Soviet occupation in the late fall of 1939, I believe. They tell us of the death of Mrs. Halbersztat and her older daughter during the September 1939 bombing of Warsaw. The Minc family comes next, and they become quite friendly with us. Julek Minc attends the Druskin Gimnazjum with me, and he and I will later join the underground of the Ghetto of Bialystok. Kraina Szklar's oldest sister, a seamstress by profession, stays for a while at our house during the Soviet years and does some sewing for us. But most memorable is the coming to Bialystok of the boys of the "in crowd" of Grudziadz's *podworko*.

It is the late fall of 1939 and I am sitting on the balcony of our fourth floor apartment at #91 Sovyetskaya Street. With me are seated my old beau Kuba, Jozek Szydlowski, and handsome Max himself, all part of the "in crowd." They stay in Bialystok but for a short time and later share the fate of other refugees who came from the German-occupied territories of Poland—they will be sent East into the Soviet Union. But now, on our balcony, I feel great because they have come to see me, and they joke and flirt with me the way they used to kid around with the "in crowd" of Grudziadz. I now know that I am one of them after all.

Another one of my Grudziadz friends, Heniek, also comes to Bialystok during the early winter of 1939, and he enters the senior class of our school. He is staying with the Minc family whose roots are in Bialystok and who, before the outbreak of the war, had returned from Grudziadz to Bialystok. Heniek and I become inseparable friends all through this frosty "Russian" winter. When he comes calling for me in the late afternoon, he always finds something to help my mother with, usually something that I had previously refused to do. ("Shame on you," Heniek says when we are alone.) In this way he wins over Mom's heart.

Heniek is worried about his family, whom he left in Warsaw. We discuss his problems, but I don't know how to show my sympathy for his concerns. I just help Heniek carry packages to the smugglers, who will deliver them to his folks. And I wish I could give him the dollars that his older sister needs for the now illegal entry into the Soviet territory, but my family has no foreign money of any sort. I also worry that Heniek may follow the example of the many other lonely young boys who have opted to leave the safety of the Soviet Union and return to live with their folks in the hell of the Nazi occupied territories. Perhaps if Heniek and I weren't just friends, my parents would take Heniek in to live with us.

Unbelievably, my mom and dad don't mind my almost daily walks with Heniek, not even when we return home from these walks quite late. I guess my parents see in Heniek an "older brother" type of friend, one who can be trusted. And Heniek, indeed, proves that his friendship with me is purely a brotherly one. He soon finds a proper (red-haired!) girlfriend and stops asking me to go for walks with him altogether. But I don't mind; Heniek has convinced me earlier that I truly am one of his people from Grudziadz, and that is enough for me.

The smuggling in of goods goes on as long as the border crossings remain, unofficially of course, open. The smugglers who get caught are either jailed or exiled into detention camps in the interior of the Soviet Union. Such is the fate of the few of my friends who come to us from Grudziadz and who later get involved in the sale of smuggled goods. It is fun to have the *podworko's* Max, Kuba, and Jozek come to see me, but later on it is terribly upsetting to discover that they have been arrested for smuggling and are about to be sent to Soviet punitive camps. I don't yet know that when the Germans reoccupy our territories in 1941, the exile of my friends into the interior of the Soviet Union will save their lives.

Many of the refugees are of high school age, and most of them come here without their families. Classrooms in our school become overcrowded with the influx of these *bezhentsy* (refugee) teenagers. Our former shop-shack becomes a refugee boys' dormitory, but the girls who have no one in Bialystok are placed with local families. The school soon institutes an early and a late session of instruction to deal with the overcrowd classes. The senior classes, including mine, are scheduled for the afternoons. Doing homework early in the morning and going home from school in the dark gives one an eerie feeling. My classes end before dark, but the school now offers lots of opportunities to hang around and do fun things after classes. To begin with, I've become the editor of the Students' Weekly Wall Bulletin posted opposite the teachers' room. My staff and I haggle for hours over the choice of items that should be reported, items that are likely to pass the censorship of the principal and the political guidance agent. We learn to hide our true feelings about sensitive matters behind the safety of satirical writing.

In addition to the editorial meetings, I often socialize after classes with the refugee boys who congregate in the empty classrooms before their dormitory curfew. It is from these boys that I learn the latest satirical songs of Warsaw's Jewish vaudeville. Some of these songs touch upon the anti-Semitic policies of Poland, others on the Italian campaign against Ethiopia (then known as Abyssinia), but most are meant to make you feel good by poking fun at yourself.

I befriend Samek Pewzner, a very intelligent and friendly boy from Warsaw who is soon appointed to serve as temporary president of the Student Organization. Samek often seeks me out to talk things over.

Influenced by Warsaw's vaudevillian satirical songs, I dub in my own satirical lyrics on current political themes into popular Jewish songs. My old choral ensemble group, the Revelersy Girls, perform these songs, along with the songs of Warsaw's vaudeville. One of the vaudevillian songs mockingly decries the former dangers of Jewish presence in Polish political life and ridicules Polish fears that "the Jews can be found everywhere, even in the Polish families!" The lyrics that I dub into a popular crooning song projects the politically correct, negative view of the Chamberlain-Hitler affairs. In this song, the British prime minister sweetly croons to the German chancellor and finally assures the Fuehrer that, "if need be, there is always Poland that we can sell you…"

At the time of our premier performance, it isn't my father whose sensitivities are hurt by our hodgepodge musical creations. This time, we manage to injure the sensitivities of a Marxist teacher. After our performance, this diminutive woman rages on and on about the outrageous decadence of our "art" and about the insult our lyrics have inflicted on the Soviet "socialist realism." The look on the faces of our audience reassures us that we needn't worry, because who the hell knows what she is raving about?? And when we notice that our Communist principal is hiding a chuckle, the five of us (Ewa, Tusia, Maszka, Sonia and I) wink at one another and triumphantly descend from the stage. We know that, for the time being at least, all is well.

Apparently the double-session instruction schedule does not work out too well and, starting in the early months of 1940, we go back to the 8:30 AM to 1:30 PM single session classes. This daily schedule is coupled with the weekly schedule of five days of classes followed by one day off, currently in use throughout the Soviet Union. With this design, the weekly six-day schedules of schools, factories, and stores don't necessarily coincide—members of one family may have a different day of rest each week. Because of this, my poor father who, as always, works in several schools, seldom has a day of rest. The nightmarish situation eventually registers with the Centralized Planning institution in Moscow and in due time they reinstate the seven-day week with six working days plus Sunday off. Extracurricular activities can now be planned and coordinated with other schools and institutions. The normalization of the school week is especially welcome when a director-actor from the Warsaw Theater comes to our school to stage plays and poetry readings with us.

The performance of *Parisian Commune of 1860* doesn't work out well because the actors start to giggle during some tender love scenes in the play. The play *Puss in Boots,* performed in Russian, is distorted by an *udarenye* (stress of syllables) characteristic of the Polish language but inappropriate for the Russian language. That, of course, offends the ears of the Russians and the Russophiles in our audience. But our poetry readings are great. Tusia and I read Russian poems by Mayakowski and Polish poems by two well known left-wing Jewish poets, Tuwim and Broniewski. (One day I will recite the English translation of Mayakowski's "Soviet Passport" at Hunter College in New York City.)

Our drama instructor is an incredible dynamo of a man. He inspires us to imbibe his drama and recitation techniques to a point where we begin to believe that we belong on the stage. When Tusia and I begin reciting the Tuwim's famous children's poem, "The Locomotive," our motions and sounds mimic those that are true of a locomotive at rest. Then, our locomotive slowly takes off and goes on speeding up along the tracks until it finally disappears, sounding off in the distance. In all of this, Tusia's theatrical giftedness outshines the acting abilities of us all; it is also Tusia who always makes us feel as if she were on the stage, even when she speaks about ordinary matters.

(Oh Tusia, I will always wonder if you recited to yourself the Broniewski's verse about the execution of Parisian Cummunards of 1860 when the bullet of the German executioner hit you...)

The Red Army steps into our school life, something entirely novel for us. We have become the so-called *podchastnaya shkola* (division's ward school) of one of the artillery divisions of Bialystok. This simply means that the soldiers of that division are to play the role of our "big brothers." A few soldiers come to help us with the Russian language of our written assignments, others bring us gifts of paper-mache figurines and handmade simple gadgets. But we enjoy most of all their division's choral, dance, and theater ensembles that come to perform in the school auditorium. They refer to many of their performances as *shutochnyie* (comic), and as soon as we discern some of the finer points of the Russian language, we begin to catch onto the meaning of their jokes. Soviet military comedians may not live up to the vaudevillian standards of Warsaw, but we appreciate the novelty of it all anyway.

The 1939-1941 "Russian" winters are brutally cold, yet our military instructor coaxes us to get up before dawn and participate in military campaigns, games, and exercises on winter Sundays. As we traipse in the snow, we envy the *valenki* (felt boots) of our Russian commanders, which aren't sold yet in Bialystok's budding State department stores, the *Univermags*. But the field exercises are exhilarating enough so that we go along with the pretense that we are soldiers of either the Red Army or the White Army, searching for the enemy in the wooded hillocks of Bialystok's hinterland.

Except for the usually enjoyable Sundays of playing games, the winter days are generally uncomfortable. Schools and homes are so poorly heated that the water often freezes in the pipes, and quite often the toilet in our apartment cannot be flushed. Furious that nobody complains about it, I finally run downstairs one day and holler at our former landlord, Mrs. Gwin, who I assume is responsible for the maintenance of our utilities. As if I were under the spell of Soviet indoctrination, I bawl out the "capitalist landlord." I threaten her that, if she doesn't fix the toilet, "the people will nationalize this lousy building and service it themselves!" Mrs. Gwin meets me at her door and, very quietly, says in Yiddish, "*Der Gwin's Moyer is nit mehr a Gwin's Moyer* (the Gwin's apartment house is no longer theirs)." Our building has apparently been already nationalized, which means that "the people" are now taking care of it themselves. Whom do you complain to now? Stupidly, I cause my parents to be ashamed of me.

Spring brings a thaw to the water situation, but the heating remains so poor that I must wear gloves to play the piano in our unheated living room.

What makes it a little more pleasant is the fact that I now often have at my piano an eager listener, a cello player from Lodz named Marek. He is much older than I, is very lonely, and is eager to find friends. A Grudziadz refugee in Lodz had given him our address, and he has since become a daily guest at our home. He did not manage to bring his cello across the border, but he can imitate the sounds of his instrument so well that the two of us can play cello-piano duets in our unheated living room. Marek has so-called "absolute pitch" and claims that, under his tutelage, I will develop absolute pitch as well. But I don't come quite close enough to it. Anyway, Marek leaves us one day for one of the smaller towns east of Bialystok where he supposedly does play cello in the town's orchestra.

In due time, a bona fide musician of the budding Bialystok Symphonic Orchestra sublets our spare bedroom. He plays the viola and shows little interest in my piano skills. The sublet is arranged by the Soviet Housing Authority and the only thing we get out of it is an increased allotment of wood and coal for the two great stoves that heat our apartment. Gone are the days when I practiced the piano and did my homework wearing gloves, but that is not to say that life is becoming as comfortable as it used to be before the war.

Before the war, there had always been a domestic helper in our home and my mom's housework was limited to cooking and baking, but now domestic helpers are allowed in exceptional cases only. My dad, my sister, and I help my mom with the house chores, but that help leaves much to be desired. Eventually the Soviet Health Center, where my mom is treated for her heart condition, allows her to have a domestic helper. Sometime in the fall of 1940, a Bielorussian country girl, slightly older than I, comes in the afternoons to clean our apartment. The girl attends our high school in the mornings and I am beginning to understand the egalitarian nature of the Soviet society. A year ago, it would have been unthinkable for the well-to-do students of the Druskin's Gimnazjum to sit on the same classroom bench with their maids! But my left-wing Zionist leanings help me welcome the social changes, and my parents appear to support these changes as well.

Providing the family with adequate food has also become a chore, in part because of the poor supply of produce. Difficulties with the transport of produce across the former Soviet-Polish border persist because of the differences in the rail gauges in the two countries. Poland's rail tracks are as narrow as the rails in the rest of Western Europe, but the Soviets have inherited the wide tracks of Tsarist Russia. Thus all imported materials must be reloaded from the Soviet to the Polish rail cars. In addition, there are few insulated rail cars on Polish trains, whereas the gigantic centralized Soviet shipments must, of necessity, rely upon a large number of insulated rail cars to transport ice containers with fish, meats and other perishables. The transport and distribution of produce is further impeded by the sluggish bureaucracy of the centralized Soviet institutions and by the epidemic theft of goods delivered to warehouses and stores. It is a small wonder then that long *ocheredzi* (queues) spring up at dawn at stores at which delivery trucks have been spotted.

It takes hours to stand in these lines as well as stamina to defend your spot in line from "spot-poachers." And it is a heartbreak to learn, just before reaching the door, that the supplies of the coveted goods are all sold out. This state of affairs promotes a class of professional "queue-sellers" from whom you can buy, for an exorbitant price, anything at anytime. Sometimes, my sister or I get up very early and stand in line until Mom comes to take our place in time for us to go to school. But when strict rationing is established for many household goods, these goods become available throughout the day. The lines remain long but it is now less likely that stores soon run out of their supplies. In this way, all of us in the family can do our share of standing in line, mostly in the afternoons. And, at times, dear old Mrs. Tartacka shares with us what she manages to acquire via her store-manager friends or her skillful maneuvers in the queue.

Our domestic helper's country people often bring into the city fresh vegetables, dairy products, and poultry. We either buy these for rubles or barter for them with vodka, cigarettes, soap or sugar, all of which we accumulate by taking extra turns standing in the queue. One way or another, there is always soup and a modest main dish at our dinner table; we continue to use saccharine to sweeten our tea, baked goods and jam, because sugar is usually in short supply.

As before the war, my Father has to hustle to make a living for the family. Because of her heart illness, Mom is exempt from work, which leaves Dad to be the sole bread winner in the family. He continues to work in the same schools, but now two of his schools pool their talents into a *svodnyi* (combined) music program. Besides his choral and orchestral work, Dad now organizes the so-called *khorovody*, the popular ensembles of folk songs and dances performed to the accompaniment of *balalaikas* and *gharmoshkas*. (The *balalaika* is much like a triangular mandolin; the *gharmoshka* is similar to an accordion with button-keys.)

Soviet Republics hold the so-called Olympiads (competitions) for their juvenile performers, and the winners compete in the All-Soviet Union Olympiad in Moscow. Locally, the music and dance ensembles compete with each other. The winning sets are sent to their Republic Olympiad, which in our case is held in the Belorussian capital of Minsk. In addition to the directing and rehearsing of his *khorovody*, my father arranges their music, which together takes hours of hard work. His routine choral and orchestral work is just as time consuming and just as taxing, but the preparation for the Olympiads is truly nerve wracking. There exists a thinly veiled expectation that Dad's "combined ensembles" must out-perform ensembles of schools that vie with us for entry into the Minsk Olympiad. With all that, my father earns less than an industrial worker!

I do my share to help my dad. As before, I remain his faithful accompanist, which includes my *pro bono* piano playing for his Red Army Division's band. I also get some paying jobs. I used to tutor a little girl in Hebrew and Polish during the 1938-39 school year. Now my former pupil again needs tutoring—this time in Russian and mathematics—and all the rubles I earn go towards the needs of my family. Luckily, I also land a junior counselor's job at a children's day camp. The camp is maintained by the Workers' Union of a textile-mill complex during the spring and winter school recesses. The job includes breakfasts and lunches and I am paid relatively well. Some of my earnings pay for my graduation dress, the only dress of the lean Soviet years that hasn't been remade from one of my mother's old dresses.

Back in school, I perform as well as I always have, and I find that the curriculum of the Soviet school requires little effort in order to excel. With the old "cool" of the Druskin "brats," most of us hold the Moscow-mandated Bielorussian and Yiddish language classes in low regard. The "commit to memory and recite" history of the Soviet Communist Party, the Soviet Constitution and the writings of Comrade Stalin are all held in benign contempt. It is truly funny to see the very pregnant, docile Soviet teacher who is totally oblivious to our shenanigans, rattle off these holy scriptures verse after verse. Her attention seems to fade except when, during someone's recitation, we come to the obligatory phrase, "*tak skazal Tovarishch Stalin* (so said Comrade Stalin)," after which she applauds and we vehemently join in.

There appears to be no political conversion of our bourgeois youth during the first year of the Soviet regime. There are some newcomers with Marxist leanings, but only one of them is adamantly vocal in her convictions. We are flabbergasted by this girl whose family has volunteered to work in sub-Arctic Siberian agriculture projects at the same time that less fortunate families are forced into Siberian slave labor. And we hear of many such exiles during the course of the 1939-1940 school year. We learn that textile-mill and other factory owners are imprisoned and their families are exiled to the Far East. Some of these exiles are the families of Druskin students. Our class is personally affected by the loss of Erka's and Niura's families, and my sister also loses several of her classmates. But strangely enough, the letters that come from these classmates do not depict the Siberian horrors we've expected. Their letters depict discomforts of daily living—they must walk a long distance to buy milk, to get to school, to go to the post office and movies, along with other such hardships. Somehow, these hardships become less awful when we think of the stresses of the daily life here in Soviet Bialystok. And it is comforting to know that the textile-mill owners who have been given a vote of confidence by their own workers were not imprisoned, and that some of them were even asked to manage their now nationalized mills.

My family and I harbor no ill feelings toward our Soviet "liberators"(as they typically call themselves). There is no sign of anti-Semitism on their part and they make us feel equal to the other nationalities of the Soviet Union, a status the Jews of Poland did not have. It is comforting to know that there is a Department of Yiddish Culture at the University of Minsk. It is comforting to have Yiddish schools, a Yiddish theater and a Yiddish library here in Bialystok. The luxuries and niceties of life remain very limited, but for us the teenagers, there are ample opportunities for healthy and safe fun in this Soviet way of life.

In the distant future, I will be repeatedly attacked for my rosy view of the Soviet way of life and I will become defensive about it. Perhaps the dismal years that follow my life in the Soviet Bialystok will shed a rosy glow on that life. But maybe my defensiveness will be justified, after all. Maybe my life during the Soviet years really wasn't that bad...

"FROM EACH ACCORDING TO HIS ABILITY AND TO EACH ACCORDING TO HIS NEED."

Whenever we got together with our doctrinaire-Marxist friends, I found reasons to attack their views. Only in the so-called "left-wing" crowd did my arguments tend to remain anti-Soviet. Why then, ever since I came to the United States, did I seek out these left-wing, or progressive, acquaintances and friends? And why did I always love to sing the old Soviet songs and see the old Soviet films? Was it perhaps true that my Soviet years had left echoes of their world views in my psyche? Was I perhaps enamored of what I perceived to be the Soviet peoples' way of life?

In the concentration camps, I hung around Soviet inmates, I sought to speak Russian with them, to hear their life stories, and to "connect" with them. After my liberation from the camps I briefly wore on my blouse a little red flag, as if I wanted to hang on to my transient citizenship in Soviet Belorussia. And my "Soviet hangover" showed up at other times as well. Before I discovered that Bialystok was given back to Poland, I apparently coaxed my fellow survivors to go back to what I thought was the Soviet Bialystok. That, of course, happened before I actually went to search for my sister in the Soviet Union and in Poland and learned that neither Poland nor the Soviet Union held promise of a hospitable home for me.

What then transpired in the latter part of the two years in the Soviet Bialystok that left within me shards of nostalgia for the Russia of my teen years?

In the late spring of 1940, we get a preview of Soviet politics that isn't auspicious for us at all. The arrests of former Polish policemen, army officers and local and regional officials become commonplace. Some people are issued passports annotated with the *odinadtsatyi paragraph* (eleventh paragraph) of the Soviet constitution, and we know that the eleventh paragraph severely limits the civil rights of those who are thought to be politically untrustworthy.

My parents go through a few uneasy moments with their passports themselves. Since my dad's military papers show that he fought against the Soviet armies that invaded Poland in 1920, Dad suspects that he also may get the "eleventh paragraph." He panics when he is asked to surrender his military documents and tells the passport-issuing authorities that he lost them during our move from Grudziadz. The issuing of Dad's passport is delayed; we live in fear about the threatening annotation and in fear of perhaps another repercussion on the part of the Soviet NKVD (KGB in later years). And the NKVD does indeed appear at our doors!

As we often do on Sundays, my friends and I go to the movies on the Sunday following Dad's application for his Soviet passport. Unexpectedly, the film is interrupted, the lights go on, and standing in one of the doorways is an NKVD officer accompanied by a big German shepherd dog. I notice that he is showing a photo to the girl at the door, the girl points in my direction and then comes to get me. The frightened faces of my friends confirm my own fears: I am wanted by the NKVD. I am in trouble because of Dad's lost military documents. But to my amazement, the NKVD officer holds out my photograph and shakes his head in disbelief when I approach him. I recognize the photo—it is the "sexy" photo from the 1939 summer camp taken by the girl-photographer who used trick-photography to make me appear tall and voluptuous. The officer appears to be puzzled by the reality of my looks because he asks if I am sure that he is holding a photo of me, and finally he shakes his head and goes away.

I see fear in my mom's face when I come home after the movies. She tells me that an NKVD officer came to our house earlier and that she told him where he could find me. Later the same day my parents pack our knapsacks, just in case the NKVD comes to take us away.

The mystery of my photo is soon absolved from having any connection to Dad's passport. The girl who had taken my photograph at the summer camp soon shows up in my school and tells me what had actually happened. It appears that an NKVD officer stationed at their home saw my photograph, insisted on getting my address, frightened my poor mother, and ended up seeing me at the movies. As for my family, we unpack our backpacks and wait to see what the future will bring.

A few days later, another NKVD officer appears at our door and asks my mom to send me after classes to their headquarters "just to help the NKVD" complete my files. This time we are sure that it is the affair of my dad's lost military documents, and this time they do interrogate me.

"Did your father hide his military documents, and if so, where?" they ask me time and time again. "Tell us what you know about your father's military service, especially when and where he served," they continue. "We assure you that the NKVD understands the predicament of the Jewish soldiers who were forced to fight against the Soviet efforts to liberate the Belorussian and Ukrainian territories. We want you to reassure your father that he doesn't need to fear handing in his military papers."

The interrogation lasts the whole afternoon and my ordeals are sweetened by lots of candy. There are no threats of any kind. "My dad never lies," I keep repeating, "and if he claims that his military documents are lost, then this must be true." I go on to offer my own assurances to the NKVD. "My dad was a musician during his military service, as well as later during his civilian life, and has no reason to lie about his military service. He even swore to my grandfather that he would never kill a man and that he never used a gun during his military service. I know he participated in Russia's civil war in Siberia and was released by the 'Reds' from the Austrian POW camp in Chita (in Siberia). In fact, he was promoted to be a 'Red Commissar' whom the 'Whites' tried to kill, and managed to escape from the 'Whites' by joining the Pilsudsky Siberian Legion." I pause for emphasis. "Do you know that I saw 'tears of joy' in my dad's eyes as he watched the Soviet Army enter Bialystok?" At last they let me go home, but I wonder if they believe my stories.

We pack our backpacks again, but to our relief my dad gets his passport without the eleventh paragraph. His passport will be validated each year, but only after a favorable review of his and his family's "civic activities." Now we can unpack our backpacks for good.

Early in June of 1940 we hold elections for the next school year's membership in the *UchKom* (Student Committee). The candidates are both nominated and elected at a Delegate Assembly and they present their platform at that time. I have known for some time that the delegates will nominate me for the position of the *"Predsiedatel UchKoma"* (the head of the Student Committee), and I have prepared my electioneering speech ahead of time. Since the NKVD seeks to review my family's "civic activities," I decide to use my left-wing Zionist background in composing my speech. This will surely impress the principal and the NKVD. Besides that, I hope to show honest sympathies with the Soviets' promises for the future and with the social benefits that are already here.

The incumbent head of the Student Committee, Samek Pewzner, is the alternate nominee for this office. The delegates loudly applaud his endearing speech and the principal smiles with approval. Now comes my turn, and I proceed to proudly tell my audience that I am a former member of a Zionist organization of the Jewish working people, the Hashomer Hatzair. The Hashomer Hatzair aspires to the creation of a socialist society in Palestine. I passionately advocate that all national Socialist Youth organizations ought to work hand-in-hand with the Soviet Komsomol to build in each country its particular brand of Socialism. As for my platform, I promise to steer my Jewish schoolmates toward extracurricular activities that are appropriate for life in either the Soviet Union or Eretz Israel.

The Delegate Assembly meets my speech with dead silence and all eyes are on Principal Tykocinski, whose pale face seems to have been totally drained of blood. I cower within myself as Tykocinski finally faces the students and proceeds to demolish my speech, my ideals, and me. I learn that my Zionist ideas are counter-revolutionary and that Zionism serves to delude the Jewish workers from their true course towards international Socialism and Communism which has been charted by Marx, Engels, Lenin, and Stalin. The principal implores the students to steer away from my counter-revolutionary ideas and to reelect the trustworthy Samek Pewzner to head the Student Committee of our school.

The Delegate Assembly votes by a show of hands. Sure of his persuasive powers, the principal confidently asks the delegates to vote for me before voting for Pewzner, but so many hands go up for me that he doesn't even bother to either count my votes or call for a vote for Pewzner. I win, the Delegate Assembly goes wild, and the principal and his ideological soul mates walk out of the auditorium.

The news about my speech reaches the students of other schools and some of these students tell my dad that he ought to be proud of his brave daughter who stood up to the Soviet power. My parents tell me to pack my backpack again, and this time we are sure the NKVD is coming to take me away.

But they never come. Were they impressed by the "bravery" of my confrontation with the authorities, or did they simply find my juvenile concoction of ideologies unworthy of their attention?

As is true of all Soviet schools, our final exams are given around the middle of June of 1940. This is the first time in my school career that I have to study for standardized written tests. There will be some essays and some short answer questions. The tests in different subjects follow one another after a break of two or thee days, and these days are spent on concentrated cramming. Two refugee girls, Mirka and Dasa, often study with me for the tests. These two Varsovians are the most appealing and intriguing girls I've met during the Soviet times. Mirka is a cute curly-haired blond with blue eyes and Dasa is a ravishing brunette. Both girls come from families of former Jewish-Polish communists who transferred their allegiance to the Jewish Bund when the Polish Communist Party was disbanded.

During the breaks between our exams, Mirka sometimes sings her Yiddish folk songs for me, and I find these to be entirely different from the "schmaltzy" vaudevillian songs I heard in Grudziadz. Mirka's Yiddish songs speak of the hardships, joys, and aspirations of Jewish working people, and there is a harmony between these lyrics and my social consciousness. I sing for my father one of these songs, "*Katie, Katie, Katerine hot sikh mit a Yad bakent, mit a Yad mit a Tshuprine, mit Mazoles oif die Hend* (Katie meets a boy who has a mop of hair and callouses on his hands)." He is intrigued by this and other "working peoples' songs" but does not include them in his choral repertoire. But I will surely some day include many of

Mirka's songs in my repertoire of Yiddish folk songs.

Dasa and I form a special relationship; we talk about social issues, about the causes of wars, economic depression, discrimination of national minorities, and exploitation of man by man. This political consciousness-raising is new to me because it comes from a popular and well-liked classmate and not from a political demagogue or a textbook. Dasa remains my soul mate throughout the good and the bad times of the next few years. But in the meanwhile, I play my role of a scholastic watchdog for our trio, and we all pass our finals with mostly A's and just a few B's.

Just before finals a new person appears in our school, a Komsomol organizer, the *Komsorg*. Teenagers who apply for the Komsomol (Young Communist League) must meet the criteria established by the Communist Party. To begin with, you must come from a family of working people or intellectuals whose work benefits the masses. The *Komsorg* informs us that sons and daughters of wealthy merchants, of owners of the various workshops and factories, or of former bourgeoisie needn't apply for membership in the Komsomol. And the *Komsorg* needn't worry. None of my old friends apply.

The *Komsorg* is here in yet another role: he replaces the former *Politruk* and takes over the *Politruk's* role as a political official of our school. I become acquainted with the Komsomol organizer during an organizational meeting of the newly elected Student Committee and I am favorably impressed with him. He isn't dogmatic at all, he simply shows us how the new Soviet way of thinking could be comfortably substituted for the old "bourgeois" guidelines of the student self-government. He never uses the Soviet cliché, "and so said Comrade Stalin," and he doesn't quote the Soviet Constitution or the writings of Marx and Lenin to justify his contentions. It is easy to listen to *Tovarishch Yevseyev* (Comrade Yevseyev) and to follow his advice; and it is on his advice that I become a music counselor-in-training in the summer camp for Young Pioneers (children of pre-Komsomol age).

The summer of 1940 is absolutely marvelous, and the summer resort of Dzikie, where the Pioneer Summer Camp is located, has all that is needed for a great vacation. The Army transports the kids by trucks to the camping bunkhouses in the woodlands of Dzikie. The boys' counselors, the athletic director and the head counselor share one room and the girls' counselors and I share another room in the staff bunkhouse. The camp's cook, the kitchen help and an older married couple who are the camp's accordionists, are rooming with local families. The counselors are all *vostochniki* (easterners) from the USSR and all of them members of the Komsomol, as is our Comrade Aliosha Yevseyev who is now the head counselor of the camp. The athletic director, the accordionists and the kitchen workers are all *zapadniki* (westerners) from the former Polish territories.

The camp life here is much like that of the summer camps of my past in that it has athletic, cultural, and nature programs. We have a lovely lake with a sandy beach for swimming and boating, lovely woods and meadows for nature studies, and an arena where the children's *samodeyatelnosc* (amateur performing arts program) is held. I am amazed at the variety of skits, dances and comic songs that are created by individual bunkhouses, and I am taken aback by the artful costumes they make. As the music counselor-in-training of the camp, I am limited to conducting the daily sing-outs and performances of my little choral group, but I am also asked to help with the creative efforts of the bunkhouses themselves, and I like that most of all. At this time I become friends with Simka, a younger student from our school and a sweet soprano. (Her dad was the head of the Fire Department in whose building we had our first apartment in Bialystok.) Simka will soon become my dad's lead singer and my friend in the years to come. I also become familiar with the children of my sister's age, which helps me appreciate my talented sister. I vow to let her know about it. (My sister will surprise me much later in life by claiming that it wasn't her dancing talent but her academic giftedness that I did not appreciate!)

My folks come to camp on Visiting Day and my mom takes me aside to tell me that my choral work may jeopardize Dad's chances for getting a paid summer job as a music director in the Pioneer's camp next year. I feel ashamed that I did not think of it when I started my choral group, but it is now too late to make a change. But when my choral group performs for the visitors, out of tune with one another and out of sync with the accordion, the expressions on my parents' faces tell me they no longer fear me as a potential competitor of a professional choral master like my dad.

I enjoy the camp life best in the evenings and during the campers' afternoon rest periods because I can socialize with the counselors at that time. This is the first time I come in contact with young Soviet Jews who, as members of the Komsomol, are obviously Communists. Misha is a co-median among these Soviet Jewish guys. Misha's jokes remind me of my Polish Jewish friends' jokes, and so do his funny ditties, such as this one: "'I'll see what I can do,' said the blind Yosl to his deaf brother Shmul." And I find much of the *podworko's* humor in Misha's song about Masha, who waits for her Yasha at the drugstore, while he waits for her at the grocery store, and when the two finally find one another, they decide to meet again next day at the same time and in the same place.

It is quite illuminating to listen to these "easterners" when they talk about their life in the Soviet Union. I learn that the red-haired counselor Riva will be married by a rabbi and that her grandma will make a real Jewish wedding party for her. After that, she and her husband will volunteer to recruit the Ural miners for the Party. Seriozha tells us that he will study Agricultural Technology instead of Electrical Engineering because there is a greater need for agrarian technologists during the current Five-Year Plan. They all agree that the country's needs are more important than their personal whims. Finally, it is our Komsorg Aliosha Yevseyev who tells of his satisfaction when he changes self-indulgent "bourgeois" youngsters into productive members of a socialist society, productive according to their ability. I wait for the "and so said Comrade Stalin," but it does not come, which leads me to believe that maybe my Komsorg is a sincere Communist and perhaps the others are, too. I marvel how the Jewish Komsomol members seem to find no contradiction between their Judaism and the anti-religious teachings of their society. Indeed, what the young Soviets project in their person-to-person talks is that they like it there back home.

I am 15 years old at the start of the 1940-1941 school year, which starts with a bang: Principal Tychocinski is gone and Comrade Ivan Ivanovich Bukharevich from Minsk becomes our new principal. (In my later life, I will watch the televised performance of Comrade Khrushchev who provokes in me a feeling of deja vu in the person of Comrade Ivan Ivanovich Bukharevich.) But in Bialystok in September of 1940, it is the new principal who provokes flashbacks of the old Principal Tilleman. Tilleman used to yell at the top of his lungs, "YOU get going to your class

IMMEDIATELY!!!" Bukharevich replicates this command in folksy Russian saying, *"TY poshol v clas, NEMEDLENNO!!!"* Within a week, the strict discipline of Tilleman is restored in this Soviet variant of the Druskin's Gimnazjum. Being called to the principal's office now gives you the pre-death penalty chills. After the bell, a deadly silence reigns in the empty-of-students corridors, and even the voices of teachers in the teachers' room are subdued. Fortunately for the members of the *UchKom*, only the introductory meeting takes place in the principal's office. His disjointed and confusing sermon convinces us that, as much as possible, we better stay away from him. Fortunately, Ivan Ivanovich does not aim at playing the role of either an educator or of an instruction supervisor, so peace reigns once again in our classrooms.

We have another eastern addition to our teaching staff, Nadezhda Sergeyevna Pavlova, and she proves to be an excellent instructor of Russian literature. Nadezhda Sergeyevna is an intelligent and well-read teacher who is so well versed in Russian and Western literature that her classes are as challenging as the classes of the old Druskin vintage. Then, at the beginning of the second term of 1941, another Soviet educator comes to us, a mathematician, the likes of whom we never encountered even at Druskin. His name is Zigelbojm. He is a math instructor at the Bialystok Pedagogic Institute and therefore only has time to teach senior classes at our school and at another secondary school. Zigelbojm knows his math and he is tough; our wise guys learn that with him and with the likes of Pavlova, our finals will require serious cramming.

There are also changes in the student roster of our classes. Gone are the refugee boys of the dormitory at the shop-shack, and so is my Grudziadz friend Heniek, all of them apparently resettled in the interior of the Soviet Union. Apparently, the refugees who have roots in Bialystok and those who live with their Bialystok relatives are not being resettled, at least not yet. There are also several new students with us, one of which is Vasiliy, a Soviet boy. Of the other new students, only Lovka Lewin comes from the outlying northeastern territories; the rest either come from the German Occupation zones of Poland or else are simply transferred to us from other high schools. Lovka Lewin and Monia Wajsenberg, who come from Warsaw, soon become close buddies, and our Sonia soon becomes Monia's girlfriend.

Several of my classmates and I now find it gratifying to talk about the politically changing times of our young lives. We wonder who we are and what our attitudes toward the Soviet regime should be. Of course, there are among us those who have been programmed by their families to favor the Left-Wing ways but I soon learn that there are other formerly non-committed "westerners" who, like myself, begin to be attracted to the promises of the Soviet way of life. Ewa and her close friend Tusia both show interest in the possibilities of studying and of reaching professional goals in the Soviet Union. But what about Eretz Israel, which I will always love?

There is also a change in my music education. My piano teacher has joined the newly organized *Muzikalnoe Uchilishche* (School of Music) which I now attend. It is teeming with all kinds of musical activities. My friend Dasa is wooing a cellist who both teaches and plays his cello at the school, and so she and I begin to attend most of the performances there. In addition to these performances and my regular piano lessons, my teacher makes me practice for our competitions at the School of Music. The rules of the *Uchilishche* call for the students' vocal and instrumental competition at the end of each semester and I am forced to practice the piano like never before. I practice more out of loyalty for my teacher than for my own needs. My teacher aspires to be named "the best piano teacher" of the school, a status that is predicated upon the winning performance of her students. At the end of the first semester of 1941 I play, accompanied by my teacher's second piano, the Mozart *Piano concerto in C major* and my mind draws a blank on one of the key passages. In the audience, Mom and my sister are clearly commiserating with me while my dad's face tells me, "Haven't I told you a hundred times that you should practice more?"

To soften my downfall, my teacher recommends me for one of the school's ensembles of chamber music. I end up in a trio with a violin and a cello, playing a Hayden sonata and a Tchaikovsky waltz from his ballet "The Swan Lake." Dasa goes to the practice sessions with me since the cellist on whom she has a crush supervises them. The trio is scheduled to compete at the Minsk Olympiad and my mom has my fanciest dress remodeled for this occasion. But things don't work out for me after all. At almost the last moment, the Soviet director of the *Uchilishche* prevails upon my teacher to allow her daughter to replace me at the piano, and I don't go to Minsk. In protest, my dad resigns from the School of Music at the end of the spring semester. My principal, Ivan Ivanovich Bukharevich, protests even louder, but in private. He calls me into his office, bangs his fist on the desk and hollers that the Director of the *Uchilishche* is a *"glupaya korova* (stupid cow)." But I think the "stupid cow" is just a bully.

Early in 1941, the bedroom where my sister and I sleep is requisitioned by the Red Army. Since our cellist continues to occupy the spare bedroom, we have to be transferred into the bedroom of my parents. They, in turn, move into the living room. A Russian colonel stays in the children's room from January until the spring of 1941 and, since he is Jewish, my parents invite him to sit at our Passover supper, the Seder. I like this colonel and I talk with him about his family whom he left in Minsk, and he asks me about school. But we become less friendly in the aftermath of the Seder because I choose to excuse myself from the table soon after the beginning of the prayers. In keeping with their anti-religious propaganda, the Board of Education decrees to hold on this night school-wide dances. My principal asks me to come to school that night to help out with the dance. My parents become visibly upset but, in the presence of a high Soviet officer, they don't dare stop me from leaving the table. It is the Soviet officer himself who drags me back to my seat. He is livid with anger and tells me that he, an old Communist, would have never thought of leaving the Seder table of his parents to go to a school dance—who am I to do such a thing? The colonel goes on and on lecturing me about the right and the obligation of the Jewish people to maintain their traditions, and I end up staying. Next day, I ask the *Komsorg* to help me out and explain to the principal why I didn't come to the dance, and the principal lets it be.

When the Colonel leaves, a young Soviet Lieutenant and his bride move into his room. They both work at the local Army base and come home late in the evening. These two newlyweds keep to themselves most of the time so that we don't get to know them very well.

The Student Committee holds weekly meetings with the *Komsorg* and I learn how difficult it is for a girl to head a committee whose members are boys. I have never mastered the girlish mannerisms that could help in getting the support of these boys and I keep provoking their macho negativism, no matter how good my suggestions are. At this stage of my adolescent development, I am so much down on myself that I hardly put up a fuss when I am stepped upon, so the boys get their way, time and time again. Finally, Aliosha Yevseyev steps in and gives the boys a sermon about the sinfulness of sexism in the Soviet society. In fact, his sermon is followed by the reading of a very cute children's poem by Kolchak. In this poem, a bunch of children argue with one another as to whose mom does a more important job. It mentions Soviet moms who drive tractors and buses, moms who are electrical engineers and auto mechanics, and finally, moms who sit in the Supreme Soviet (but what about the Politburo, I wonder). Perhaps the boys weren't impressed with either the poem or the sermon, but they surely knew that they had made an unfavorable impression on someone in authority, and they behave themselves after that.

My friend Hela's cousin, Lieberman, who serves on the Committee, later tells me that the problem with me isn't that I am a girl but that my ideas are too immature for a leader. Toward the end of the spring term of 1941, the junior class elects a boy to serve as Head of the Student Committee next year.

The Komsorg talks with me about joining the Komsomol when I feel ready for it. We discuss my Zionist background and I am asked if perhaps I could be persuaded that Socialism is more likely to better human lives than is Capitalism, with all its nationalistic and individualistic contradictions. I answer in the positive, but I feel like a traitor. Whatever happened to my dreams about our own land, the Eretz Israel? How could Socialism cure the world's 2000-year-old hatred of the Jews? We talk about my fears and I am told that, in the Soviet Union, anti-Semites go to jail for calling the Jews the derogatory name *Zhid* instead of *Yevrey*, that Jews hold important positions in the Soviet Government and in the Armed Forces, and so on. I find myself looking for excuses as to why I am not ready to join the Komsomol and I mention that I wish to devote myself full heartedly to the study of architecture at the Leningrad's Academy of Art and so will hardly find time for the Komsomol. I am advised that Komsomol would not limit my academic life as much as would the Communist Party, if I ever join it. Yet, says Aliosha Yevseyev, the day will come for Communism to displace Socialism and then it will be, "From each according to his ability and to each according to his need." Things will be different then.

I go home completely charmed by this soft-spoken Communist and decide to talk with my parents about applying for the Komsomol after my final exams and before summer vacation. (I don't yet know that this is not to be.)

On the 1st of May, Workers Day is celebrated with a spectacular parade of the army and the working people of Bialystok. The marching goes on until the afternoon, and in the evening the pubs and cafes are crowded with the holiday makers. But soon after this most important Soviet holiday, ominous things begin to happen. We hear of nightly visits by the NKVD to homes of various people, among whom are those who hold passports with the "eleventh paragraph," clergymen, and refugees who have been, until now, allowed to remain in Bialystok. Those who are visited are given but a short time to pack. They are then taken into detention centers and shipped in "cattle cars" to the interior of the Soviet Union. People of Bialystok become terribly uncertain of what their tomorrows will bring. We learn of friends and acquaintances who have been resettled and of others who go into hiding to avoid the transport. People whom we know, my French teacher's husband among them, no longer sleep in their own homes in an attempt to evade the NKVD. I am beginning to have a hard time with my shaky pro-Soviet ideology, but a talk with Aliosha helps a bit. He explains to us at the *UchKom* that because of the proximity of the Germans to our territory, our territory must be peopled only by those who are totally trustworthy. Having potential spies and traitors so close to the Soviet-German border could be disastrous. And so, the transport of the "undesirables" goes on until the German invasion in June of this year when, not far from the outskirts of Bialystok, some of the resettlement trains are strafed by the Germans, allowing the exiles to go home.

During these ominous times, Rachelka becomes my study-mate for the finals. She comes from a small town nearby and lives here with a family whose home on Polna Street has a quiet backyard where we can study, shielded from the street noises. Rachelka is sweet, gentle, and fun to be with. We grow very fond of each other and we spend all daylight hours together. I get to know the family with whom Rachelka is staying, their two expectant daughters, and their young son who has a sweet tooth for Rachelka. When I see them around their evening dinner table, I feel the warmth that radiates from this family of hardworking, simple people, and I envy them their warm togetherness.

Rachelka and I do extremely well on our finals. She has many A's and I, now a complete *otlichnitsa*, have all A's on my report card, which will be registered in the Republic's Archives in Minsk. Because of this I will be absolved from having to take entrance exams at the Leningrad Academy of Arts next fall.

My sister, who has been sick with a lingering bronchitis, has a hard time preparing for her sixth grade finals, and I have to help her with her studies. Magnanimously, I forgive and forget the taunting gestures that were routinely directed at me by my sister and her cronies, and I spend hours at a time diligently studying with her. This is the one time my mom does not need to plead with me to help my sister. Perhaps this is because I have a premonition of soon parting with my sister for a long, long time…When her June 1941 finals are over, my sister leaves for the Boryslaw home of our aunts in the Carpathian mountains. My parents believe that out there, the mountain air will help cure their little daughter's bronchitis.

The war between the Soviet Union and the Germans starts on June 22, 1941, and my sister never comes back to her home and family.

Rachelka somehow returns to her small hometown just before it is occupied by the Germans. She will be killed there with the rest of the towns' Jews. From my home on Polna Street in the Ghetto of Bialystok, I often see the daughters of Rachelka's host family wheel their babies in their carriages. I enjoy seeing these cute babies, but only until the violent February 1943 roundup of Jews for the extermination camps, after which time I occasionally see the mothers—alone. I am told that, to protect its occupants, the crying babies had to be smothered in their basement hideout. The younger brother, who had a sweet tooth for Rachelka, is taken into the woods of Pietrasze along with thousands of other men and executed during the infamous Sabbath of July 12, 1941. The other members of the family perish in Treblinka with the rest of the Ghetto Jews in August of 1943.

The day will come when I will learn about the purges, the atrocities against the "kulaks" and the murder of millions of innocent people in the Soviet Union. The day will come when I will learn that Stalin was a pernicious criminal. I will find it hard to believe that my naive perception of "dorogoy towarishch Stalin (dear comrade Stalin)" as a benign father figure was based on pure hoax.

I will some day go to Russia and look for the embodiment of my rosy memories of the prewar Soviet life, but find nothing of the sort. And I will always wonder about the reality hidden beneath my rosy memories of an easy life in Soviet Bialystok from 1939 to 1941—why hadn't I seen the reality?

"YESLEE ZAVTRA VOYNAH, BOUDZ SIEVODNIA K POKHODU GOTOV..."

(IF WAR COMES TOMORROW, BE READY FOR IT TODAY...")

Ever since I made my home in the United States, I've been addicted to watching World War II movies and television reruns. Vicariously, I lived through the sea battles in the Pacific and the Atlantic Oceans, the Allies' invasion of Normandy, Africa, and Italy, and the Russians' rebound after their heroic defense of Stalingrad. In my imagination I lived through the ordeals of the American soldiers and I grieved after them in the military cemeteries of France, Belgium, and the Philippines. And I cried bitterly when I laid flowers on the mass graves of the thousands who starved to death during the siege of Leningrad. All this was simply part of my catching up with the history of World War II—the war that was taking place while I lived in ignorance about its course, and in isolation from its happenings. Yet there was a small segment of World War II in which I could revisit my own memories, the revisiting of the shadows of the German invasion of the Soviet Union in June of 1941. One would never expect the roar of an American plane to bring forth again these shadows, yet it happened to me quite recently.

We were at dinner in a lovely restaurant in West Palm Beach, Florida, called "The 57th Battalion of the Bombardiers." The restaurant had a small landing field connected to the hinterlands of the West Palm Beach airport.

It was during dinner that I suddenly heard the roar of a vintage World War II bomber, a bomber that was the restaurant's piece de resistance. It idled for a while and then took off and circled, roaring above the hinterlands of the airport and above our restaurant.

The roar of this plane made me cringe and flooded my heart with memories of the German bombers that strafed us as we walked toward the Soviet border...

My new French-blue woolen dress is ready for me and I put it on just before I leave for my Graduation Ball. It is the first time I use eye shadow, a bit of face powder and lipstick, and the mirror tells me that I am a good looking teenager after all. My parents come to see me receive the straight-A report card and the principal's congratulations.

After the awarding of the diplomas, we stay on to dance to the live music of a real jazz band. I don't know how it happened, but a serious boy, whom I hardly ever noticed in class, asks me to dance and continues dancing with me throughout the evening. We are both novices at this so we do not talk very much, especially since some of my classmates look at us with obvious curiosity. I've never noticed before today that this quiet boy is quite handsome. I know that his name is Klaczkin, that his dad is a dentist, and that Klaczkin never volunteers in class to either answer or ask questions.

A lovely pastel dusk delicately colors the early evening skies, when the two of us leave the dance and go to the roof for a view of the city lights. Again, I don't know how it happened, but Klaczkin kisses me and tells me that he didn't notice earlier how pretty I am, and he regrets that. Stupidly, I say that maybe he didn't look at me because S.O. presidents aren't supposed to be pretty, and just as stupidly, Klaczkin says that smart girls aren't supposed to be pretty either. We kiss again, timidly and gently, and we go down to join the party and dance some more. This time, the other boys from my class ask me to dance with them, too. And, when I notice Dad dancing with one of his students, I ask him for the next dance. It is a slow waltz that Dad and I have, on occasion, danced together very well. A few dances later I discover that Klaczkin is no longer here—perhaps he has gone home.

On the radio, the clock of the Kremlin Tower chimes twelve times and we stand at attention to hear the Kremlin's INTERNATIONALE. The graduation ball ends soon after midnight, we say good night to each other and I pretend not to notice the inquisitive looks of my girlfriends. My dad has been asked by his choral group to go for a midnight walk with them, so I walk home with Murka and Maszka who excitedly gossip about this one boy and that one. Mercifully they ask me no questions about Klaczkin.

I fall asleep wondering if I should have looked for Klaczkin after my dance with Dad. Would he have taken me home? Will he ask me for a date this summer? I don't yet know that from tomorrow on, Klaczkin and I will never have a chance to have a date...

Dad wakes us up when he comes home from his walk just before dawn. He excitedly tells us that during their walk near the military airport, he and his students heard antiaircraft guns shoot at planes that were flying over the fields. Not quite sure that his story can be believed, I go back to bed. Soon after I fall asleep again, I hear a thunderous noise and feel the house shake. Now everybody is up. Our Soviet lieutenant dashes out of his room, hurriedly puts his uniform on and runs downstairs. From the balcony, we see a few Soviet officers dashing toward the corner of Kosciuszki Square, and soon we also see a military vehicle approach the Square from the opposite direction. Then a night-shift factory worker comes in sight and yells to us in Yiddish, "*S'is a bombe, oy an emese bombe is gefallen oif a moyer in die Sienkiewicza Gass!* (a bomb fell on an apartment house in Sienkiewicza Street)." How could a bomb fall on one of our houses? How could there have been an air attack without the air-raid sirens going off? I wonder if Dad's story about the antiaircraft guns could have been true. But our Lieutenant comes back and tells us that there is no reason to panic, because neither he nor the other officers had been put on alert that night. He confides in us that the only explanation for the bomb that anybody can think of is that air maneuvers were held at dawn and that a bomb was accidentally released during these maneuvers. With that, the young lieutenant collects his belongings and he and his wife leave for the army headquarters.

It is a tense day for us. We meet with our neighbors and speculate about the possibility of war between the Soviet Union and Germany. We argue about the reliability of the non-aggression pact that Ribbentropf and

Molotov signed in 1939. We reanalyze the story that has been circulating since the day before yesterday. According to the story, someone was accosted by a man who sneered at the gigantic portraits of the members of the Soviet Politburo and said, with a German accent, "These portraits will not be here by the day after tomorrow."

We hastily shop for rice, flour, and as many other non-perishable foods as possible, just in case. And we anxiously eye the many military vehicles that seem to be heading toward the Wolkowysk Highway leading east. We wonder what is going on. But we stop wondering when we hear Molotov's radio speech to the citizens of the Soviet Union: "On this night of June 22, the dastardly Germans have launched a perfidious attack against the Soviet Union and have at multiple points invaded the Western Soviet lands."

We are now at war.

The next two days remain chaotic. People mob the stores in search of wartime supplies and fight for goods that are sold out in no time at all. Dad and I find it almost impossible to buck the crowds, but we manage to get some soap, groats, and canned fish. And the domestic helper who has worked for us for the last two months brings in some farm produce. We hide the most valuable food supplies. The lengths of fabric that we can barter later for food are placed out of sight. We also pack our backpacks for a quick getaway, if needed.

On the second day of the war, a military vehicle stops in front of our house and an officer in charge of Dad's Red Army Band comes to get Dad to join his evacuating army division. I overhear the officer say, "The Germans will be here within days—they caught us unprepared and we can't stop them. Comrade Ghass (Hass), you do know, don't you, what the Germans will do with you Jews? Pack up and come with us. We will try to get you and your family into the interior of the Soviet Union." My parents stand numb and I can read in their faces that they are afraid to take the chance the officer is offering. My dad finally tells the Russians that he will not travel with his family at this time because his father has always warned him against the travel during wartime. And that is that! This is the last day for the Soviet personnel to evacuate from Bialystok and my dad refuses to go with them! So we remain in Bialystok.

A day later, there are no Soviet soldiers in the city. In the meantime, the people of Bialystok, mostly Jews, have since yesterday begun a mass exodus to the east. Some are going by horse-drawn wagons, others by cars or trucks, but the majority go on foot. There is a rumor that evacuation trains have been lined up on the former Polish-Soviet border at Wolkowysk around forty miles east of here. Tusia comes early in the morning and asks me to help her with the disposal of incriminating documents, in case there are any at our school. Lowka and Monia are at the school office when we get there, and all of us begin shredding applications for the Komsomol and any other papers where specific students are singled out for their "politically correct" thinking. We also give in to a juvenile impulse and change the registered grades of several classmates who flunked out or did poorly this year.

On our way home, we discuss our uncertain future. The boys have heard that there indeed are some evacuation trains that are stuck on the wide Russian tracks, past Wolkowysk. Apparently, these empty trains are there because the exiles traveling in them were allowed to go free. Lowka and Monia urge Tusia and me to get our knapsacks and join them for the eastward trek to Wolkowysk. Tusia is quite ready to go because she has no problem with leaving her host family and going back to her father's home near the town of Wolkowysk. But with my father's strong feelings against wartime travel, I couldn't openly leave my parents. I would have to sneak out somehow.

We finally decide to go home, get our backpacks, and meet in front of my house. Dad isn't at home when I get there. He is apparently expecting the Germans to come at any moment and is feverishly revamping his hideout in the attic. I cuddle up to my mom who is resting on her bed. She kisses me and says, "How could I protect you, my child." Then with my knapsack on my back, I climb onto the upper walkway through the kitchen window and take the staircase leading to the street. Downstairs, the four of us join the stream of humanity heading east.

The marchers become a spectacle for the suburbanites who look at us in dismay and yell, "Where do you think you are going? The Germans are already ahead of you!" A Gentile boy, a bit older than I, catches up with me and asks me to turn back. "You could easily pass for one of us. Don't go, stay here with my family," he says. But we keep going, and we soon join the civilian and army vehicles heading for Wolkowysk along the highway littered by smoldering skeletons of trucks and tanks. Suddenly, there comes a distant drone of planes, and instantly soldiers and civilians abandon their vehicles and follow the pedestrians onto the high road banks. We all quickly hide there in the underbrush, among the trees, and behind the abandoned farm equipment. The drone of the planes gets louder and louder and they come closer and dip lower, their machine guns strafing the road with a blanket of bullets and explosives. And then they are gone. More burning and smoldering vehicles are added to those already on the road. Now the fleeing civilians and soldiers come back to the highway and the march resumes. Some of the refugees stay behind and try to get their damaged trucks or tanks to work. Others walk back and forth, looking for lost friends and relatives. A few walk back towards the city. Every few hours until dark the planes come back. Eventually, their strafing patterns include the road banks so that we must hide farther away from the road. And now there are wounded and dead on the side terrains as well.

We lose Tusia in the chaos of the last strafing of the day. Hungry and exhausted, I fall asleep huddled between Monia and Lowka. The strafing starts the next morning at dawn and this time we have the comfort of hiding in the woods on both sides of the road. Somehow, I lose the boys as well.

I end up in the woods alone, and I find a spot for myself next to two friendly Soviet soldiers. Now the first wave of strafing is followed by another, and then yet another wave, and the incessant noise puts me to sleep—or perhaps it is the fear that makes me conk out. When I wake up after the air-raid, I see that many trees have been felled. I hear all around me the cries and moaning of the wounded, and I curl up inside the army coat the soldiers covered me with and cry. "*Ty odna, dievushka?* (Are you alone, girl?)" one of the soldier asks in his folksy Russian. "Yes, I am alone," I hear myself saying. "I have lost my friends and I am hungry and scared." The soldier gives me a piece of dry bread, a drink of water from his canteen and an invitation. "*Davay poydem v partizanku, dievushka* (Let's go and join the partisans, girl)!" The soldiers' situation indeed is precarious: they have lost contact with the rest of the retreating divisions and they can't surrender because the Germans most often shoot the Soviet prisoners they take in this campaign. The two soldiers have therefore decided to comb the dense woods in the area and find other stranded soldiers. In this way, a partisan unit could well be formed.

I thank the kind soldiers for asking me to join the partisans. I describe to them my own plans and I go on to Wolkowysk. It is my third day on the road and the planes keep on coming, and now the road is truly littered with burning derelict vehicles whose gas tanks and ammunition boxes keep on exploding, scaring the daylights out of the marchers. I hang on to the mainstream of the marchers, both on the road and in the hiding places along the sides of the road, and my luck is finally with me—I bump into Dasa and her parents while I seek shelter in the village barn where they lie hidden. Dasa's folks, who are also heading for Wolkowysk, take me under their wings. It surely feels good to have the fatherly protection of Dasa's dad. Bedraggled and sweaty, we drag ourselves ahead on our blistered legs until finally Dasa's mom declares that she cannot walk anymore. We must have covered a distance of at least twenty miles from the city, and now we decide to take a side road to look for food and a place to rest.

It is almost nighttime when we approach farmhouses clustered around what appears to be a community house. Dasa's dad knocks on the door of one of these houses and we disbelieve our ears when we hear a sleepy voice answer our knocking with a *"Ver is do* (who is there)," in Yiddish. Who would have thought that a Jewish collective farm, a *Kolkhoz*, would be in the vicinity of Bialystok! "This Kolkhoz has been barraged for three days by pleas for food and shelter," the sleepy woman tells us. "The farmers have to sleep during the day and work at night because German parachutists come down at dawn to search for the marauding Russian units."

We thankfully accept a dish of buttermilk with boiled potatoes and a bale of hay to sleep on in their community house.

Still in the dark, there is a wake-up call of *"Oif! Oif!* (Up! Up!)" We start traveling along a dirt road parallel to the main highway. We walk alongside fields of early wheat, away from the strafing planes. We head for the large village in front of us. Just as we reach the village, a hail of gunfire breaks loose. Braving the gunfire, we run down the village road and into an open door of the village church. We immediately realize that the church is caught in a crossfire coming from the houses and barns of the village, and it feels as if the bullets are aimed directly at us.

We quickly climb the staircase to the landing of the bell-tower and can see from here that German and Soviet soldiers hidden inside village barns and houses are shooting at each other. We can even see the bullets ricochet against the whitewashed walls of the village houses and the strings of bullet holes along the wooden fences. We watch the Germans shoot down the Soviet soldiers as they dash into the fields of yellow wheat. We watch the Soviet soldiers disregard the barrage of bullets, disregard the German commands of "*Haende Hoch* (hands up)," and disregard their fallen comrades. We watch them dash into the wheat fields, no matter what…and in the end we see that which we cannot believe to be true. We see Asian-Soviet soldiers take out their short bayonets and commit hara-kiri, cutting open their abdomens in full view of the surrounding Germans.

Dasa's dad pushes us head-down to the floor of the landing where we stay, numb and bewildered, until we are told that it is all over. After a while we leave the church, the village and the dirt road to rejoin the main road again. At one point we cross the railroad tracks and see swollen cadavers of farmers whose meager belongings are spilled all over the tracks. A few Jewish fugitives are searching the pockets and document pouches of the dead villagers and we will soon appreciate the reasons for which these Jews were looking for the Gentile farmers' documents.

In the evening we reach the village Walily, where my parents used to spend their vacations while I was away at summer camps. With a bit of inquiry, I am able to locate the farmer whose bungalow my parents used to rent in the summer. We learn from the farmer that German "pincer" armies invaded eastern Belorussia and "swallowed" the Wolkowysk region. This means that our route of escape into the Soviet Union has been cut off. Of course, we could attempt to cut through the German lines, but Dasa's plea to attempt this merits a firm no from her father. We will rest for a day or two in Walily and then head back to Bialystok. That is the final decision.

In the darkness of the night, somber-faced Dasa and I bury a cigar box with Dasa's Komsomol booklet. We bury it under an old oak tree in front of the bungalow where we will spend the night. We carve a "D" in the bark of the tree and vow to come back one day and reclaim the booklet.

We are awakened at night by the sounds of the heavy German trucks. Yes, they are here, in Walily. Knowing that the Germans always impose a strict sunset to sundown curfew for civilians, we fidget on our straw mattresses until it is light enough to safely wash up and get going home. Just as we prepare to leave, two German soldiers walk in and ask to see our papers. Since they can't read Russian, our Jewish identity is not discovered, and the soldiers treat us politely enough. But they keep eying Dasa and finally grab her by the hand and declare that they are going to take her with them. Dasa's dad speaks excellent German and proceeds to dramatically implore the two soldiers to live up to the time-honored chivalry of German soldiers vis-à-vis innocent young ladies. The young Germans relent and leave Dasa alone. We can now go home.

We follow the rail tracks to avoid the German armies moving along the main roads to Bialystok. I walk behind Dasa's family and let the images of the last two years, the Soviet years, crowd my sorrowed soul. I hum the many Soviet songs I sang along with our chorus: "From Moscow to the Distant Borders," the "Katiusha" and the "Poliushko, Polie" (Meadowland, Meadowland) songs. But there is one song that stays with me till we reach Bialystok. For it was in that song that our Soviet "liberators" told us that if war comes tomorrow, they will be prepared to fight and win that war today. They told us that on land, on the seas, and in the air, from Kronstadt to Vladivostok, the Soviet people will rise and their mighty forces will mercilessly beat the enemy! "*Yeslee zavtra voyna yesli zavtra v pokhod, boodz sievodnia k pokhodu gotov.*" I hum, "If the war comes tomorrow, and if tomorrow you must go, be ready for it today." With disappointment and anger, I silently ask the Soviets the unanswered questions: "Oh, look at how terribly your people are doing! Why didn't you prepare for this lousy war? Why did you promise us a better life and then allowed this to happen? What will become of us tomorrow?"

In August of 1943, trains bring the remaining Bialystok Jews to the train station of the extermination camp of Majdanek at Lublin. Along with Mirka and my other classmates, Dasa is marched off toward a windowless van that will supposedly take her and others to work. Dasa looks me in the eye, I recall our vows to search for her Komsomol booklet, and I nod my

head in a silent affirmation of our vows. Before I am marched off into the concentration camp of Majdanek myself, the windowless vans return without their cargo and heavy steel poison gas cylinders are hauled out. I never see Dasa or my other classmates again.

Part Three

THE GHETTO OF BIALYSTOK

"Vail in Bialystoker ghetto, a gevalt un geshrai,
Vail in Bialystoker ghetto, yeder harts tut er vai...
Mir zitsen un mir kleren, vos vet mit uns veren?
*Mir vissen nit vos vet mit uns zayn..."**

(There is a cry of woe, in the ghetto of Bialystok ,
And every heart is in pain, in the ghetto of Bialystok...
We sit here and wonder, what will be with us?
We have no idea what will happen to us...) **

*A Yiddish song of the beggars in the streets of the Ghetto of Bialystok (author unknown).
**English translation by the author.

A SUMMER MONTH OF FORBIDDEN FREEDOMS

My American family and I diligently searched out the memorable sites of the ghetto when we visited Bialystok in 1965. In the ghetto cemetery on Zabia Street, my children placed flowers on the graves of the many victims; at the commemorative plaques in other areas, we paid homage to the heroes and martyrs of the ghetto. But I vowed to myself that I would return to this adopted hometown of mine and revisit, at that time, the streets outside the area of the former ghetto. And I did return, alone.

Regretfully, I did not know Bialystok as well as I knew my primary hometown of Grudziadz. After all, I lived in Bialystok outside the walls of the ghetto for only three years. But I shared the fate of the native Bialystokers, and that cemented my allegiance to the city so that I thought of Bialystok as my adopted hometown. And, most importantly, the last month of my freedom (a forbidden freedom to be sure) was spent in and around our home, just outside the Jewish area destined to become the walled-in ghetto.

So, I came again to Bialystok and checked into a hotel on the same Pilsudskiego Street where our house had stood. From the top floor of my balcony, I eyed the entry to Kupiecka Street where the guard house of the ghetto gate had been located. Who would have believed that the girl-laborer who used to go through this gate to work, would defy Hitler's sinister designs and stay alive? Who would have dreamed that the same slave-laborer would come back and look into the defunct prison as a free woman?

Our house was no longer there, demolished most likely by the advancing Soviet armies. Just the same, I stood at the spot where the house used to be and thought of the happenings that had centered around that house during the memorable July of 1941. Beyond this spot, I stood at a plaque commemorating the Great Synagogue of Bialystok that had been burned out of existence and thought of the thousands who had perished in that fire shortly before I returned home from my eastward trek.

On and on, I walked the areas where I had tasted freedom, limited though it was, for the last time in July of 1941. I walked the former Jewish working class area of Piaski and Hanajki, up Pilsudskiego Street toward the fabulous Cathedral of St. Roch, and down Sienkiewicza Street toward the suburbs where Stela had welcomed this bedraggled wanderer and had sent me back to the German occupied city. I even ventured into the ancient Jewish cemetery and scanned the neglected gravestones to read the typical Bialystok names of the Wasilkowskis, Krynskis, Pruzanskis and such, and to feel that I was part of that, too.

Finally, I walked the street that lead to our escape route to Wolkowysk, a road which, all through the last days of our freedom, Monia and I took when we went bartering for food. This time around, I had come to Bialystok to find the shadows of the last month of my life in Bialystok spent outside the walls of the ghetto...

July of 1941 is here and with it comes, one after another, life-threatening events that we must somehow weather. It is the dawn of the 1st day of that July, and Dasa's family and I are nearing the end of our unsuccessful escape from Bialystok to the Soviet Union. Wearily, we walk along the railway tracks and come closer and closer to home. Soon we can see the distant outlines of Bialystok's eastern suburbs, but the southerly center and the outskirts of the town remain invisible; they are covered by a dense cloud from which emanates a strong smell of smoke. My heart starts pounding when I hear Dasa's dad whisper, "The Jewish areas...Oh, God, they burned the Jewish areas!" All I can think of is our house at #91 Sovietskaya Street (the former Pilsudskiego Street), a street that opens into two Jewish areas. And all I can think of are my parents, trapped there! As I drag my feet along the track, I almost wish for a train to come at us from behind at full speed. But of course no trains are running, and as we enter the eastern suburbs of Bialystok we know that we will have to face what awaits us in the city. Dasa's folks decide to head for their home on Polna Street, but I haven't the guts to return to my home alone, so I decide to stay here in the suburb. My friend and classmate Stela lives here, and I find both a welcome and a shelter at her home.

Stela tells me that the Germans occupied Bialystok on June 27th. On that very day they executed hundreds of people in the Jewish areas of Piaski, Hanajki and the more central Jewish area around Kosciuszki Square. The Germans set these areas afire and some 2,000 Jewish men were locked inside the Great Synagogue of Bialystok. The Germans set the synagogue afire with the men inside. Those who attempted to escape from the burning building were mercilessly mowed down. For nearly three days the Jewish areas of Bialystok were left burning.

Stela and I recall the rumored German threat that they would repay the Jews for their jeering and pelting of the withdrawing troops back in 1939. But is the burning of the Jewish areas just a reprisal for past misdeeds, or is it a preview of things to come?

Stela's mom isn't sure if Pilsudskiego Street, where our house stands, escaped the fire damage and offers to go there and see what's what. Toward the end of the day she returns with my mother, who helps me hobble on blistered feet back home.

It takes me three days to tend to my blisters and to come to myself. I feel helpless and lost. I find comfort sleeping huddled between my parents, which they don't mind at all. Not one word is said about my escape from home, and no questions are asked about my traumatic experiences on the road. Gradually, I start telling them some of it and they tell me most of what had happened when I was away. One of my mother's stories about a mysterious visit by a young German soldier is hard to believe. Who was this gentle young soldier who came alone and who asked for "Herr Professor Adolf Hass"? Yes, the soldier could have found Dad's address in the Town Hall registers, but only if he knew Dad's name. Was it Plischke (as my mom thought), my dad's favorite German student-violinist from Grudziadz? If so, what did Plischke want with Dad? Should Mom have taken a chance and gotten Dad out of his hideout in the attic to face the young

German? Later events indicate that staying in the attic was the safest thing to do after all.

Early on the morning of Thursday, July 3rd, the Germans cordon off Pilsudskiego and several other streets. Accompanied by civilians and working with lists of names, they conduct a house-to-house search for Jewish men. My father and several other men go into hiding in the attic. Mom and I stay with neighbors in their second floor apartment and look out the window to see what is going on. We can see that the Germans are marching off only Jewish men and we know that many of these men are professionals, artists, musicians, and employees of various offices in Bialystok. It becomes clear at the end of the day that some 2,000 men were apprehended and taken on trucks to the village of Pietrasze where they were told to dig trenches for the military. (We will eventually learn that indeed the men did dig trenches, but not for the German military. They were shot and buried in the trenches they had dug themselves.) Thus the Bialystok community loses many of its leading intellectuals. The three hundred victims and their widows will henceforth be referred to as *Die Donershtike*—the Thursday-Ones.

In the late afternoon of the same day, Monia visits me and derides the three days of my "recuperating." Next day, he and I are going to go into the country and barter salable "stuff" for food. There is hardly any bread in town, and Jews found in the few bread lines left are beaten up by the Germans and the hostile native Gentiles. Grocery stores hardly open up at all and Monia convinces my parents that he and I must bring in some food from the villagers. He believes that we will be safe in the villages not only because we look like Gentiles, but also because a boy accompanied by a girl will make a good impression on the farm family.

Our trip to the countryside proves to be both pleasant and educational. We discover that little besides eggs, milk, salt pork, and bacon slabs can be bartered from the farmers in exchange for cigarettes, *makhorka* (Soviet coarse tobacco), soap, sugar and vodka, none of which we are carrying. We finally manage to swap Monia's girlfriend's prewar silk stockings and my mom's silk scarf for a large sack of potatoes, sour cream and some eggs. The farmer's wife treats us to buttermilk and fresh bread and that is indeed a pleasant surprise. We learn that the farmers (Polish and Belorussian farmers alike) hate the Germans and the Soviets with equal ferocity. They hate the Germans for the theft of their barn animals, they hate the Soviets for the collectivization of their farms and for their favoring of the Jews!

On Saturday, July 12th, we wake up to threatening German shouts coming from the Jewish area abutting Sienkiewicza and Pilsudskiego Streets. We can see from our balcony that the Germans are herding all pedestrians into their houses and following them there. Mom and I immediately realize that we must hide Dad, but before we can get our thoughts together and expedite Dad to his hideout, German soldiers are at our door. "Heil Hitler!" they bark, demanding to see the men of our household who are of military age. My dad doesn't budge from his bedroom, but Mom proceeds to tell the Germans, in her impeccable German, that her husband had served in the Austrian army with valor during World War I and that he now receives a pension as a disabled veteran. One of the soldiers walks into the bedroom, looks at my gray-haired ashen-faced father sprawled in his bed, checks his passport and, motioning the other soldiers to follow him, walks out of our apartment. Mom, who very seldom speaks Yiddish, whispers to Dad: "*Gott hot uns geretevet* (God saved us)."

For the three of us, that was all that happened on that day. But we soon discover how much more happened on this infamous Sabbath to other Jewish families of Bialystok. Three thousand Jewish men of military age had been rounded up and transported to Pietrasze. They had been executed and buried in the graves which they had been forced to dig. The victims and their wives and mothers are henceforth referred to as *Die Shabesdike—* The Sabbath-Ones.

Monia and I go on two other forays into the countryside, venturing into several new villages. This time, we come well supplied with *makhorka* (cheap Soviet tobacco), cigarettes, several bars of soap and even the heavily scented Soviet *dukhi* (perfume). This time we come home not only with bags of potatoes and loaves of bread but also with slabs of salt pork and fresh milk.

On the last day of our country ventures we encounter German road patrol soldiers and are asked to show our papers. I look young enough to justify my not having an ID passport on me, but Monia is ordered to show his documents. Thanks to his foresight, Monia always carries on his person the papers which he found on the body of a dead villager during his east-ward trek. The Germans let us go but they warn that an *Ausweis* (a German ID booklet) will soon be required; we know that this ID will carry a J, P, or B, for Jews, Poles, and Belorussians, respectively.

Monia and I become quite friendly during our vagabonding days. He fills me in on the particulars of his trek to Wolkowysk when he and Lowka became separated from me. I discover that he went back to Bialystok after he found and kept Christian documents for himself and his girlfriend, Sonia. But Lowka went farther east and was never heard from again. We ponder the fate of Tusia and wonder if she ever reached her dad and her home-town.

During our last day together, Monia and I decide that as soon as the ID and the dreaded yellow star are required of us, we will discontinue our bartering with the villagers. And indeed we have to discontinue it quite soon.

All this time, my parents have continued to hibernate inside the house and I become their sole liaison with the world outside. Thanks to my "Aryan" (non-Semitic) looks and thanks to the fact that practically none of the Gentiles of Bialystok know me, I stand in bread lines near our home and even shop for vegetables outside of our area and get away with it.

But my activities will soon be severely restricted. Several days after the Saturday execution of the 3,000 men, wall notices issued in the name of the Chief Rabbi, Dr. Rozenman, inform the Jews of Bialystok that the German authorities have ordered the Rabbinate to convene the Judenrat (Jewish Council). Even more threatening than this order is that starting on July 27,

Yellow Star of David

1941, all Jews will have to wear yellow Stars of David on outer garments, and by August 1 they must move into the ghetto. The Jewish Ghetto is defined as a walled-in area where the Jews are to be limited to three square meters of apartment floor space per person. As soon as all the walls and the entrance guardhouses are completed, the ghetto will be guarded both by the Jewish and the German police.

Mom and I scrounge among our fabric remnants for yellow scraps, and we do find a few of these. I design and cut out a paper pattern of the Star of

David and replicate the pattern on our scraps of yellow fabric. My yellow Stars of David look quite elegant but they are not meant to signify our national pride. As of July 27, these patches will be sewn onto the left front of our coats, jackets, and sweaters. As of that day we will be conspicuously singled out as members of the inferior "race" of humans.

Meanwhile, Mom asks her brother to help us find a place to live in one of the streets where the ghetto will be formed. We know very few people in that area, but a few of my uncle's fellow teachers from the Hebrew Gimnazjum do live there. He introduces us to Mrs. Adler, the widow of one of those teachers, and to her daughter Raszka. We are invited to share their five-room apartment, its kitchen and bathroom, its backyard woodbin, and its attic storage space—with four other families! And since one of the other bedrooms must be entered through our room, we will have to line up our furniture to form a passageway to this bedroom.

Back at our home, we feverishly pack our clothing, linens, and bedding into the large armoire that will be taken into the ghetto. We pack the wrapped-in-cloth dishes and our food supplies into the long credenza that will go with us, in addition to my parents' bed, a table, four chairs, and my cot. To build a room divider for the needed passageway, we will use the long credenza, the large armoire, and a set of heavy curtains.

Two days before the closing of the ghetto, Dad and I begin carrying the tightly packed pieces of furniture, one at a time, down the four flights of stairs. We hoist each one of them on top of the flimsy borrowed cart. We then drag this lopsided old cart along some seven or eight street blocks to Polna Street where the two of us carry each piece of furniture up the two flights of stairs into our room. From all corners of Bialystok come carts similar to ours, and these similarly disgorge the meager loads of Jewish possessions into the shared apartments of the ghetto. But there also are the refugees who come into the ghetto from the burnt-out Jewish areas of Bialystok and from the outlying small towns and villages, and those people come into the ghetto without any possessions at all. Most of these refugees settle in the unoccupied factory and school buildings where they will become wards of the Judenrat.

During the last day of our moving, a German soldier snatches the violin case with Dad's fine violin (possibly a grade or two below that of the

Stradivarius!) from his hands, and no amount of pleading can persuade the soldier to give the violin back to Dad. Evidently, the German doesn't relish stealing the guitar, the mandolin or the cornet, and that is indeed fortunate for us because these instruments will later be sold for a good price. Luckily as well, Dad's handmade gypsy fiddle is well hidden out of sight so that he will at least have one of his beloved violins, as well as his guitar, mandolin, and cornet.

We cast a sorrowful eye on the apartment we are about to leave, at the remains of our furniture, the pictures on our walls, and, of course, the empty spot where my baby grand piano used to stand. I rehash in my mind the scene of the "requisitioning" of the piano by the Gestapo and I bemoan the fact that we didn't store it in the home of our Gentile house helper before the Gestapo took it away. At least Dad's precious sheets of music are not left behind—he and I carry cart loads of these sheets into the ghetto and store them in the attic of our new house. (In the future, I will return to Bialystok and search the attic for these sheets but to no avail; they were apparently used instead of kindling wood!)

It takes us two full days to move into the new place and a full day thereafter to organize our living space. One third of our room is closed off by a drape and by the lineup of the long credenza and the armoire. A small iron stove is installed near the door. Its long chimney-pipe goes across the room divider and the balcony door. The table and chairs stand at the window to the left of my parents' bed. My cot stands at the door across from the iron stove.

During my back-and-forth walks to the ghetto, I bump into Monia, who is not wearing the yellow patch on his clothing. He tells me that he has helped Sonia move into the ghetto but that he will stay with his Gentile friends on the outside. He sounds very enterprising and sure of himself. Apparently he has lined up various contacts that will help him trade people's valuables for food. He plans to supply Sonia's family with necessities of a fairly comfortable life in the ghetto, but he hopes to eventually take his girlfriend out of here and seek a safe haven with her in Warsaw. Monia also advises me to seriously think about obtaining "Aryan" papers and getting out of the ghetto. Alas, I have no such plans or hopes...

Monia and I bid each other a Polish *dowidzenia* (I will see you soon), but I have my doubts about seeing each other again...

Time and time again I reminisce about my long-lasting friendship with Tusia, and I always hope that she somehow survived the journey to her village at Wolkowysk and that she might be alive after all. But I soon learn that Tusia did not make it. She did have a chance, though. During a Soviet-German skirmish on the road to her hometown she was wounded. She survived her wounds, but not for long. Tusia died from a bullet of a German soldier who summarily executed the wounded girl.

I recite Tusia's "Parisian Commune" and "Locomotive" poems in memory of her. And I remember the way we were in 1941...

As for Monia, I do not see him again until I visit him (now Mietek) and Sonia at their home in Melbourne, Australia, in 1987. I learn about their escape from the ghetto of Bialystok to Warsaw where, shielded by their Christian documents, they both survived the Holocaust. The enterprising Monia had managed to get Stela a proper set of Christian papers and had also gotten her out of the ghetto!

In September of 1998, I learn that the invincible Monia-Mietek died a few weeks earlier, on August 19. I hold in my hand a letter from Sonia, a letter that tells me that Mietek went to take a shower and just fell to the floor, apparently a victim of a massive heart attack. Sonia writes that she cannot believe Monia is dead. She writes, "I see you two coming from the country, you with some stuff in your bags and my Mietek with a sack of potatoes and a jar of sour cream. And I cannot cry."

I make a donation to the Bialystoker Home for the Aged in New York and plant a tree in Israel in Monia-Mietek's memory. And I remember the way Monia and I were in 1941...

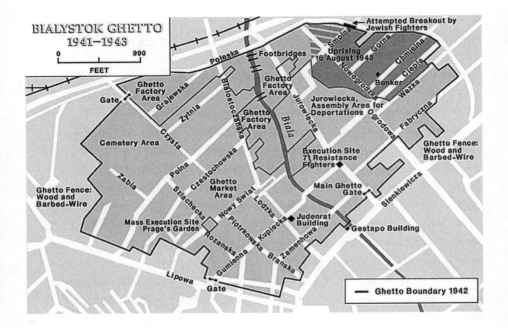

BIALYSTOK GHETTO
1941-1943

0   990
FEET

Attempted Breakout by
Jewish Fighters

Poleska — Footbridges

Uprising
16 August 1943

Smolna
Gorna
Chmielna
Ciepla
Nowogrodzka
Wezka

Ghetto
Factory
Area

Grajewska

Bunker

Gate

Zytnia

Bialostoczanska

Ghetto
Factory
Area

Ghetto
Factory
Area

Jurowiecka,
Assembly Area for
Deportations

Fabryczna

Czysta

Biala

Jurowiecka

Ogrodowa

Cemetery Area

Polna

Czestochowska

Execution Site
71 Resistance
Fighters

Ghetto Fence:
Wood and
Barbed-Wire

Zabla

Szlachecka

Ghetto
Market
Area

Nowy Swiat

Lodzka

Main Ghetto
Gate

Sienkiewicza

Ghetto Fence:
Wood and
Barbed-Wire

Mass Execution Site
Prage's Garden

Rozanska

Piotrkowska

Kuplecka

Branska

Zamenhowa

Judenrat
Building

Gestapo Building

Gumienna

Lipowa

Gate

— Ghetto Boundary 1942

"RIVKELE DIE SHABESDIKE ARBET IN FABRIK..."

("RIVKELE, THE SABBATH-ONE, WORKS IN A FACTORY...")

My cousin Dahlia brought me a cassette of Yiddish folk songs sung by an Israeli folk singer, Chava Alberstein. Most of these Yiddish songs were familiar to me, but there were two songs I hadn't heard before. Both songs must have been created during the days of the Holocaust; the lyrics of the song "Es iz geven a Zummer Tog (it was a summer day)" told of the lovely summer day when the Germans marched thousands of Jews off to be confined within the walls of the ghetto, while thousands of their brethren were led to be executed in a place called Ponary. The second song, "Rivkele die Shabesdike (Rivkele the Sabbath-One)," told of the sorrows and loneliness of Rivkele, a weaver at the ghetto knitting factory, whose husband was taken away by the Germans on the never-to-be-forgotten-day of Sabbath.

The name Ponary brought to mind the great enclave of Polish-Jewish cultural life, Vilno (Wilno in Polish). Yes, it was at Ponary's ravines that most of the Vilno Jews had been gunned down by the Germans. But what about the second song—why did it suddenly sound so familiar? No names of places were given on the cassette's blurb, but the reference to the "Sabbath-One" tore at my heart.

I realized that the song "Rivkele die Shabesdike" must have been composed in the ghetto of Bialystok. And there was a girl named Rivke Leye who worked in a knitting shop with me...

On August 1, 1941, construction workers begin erecting wooden fences that cut off the streets of the ghetto from their counterparts on the outside. The areas outside the ghetto become off limit to us. The *Schuppo* (German police) and a few days later, the Jewish police, begin patrolling the borders of the ghetto. The construction of the fences includes the building of two heavily guarded gates, one at Jurowiecka and one at Kupiecka Street.

On the days before the fences and the gates are constructed and fully manned, we remain fair game for manhandling by German intruders and for sniper bullets of German sharpshooters. Even after the closing off of the ghetto, the Germans make us painfully aware of our denigrated position by ordering us to step aside, with our eyes downcast, when we face a German officer walking our way. And the yellow Star of David continues, in this ghetto-zoo, to be a badge of racial inferiority.

During the first few months, the ghetto is administered by the Wehrmacht. Because Bialystok has now been annexed into the Third Reich's *Ostpreussen* (East Prussia), however, civilian authorities from its capital, Koenigsberg, soon take over. The head of the East Prussian NSDAP (Nazi Party), Gauleiter Eric Koch, and his deputy Dr. Brix, assume control of the ghetto via various local channels: the *Burgemeister* (Mayor), the *Ghetto Verwaltung* (German local Ghetto Administration) and finally the S.A. or *Schuppo* (German police). After November of 1942, a local division of the Gestapo, headed by Heimbach, forms the IVE (Special Department of Jewish Affairs) and puts Altenloch in charge of the department. Altenloch, in turn, leaves the ghetto in the hands of Friedel (the beast of Bialystok!), Dibus, and Schmidt, who will personally conduct the annihilation actions in the ghetto in 1943.

In sharp contrast to the freely elected prewar Jewish self-government, the Kehila, the Judenrat of the ghetto is established by orders from the Germans, largely to help them exploit and control the Jews of the ghetto.

Dr. Rozenman is only a Judenrat figurehead; Barash, an engineer by profession, becomes the Judenrat's real man of power. The Judenrat has various departments (ironically referred to as "ministries"), all of which unwittingly serve as vehicles of assistance for the Germans. The Department of Education is limited to overseeing an industrial school inspired by the model of the Jewish ORT (Artisan Crafts &Industry) schools. It is largely run by the remains of the prewar heads of ORT. The Department of Justice regulates simple day-to-day problems. The extremely overworked Department of Health runs a hospital and health clinic, both of which have totally impossible conditions of sanitation along with medical and pharmaceutical shortages. The primary role of the Housing Department is to allocate housing to latecomers to the ghetto and to run communal housing and soup kitchens for the homeless, located in the buildings of former factories and schools. The Department of Labor maintains *Aussen-commandos* (Labor Brigades working outside the ghetto) composed of unskilled and skilled workers who are needed by the Germans for various tasks. The Department of Food Supply is responsible for the rationing of bread, margarine, flour and groats, potatoes and other "occasionals" such as jam and horse meat. These are supplied by the Germans and, to a small extent, bought by the Judenrat. The Finance Department levies taxes on the wealthier Jews of the ghetto under the threat of an arrest or deportation for non-compliance. Only a minute portion of the levies is used for payment of the pitiful wages of the Jewish police and Judenrat employees; it is the Germans who demand money, and the Judenrat always complies with their demands.

The Germans order all men aged 15-60 and women aged 16-50 to work. The Department of Industry and Employment must see to it that all eligible Jews are employed. The Judenrat thus initiates the organization of factories and cooperatives within the ghetto that employ a vast force of slave-laborers. The ghetto shops produce and repair articles of clothing for the German army; also produced are various gadgets and machine parts, wooden furniture, and paper products, all for export to Germany. The ghetto shops are jointly owned by the various local German institutions and by the German industrialist, Oskar Stephen; the larger factories are run by the army and the state. Perhaps it is because of these private and state interests that, in the face of the ongoing extermination of many other ghettos, the

Bialystok ghetto's existence is prolonged. The local administrators see to it that the economic gains, based on the productivity of their slave-laborers, remain available as long as possible. In fact, an order issued in December of 1942 for the deportation to Auschwitz of 30,000 Jews is rescinded because of the tremendous productivity of the ghetto.

Initially, the sole function of the few hundred Jewish policemen is to maintain law and order in the ghetto, but unfortunately they soon end up being subordinates of the Germans. During the deportations, it is commonly the young Jewish policeman who carries out the orders of the Germans. It is he who forces people out of their homes, hideouts and shelters.

During my first days in the ghetto, I lie on my cot facing the wall, half asleep and half daydreaming. I feel as though I am coming down with something, but perhaps I am just trying to escape from the reality of the situation. As in the old days, my mom is offering me food and drink but I pretend to be asleep. I cringe with sorrow when I hear Dad say that he is going upstairs to speak with someone about selling his mandolin, but I continue to lie still. Outside in the street the sparrows are chirping and I daydream about jumping the half-finished wooden fences and going somewhere, but where, where to? I don't know where I could go…

Toward the evening of my second day in bed, our landlady comes in with the name of a doctor who lives down the street. I don't care about the doctor, I don't care about Dad's selling his mandolin, I don't care about anything except that I want to get out of here! At night, I begin to feel hungry and devour the cold pancakes left from my parents' supper. On my way to and from the bathroom, I tiptoe through the bedrooms of our neighbors and listen to their snoring, and finally, back in my own cot, I listen to the muffled noises of the night till I fall asleep again.

The next morning, Dasa comes in with the bad news that her mom died last night. Now I have to come back to life. A quick bite of some dry bread and ersatz (roasted grain) coffee, a hasty wash-up in a wash pan, and I am off to Dasa's home. What I find there seems almost unreal. Dasa's mom is lying, uncovered, on their kitchen table. Her husband sits at the table holding his face in his hands, and then all three of us stand around the table, and nobody is crying. Dasa's mom had a heart attack. She had suffered with a heart condition for quite some time and her heart attack was not unexpected at all.

I stay in this mournful place for a while and share the sorrow with my friend and her father. Toward the end of my stay, Dasa's dad says that his wife is lucky to escape the fate that awaits us here in the ghetto. But Dasa grabs my hand and says that we must do everything to survive this ghetto. We must survive, she says, because the day will come when the Soviet armies will liberate us and we will surely see the downfall of the Nazis at their hands. Then a man and a woman come in to take care of Mrs. Lin's body, and Dasa asks me to go home.

I come home, cheer up, and go to meet the people who share our apartment with us. The old Grandpa and Grandma Szabrynski live in the bedroom that must be entered through our passageway. Their divorced daughter, Charlotte Lewinson, and her two teenagers, live in the large dining room that we must go through to get to the kitchen and to the bathroom. Charlotte's brother shares the room with the Lewinsons, but he is an official of the Judenrat and usually comes home late at night. Later on, another daughter of the old Szabrynskis will come here to escape one of the decimating *Aktions* (bloody roundups of Jews for their deportation to extermination camps) of the Vilno ghetto.

I get to the kitchen going through a passageway made from a curtain. The curtain divides a small room, so small, in fact, that it contains just two side-by-side cots and, above them, a bunch of wall-shelves. Several garments that obviously belong to the occupants of this small cubicle hang on the passageway's wall. A girl walks out from behind the curtain, introduces herself as Cyla Zbar, and tells me that she lives here with her brother Oska. At the moment, I don't dare to ask Cyla if her brother has been one of the leaders of Bialystok's prewar Beitar. I will soon learn that indeed, this Oska Zbar is none other than the Beitar solicitor who, once upon a time, stood me up.

I wonder about the paucity of clothing the Szabrynskis, Lewinsons and Zbars brought with them to the Adler's apartment. Mrs. Adler herself provides the explanation. Our neighbors are all escapees from the burned Jewish areas and, as such, they weren't able to save much of their belongings except for some valuables and memorabilia. Mrs. Adler needn't tell me that the Szabrynskis have lots of money—the meat and fish dinners the grandma cooks daily for her clan gives this away. There are no meat rations to speak of for the Jews of the ghetto, and it takes gold coins or dollars to keep buying the beef, chickens or fish that are smuggled in. As for the two Adler ladies, they have enough antiques in their room to fill a showcase in a museum; they will surely be able to trade in their antiques for dollars or gold coins that will feed them well. The Zbar siblings are soon fighting over some such purchase or sale and we assume that their dad, a dentist, left them some dental gold before he went to Pietrasze with "the Thursday-Ones."

Within a few days of her mom's death, Dasa decides to do something creative while she stays in the ghetto and awaits her liberation by the Soviet army. We both have boxes of watercolor paints, tubes of oil paints and a goodly supply of cardboard, so I join Dasa in reproducing still life paintings by various French Impressionists. We discover a bit later that a girl named Hanka has formed an amateur painters' group at her home, right across the street from my folks' apartment. Dasa and I drop in on Hanka's group and continue meeting with these congenial artistic young people. Now we paint actual still life arrangements that Hanka sets up for us. I learn that Hanka's family is from Malkinia, a small town on the former Soviet-German border, close to the place where refugees from the German territories entered the Soviet territory. After each painting session there is a lively discussion of the issues of the day, and I remain an avid participant of this group until the Germans give us a rude awakening about the realities of life in the ghetto.

For a month and a half, life has been quiet enough in the ghetto. The rations provide a weight-reduction diet, but my dad's mandolin and Soviet cigarettes (accumulated after Dad stopped smoking) buys us some dairy products and pork fat that supplements the meager rations. But on September 16 of this year, there is trouble in the ghetto. My Uncle Munio takes us with him to the Judenrat, where he works, and we have to stay there all day. Aided by the Jewish police, the Germans comb the streets and communal centers, round up "unemployable" Jews and deport them to a "warehousing ghetto" in Pruzany.

Although we are assured that the only reason for the deportation is to genuinely ease the overcrowding of the communal homes, all three of us feel threatened. None of us are protected by a legitimate *Arbeit Ausweis*

(Work ID Card) and the current deportation of the 6,000 "unemployable" Jews to Pruzany convinces us that we must find work as soon as possible. Uncle Munio helps Dad get a position as a clerk at the police precinct housed in the former Druskin Gimnazjum right around the corner from our home. Dad now wears a policeman's hat and armband. He usually works seven days a week and brings home from the soup kitchen of the communal shelter at Druskin's a large canister of nutritious soup for our daily dinners.

Mom becomes a seamstress, a home piece-worker for a sewing cooperative. She makes, by hand, buttonholes for army uniforms. I opt for the *Aussen-commandos* (outside work brigades) that gather daily at the Kupiecka gate of the ghetto. There they pick you for whatever project needs unskilled workers. My first assignment is in a Russian POW field hospital and proves to be a traumatic experience. I tend emaciated Soviet POWs, many of them with stumps from missing legs, arms, hands or feet, pathetic stumps that are covered by dirty rags. Many are feverish, many are covered by dirt and lice, and all of them are left without medical and nursing care. And there I am, a totally incompetent practical nurse who can only bring in a bedpan for those who yell "*Davaite pomochitsia, sestra!* (let me urinate, nurse)" or bring a water pitcher for those who beg, "*Vody, sestra, vody!* (Water, nurse, water)." I keep thinking of the friendly Soviet soldier whom I met on the road to Wolkowysk. Hopefully he is somewhere with the partisans and not in a POW camp as horrible as this one.

As famished as I am, I can't eat the potato soup offered me by a German guard at the field hospital. Instead, I mix this thick German soup with the watery cabbage soup of the wounded POWs. I dish it out for them and spoon-feed the few who cannot feed themselves. Among these is a boy who is not much older than I am and whose feverish eyes look at me as if he is pleading for me to put an end to his suffering.

As we march back to the ghetto at the end of this stressful day, I discover a new need within myself, a need to study medicine, a desire to become a physician and to heal those who are sick and those who are suffering. One day, I will attempt to become a physician.

On a subsequent assignment, they pick me to go outside the ghetto and dig potatoes for the German army. Just for a taste of what life used to be like, I succumb one day to the temptation of pretending that I am a Gentile. It is a lovely Indian summer day, my jacket bearing the yellow Star of David is off, and a handsome young German stops by to flirt with me. My coworkers look at me with disdain when they hear me trying to impress the young German with nonsensical stories of my life. But they cover up for me when I return to the fields and act as an "overseer of Jews." My brethren cover up for me because they hear the soldier's threat that he will check out if I have told him the truth about myself. Luckily, the Germans take us off the potato field and send us to harvest turnips and carrots in a different location, and my soldier does not appear there.

But another problem awaits me on one of my last days working outside the ghetto. Before sending us off to work, the guards send us into the guardhouse to search for illegal goods we may be carrying for a later barter. Indeed, I am carrying, in my brassiere, a pair of silk stockings that I hope to barter for a slab of salt pork or bacon. I assure the Germans I have no barter goods, but apparently I am not convincing enough. One of the guardhouse officers sticks his hand into my brassiere, pulls out the stockings and smacks my face, yelling, "How dare you lie to me !"

When I get home that day I announce to my parents, without explanation, that I will never go outside the ghetto again. I will need to find work inside the ghetto.

The factories organized by the Judenrat's Department of Industry and Labor are now working at full capacity. Uncle Munio secures a job for me in the *Strickerei*, the knitting and weaving factory owned by the German industrialist Oskar Stephen. The loom weaving is done in the mornings and early afternoons, and the hand knitting is done during the late afternoons and in the evenings. Army sweaters are loom-weaved, as are most of the knitwear orders for the wives and daughters of the Army and Gestapo officers. In addition to machine knitting, special orders for hand-knitted sweaters are left in the hands of highly skilled women. But the largest number of women are employed to hand-knit army socks. Fortunately, I have knitted a sweater and a scarf in the past so that my knitting skill is sufficiently good for knitting army socks.

A woman of my mother's age sits next to me and helps me through the difficulties of the first few weeks. I remember her daughter Sonia quite well, first because she attended the senior class during my first year at Druskin's, and second because she became very popular when she and her mother returned from the 1939 World Fair in New York. There is no end to this woman's talk about New York City where she has a married sister and a niece about my age. (One day I will come to New York and meet Dora, my ghetto coworker's sister, who learns from me that both her sister and her niece Sonia perished, with the rest of the Jews of Bialystok, in the extermination camp of Treblinka.)

There isn't enough working space for the many hand-knitters who are needed to both knit socks from scratch and to repair badly worn army socks, so part of the work has to be done at home. During the early part of 1942, I am relegated to working at home where I must fulfill a specific quota of knitted *de novo* and of patched-up, used socks. This arrangement suits me fine since, during the day, Mom works in a sewing factory and Dad at the police precinct. By working at home, I can prepare dinner. Our cooking is done on the small iron stove and dinner consists of the warmed up precinct soup and a batch of potato pancakes masterfully prepared by me. In fact, I've also become efficient at chopping the wood for our little stove so that our backyard woodbin is now well stocked with splintered logs.

I bring my quota of finished socks into our factory early each day and wait there, near the loom weavers, for the inspector to show up. I enjoy watching the skillful hands of the weavers and I listen to their elegant Litvak Yiddish small talk. Gradually, I get to know the weaver girls. They often ask me questions about myself, in Yiddish of course, questions which I can understand but can answer only in Polish or in Russian.

There is one weaver who never talks with the other girls and who doesn't pay much attention to me, either. I see her pensive, sad face turn to the windows, as if she were expecting to see someone there. On one occasion, I take a seat next to her loom and I greet her with, "*Guten Tog* (Good day)," to which she just nods her head but does not answer. Why is this young girl so sad? I would so much like to know about her but I haven't yet learned to initiate a heart-to-heart talk with anyone, let alone a stranger. This young woman is not like the friends I have. After a while I give up my preoccupation with this weaver-girl, except once during a session with my inspector when I see her cry. I quietly ask my inspector about the girl. She tells me the girl is *die Shabesdike* (the Sabbath-One). My thoughts wander back in time to Saturday, July 12, the day that will remain vivid forever in my memory…

I see my dad sprawled on his bed. I see my mother, her face covered with red blotches, as she implores the German soldiers not to take my dad away. I see my dad as he looks now, his aged face and his graying hair under the laughable police hat, and I thank heavens that neither I nor my mom were made to be *die Shabesdikes* like this crying young weaver-girl.

A few days later, I overhear one of the other weavers address the sad girl as Rivke Leye.

Could this have been the weaver-girl about whom a song is later written, a song that survives for years to come? Will the song "Rivkele the Sabbath-One" refer to the sad, young weaver-girl Rivke Leye die Shabesdike, with whom I worked at the ghetto of Bialystok?

"BUTTERFLIES DON'T LIVE IN HERE, IN THE GHETTO"

We had been able to visit our son Steve's family much more frequently when they came from Oregon to stay in Chelmsford, a suburb of Boston. My grandson Evan and I would roam around the underbrush and field around their home, together exploring the living creatures of this suburban environment. As a high school teacher, I had had no opportunity to teach science to younger children, and I therefore enjoyed having early-childhood science talks with my grandsons. Then, one day, my daughter-in-law Barbara showed me Evan's drawing of a bee sitting on a flower of a dandelion. Beneath the drawing were these words of his teacher: "Evan told his class that while the bee sucks in the nectar of a dandelion, the flower's pollen sticks to the bee's legs and the bee transfers this pollen to the stigma of another dandelion. This way, two dandelions take part in producing each dandelion fruit. Evan told the class that he learned this from his grandma, who is a scientist!" I read the inscription, looked at the face of Evan, and saw in my mind faces of other little boys...

Daniel is our youngest grandson. I have always enjoyed walking with him (and Jake the dog) in the woods, collecting "specimens" for his science projects, and helping him design experiments for his school's Science Fair. Daniel's silent hugs told me that he and I had found common wavelengths and that he had learned some science from me. I hugged Daniel and I remembered other little boys...

In the United States, I have been a high school and a college science teacher nearly all of my adult life. But back in Poland, there was a time when I taught younger pupils. Some were as young as Evan was, when the two of us were probing the nature of his backyard, some as old as Daniel when we designed his sixth grade experiments. The faces of these children are engraved in my subconscious and it takes little to view flashbacks of them. But until recently, I couldn't recall a name of even one of my young pupils. Now I remember one name, the name of Pawelek Friedman whom I taught in 1942 in the ghetto of Bialystok.

Another boy, the Czech Pavel Friedman, wrote in the confines of the Theresienstadt Ghetto a poem about his longing for butterflies. There seldom were any butterflies around him in the ghetto. On April 18, 1985, I had been a guest speaker at the Holocaust Memorial held at the school in which I taught. I failed to pay much attention to the printed program of the Memorial, but I kept it as a souvenir. When I was recently going through my memorabilia, I came across the program and Pavel Friedman's poem:

The Butterfly

The last, the very last, so richly, brightly, dazzling yellow'
perhaps if the sun's tears would sing against a white stone

Such, such a yellow, is carried lightly way up high
It went away I'm sure because it wished to kiss the world goodbye.
For seven weeks I've lived here, penned up inside this ghetto
But I have found my people here. The dandelions call to me
And the white chestnut candles in the court.
Only I never saw another butterfly.

That butterfly was the last one.
Butterflies don't live here in the ghetto.
(Pavel Friedman, Theresienstadt, April 6, 1942)

When I read the poem by the little poet of Theresienstadt I recalled the name of Pawelek Friedman, an imaginative and artistic little boy of the ghetto of Bialystok where, as in Theresienstadt, there were no butterflies. And I have seen in the eyes of my grandsons, Evan and Daniel, the eager eyes of Pawelek and the eyes of the other children of Bialystok who were my pupils in the ghetto.

Spring comes early this year and we enjoy its relatively peaceful days in the ghetto. My hand-knitting work at home leaves me with enough time for socializing with my old friends in Hanka's painting circle; and I also seek out new friends.

Dasa does not meet with me anymore; she now has a boyfriend Frankel, a handsome younger classmate whom I do not know too well. Occasionally, I visit with Dasa and Frankel and try to sound them out about any underground youth organizations they know of. Dasa tells me that since I was so terribly upset about the Red Army losses in the war, she was not going to tell me about any left-wing organizations, even if she knew about them. I assure her that I am no longer unhappy about the disappointing performance of the Red Army, that I am eager to get the current news about the Soviet-German front, and that I want to be informed about the ongoing activities of the Soviet partisans. But neither Dasa nor her boyfriend show much interest in my inquiries.

There is music in the ghetto. A young jazz musician, now a policeman, composes fine jazz pieces with timely lyrics that depict our life in the ghetto. Dad brings a few of these jazz pieces home. One of the songs begins, "In the streets, at home, and at the police precinct, we are looking for the happiness that fate has stolen from us." These are hopeless words, but the song continues with a happier theme of drowning one's sorrow in music: "So long as there is jazz, things will be OK." (On August 17 of 1943, the ghetto's jazz musician will jump from the window of the train bound for Treblinka and be killed by the bullets of the Ukrainian SS men.)

Yes, many of us reach out for music to give us a better feeling about life. Simka, the wonderful soprano of my dad's choral group, organizes an afternoon sing-out in someone's apartment. My dad comes with his violin and gets a round of applause when he starts the sing-out with some of our choral songs. We go on singing till late at night; Dad accompanies us on his violin, Simka performs a few of her delightful solos for us, and it is so hard to end the sing-out and to return to the somber reality of the ghetto. (At the disembarkation depot of Majdanek, Simka will go to "work," along with Dasa and Mirka, in a van rigged up to asphyxiate its passengers.)

During my first year in the ghetto I become friends with Rozia and Musia. Rozia is my former classmate and warmly invites me to visit her and her sister at their home. I marvel at the many members of their extended family who crowd the tiny ghetto apartment. Both Rozia and Musia have boyfriends with whom they go for extended walks and I am invited to come along with them. But, although we go for these walks to escape the crowding at their home, we usually end up there anyway. At times, a serious political discussion takes place at their house. The two boyfriends like to participate in this political discussion, but Rozia, Musia, and I do not, preferring to just listen. The sisters' cousin, Pesia, has also been my school-mate and is a vociferous leftist. Pesia would surely speak out here, but she apparently stays with the family of her fiancé and never shows up during my visits.

During one of our walks we are joined by Musia's friend, a young Varsovian whose name is Boleslaw (Bolek) Pachucki. Bolek is several years older than I am. He is well educated, mature and suave, and he writes poetry. And soon he begins to show an interest in me. Being a handy seamstress, I now set out to revamp my limited wardrobe and with a stitch here and a stitch there, my old blouses and skirts acquire a chic look, or so my mirror tells me. Spring is in the air. I tire of painting and begin to write songs instead. My dad's guitar is still here (we sold the cornet) and it can be of help in composing simple tunes. At first I set songs to Russian poems, one of which becomes a lovely folk song that even Dad appreciates. When I sing, "*Zveni zolotaya, shumi zolotaya, moya zolotaya taiga* (Ring out, you golden one, whisper out, you golden one, my very own golden taiga)," I dream of the whispering sounds of the golden Siberian taiga forests of Prokofief's poetry. One by one, the short poems acquire a melody, some better than others—none of them too good, as my father says—but I enjoy creating these songs.

It is Bolek Pachucki who encourages me to compose melodies whose music alone will convey a specific meaning or a specific feeling. Encouraged by Bolek, I write a song that I call "The Song of the Minarets," and another called "Before the Last Journey." Together Bolek and I dub into these melodies "nonsense" words that fit the beat and the inflection of the songs. This routine subsequently helps Bolek write meaningful lyrics, and these are indeed fine poetry. His words to my song churn our feelings and penetrate deeply into our young souls:

Before the Last Journey

Battered in the woe, crimes and sorrow,
humanity sinks to the blows...
Quietly, await the final journey of sorrow,
sadness and woe in our souls...
The stars shine, as always, so far and still farther,
the moon calls, come bathe as before, in the glow.
Lost, bewildered in the night, we found one another,
and shards of the time of long ago...
Come and hold my hand, there's no path to salvation,
blood and cinders lay where life bloomed yesterday.
Let's together drift in the tempest of damnation,
on the foaming waves of somber days...
The night brought us together, let's hold our hands,
and don't let the waves come and break us apart!
Hear someone say that the night will soon end,
and sunrise will blush in the dark...*
(*Author's translation from Polish.)

The words of "Before the Final Journey" are more than moving. They tell me that Bolek cares for me in a way that I cannot reciprocate. We go on spending time with the two sisters and also just the two of us at my home, but I am beginning to feel awkward in Bolek's company. In essence, I don't want Bolek to be my boyfriend. That feeling jells inside me when a fellow I used to know at school tells me, "You are too much 'with it' for a fancy dude like that one from Warsaw." When Bolek is hospitalized with infectious hepatitis for a few weeks, I send him sympathetic notes and decide not to resume our friendship when Bolek gets well. In fact, other events begin to unfold and capture my attention at the end of the summer of 1942.

The third of our room that had been walled off by our furniture no longer serves as a simple passage to the elder Szabrynski's room. A couple of refugees from Vilno and their two sons sleep there on army cots and on the floor. I often hear the boys talk with their parents before they fall asleep. It is through these boys that I learn the horrid details about the fate of the Jews around the environs of Vilno. We have heard about the formation of the Vilno Ghetto and about the mass executions of Jews by the *Einzatz Truppen* (Special Forces) in regional towns and villages. Now the two small boys fill me in on the details.

One night, one of the twins complains about the crowded conditions in our house and pleads with his mother to go back and stay with Grandma. "Grandma is no longer in Vilno," says the mother. "Where is she?"

"Your grandma has gone to Ponary."

"So why can't we go back and stay there with Uncle Abrasha?"

"Because Uncle Abrasha and his family have also gone to Ponary."

There are a few more requests for staying with other aunts and uncles who, the boy is told, have also gone to Ponary. There is a long silence on the other side of the room divider, and then the second boy speaks words that bore deeply into my soul: "Mommy, how could God allow the Germans to take away so many of our people, just to fill the hollows of Ponary?" I bury my head in my pillow to muffle the sobbing sounds I hear behind the room divider.

Since the end of the summer of 1942, my daily quotas of hand-knitted military socks begin to get smaller. Perhaps it is because of the greater productivity of the machine-knitting brigade or because of the increased size of the work force itself that now the compulsory work laws are strictly enforced. Whatever the case, I have more time on my hands and I decide to search for new activities. The wife of my uncle's former colleague, who lives above us, often stops by to share with me the latest news her husband gets at the Judenrat. The woman has taught elementary grade children and she is concerned with the idle life of our children in the ghetto. I had never given this matter a thought, but now I also begin to wonder how our children could get some education in the ghetto. Bona fide education of Jewish children is strictly forbidden. For reasons of safety, former elementary grade teachers (the few who escaped the execution of intellectuals in Pietrasze) will surely not want to hold illegal classes and risk endangering their pupils and themselves by being reported to the Gestapo. Well, what about high school graduates becoming teachers?

My landlady's daughter, Raszka, and I have a long talk about holding classes for young children. We decide that the idea is feasible and that the two of us can do it. It would be less risky for two teenagers to disguise teaching as child-care service for working parents than it would be for professional teachers to do so. In addition, both Raszka and I have a valid excuse for staying at home during work hours. Both of us hold permits to do our sewing and knitting at home. Our own rooms henceforth become the children's classrooms, and we soon find quite a few parents who are eager to enroll their children in our "school."

My morning class for the youngest pupils is followed by a combined class of 4th-, 5th- and 6th-graders. We find a few textbooks in the homes of former elementary grade teachers and a few from the homes of our pupils. My uncle brings us pencils, pens, and writing pads from the offices of the Judenrat, and Mrs. Adler, herself a former elementary grade teacher, helps us with the planning of our lessons. Our earnings are small. But they buy some victuals to supplement our daily diet—a ration-based semi-starvation diet (not withstanding the daily soup from the precinct's soup-kitchen). And, thanks to the ingenuity of the outside-the-ghetto laborers and to the ever-increasing numbers of smugglers, food can now be bought even using the German money that circulates in the ghetto. Mom pockets my teacher's "wages" while my dad pretends not to know that his daughter supports the family.

But all three of us appreciate the now ample portions of greasy potato-pancakes and the once-a-week addition of scraps of meat to our Saturday "cholent," the ageless, traditional meal of Jewish proletarians. Cholent-baking surely remains a tradition in the ghetto, and I participate in it with zest. A special pot with a tightly-fitting cover is filled with potatoes, onions, beans, peas, grains, scraps of meat, animal fat, and whatever else happens to be available. The contents of the pot are then topped with salty water. All of this gets done on Fridays, right after my pupils go home around noon. I then wrap the pot in paper, tie it securely with twine, and bring it to the baker down Polna Street. I must wait in line for my turn to place the cholent in the great oven. In time, my pot joins many other cholent pots in the baker's slow-baking oven, and it remains in that oven until our Saturday mid-day meal.

I also collect my weekly pay at the end of my teaching on Friday at noon, and it feels good to know that it is I who makes it possible for us to feast on a delicious meaty cholent on Saturdays. But the teaching itself, not the pay for it, becomes the greatest satisfaction of my young life.

We teach the older children the Russian language, mathematics, science (basically physics), Latin and ancient history. Some subjects are taught in Polish but most are taught in Russian because, except for the Latin and ancient history texts, we have only Soviet textbooks, which are written in Russian. My pupils have to do some class work and some homework each day, and I give them frequent oral quizzes. We do not discuss the current history or the happenings of the day. From the very first day of our "school," I prepare my pupils for a foreseeable future entry into the Gimnazjum, and the future entrance exam into that Gimnazjum becomes a given for my pupils. I constantly pressure the kids to study hard and tell them that they must be ready for the entrance examination, which will surely take place soon enough.

Perhaps I believe, at first, in what I am telling my pupils, but I gradually get to know that I am telling a lie. Enough information has already seeped into the ghetto to make me aware of the fate of many Jewish children during the often-violent *Aktions* (roundups) preceding the deportations of Jews from the ghettos. And I soon perceive the simple truth that Jewish children aren't worth warehousing for even a short time since no labor can be extracted from them. Thus, hardly any children can hope to survive.

There is a wide-eyed blond sixth-grader in my older group and he smiles disarmingly as he repeatedly asks, "Are you sure there will be Latin on the entrance exam, teacher?" Or: "Are you sure the physics' part of the entrance examination will be so hard? I hate physics!"

My younger group learns reading, writing and arithmetic, both in Polish and in Russian. Their children's textbooks are all in Russian but the children themselves speak Polish, so we just navigate between these two languages. We do have crayons so that the youngest ones can also do some drawing. There is among these children a blond boy with a sweet face and dreamy blue eyes who creates drawings that tell stories about imaginary beings and magic worlds. I place interesting objects in front of my pupils, hoping they will draw what they see. Most of them do, except for the boy with the face of a little angel. An ordinary cup and saucer become a magic lantern with a genie that showers goodies upon the world; carrots become space-ships and I become a giant princess of a magic land of children.

I know that one or two of these younger children have come from outlying townships and may have witnessed or experienced German cruelties. Yet here, in their "school," these children behave as if this indeed was a normal, real school. I do nothing to belie their belief. Here too, we talk about making sure that they will be prepared to pass into higher grades, once the public schools are open again.

In November of 1942, the Gestapo takes over the control of the ghetto and the mood of the Jews changes. In the streets, people hide in the doorways when they see "the beasts"—the Gestapo's Friedel, Dobus, and Schmidt—walking in the ghetto and looking for victims. People worry about the pending "deportation" of 30,000 Jews, and parents of minors know that their children will surely be among the deportees.

By November, I become seriously involved with the underground. In December, on the day of my ill-fated partisan venture, I give my pupils a short "winter vacation" and dismiss them at mid-day to go home. Since the need to permanently cancel the classes disappears later the same day, I call on my pupils' parents to let them know that classes will resume. My little artist is the first one to come back, and on that day he and I draw imaginary things together. And, for the first time, the boy asks me the "Why?" and the "How come?" questions to which I give answers that avoid the truth.

Within a short time, many of my pupils are simply kept home. At the beginning of 1943 our classes gradually come to an end. Two boys remain in my classes to the very end, the one who "hates physics," and the little artist with an angelic face. The science-phobic boy surprises me with a stick-model of a functioning catapult and tells me that he will become an engineer when he grows up. The little artist makes me a gift of his earlier picture of a world of magic, with me in the center of it.

Few children are seen walking the streets of the ghetto after February

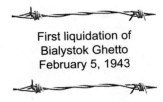

First liquidation of
Bialystok Ghetto
February 5, 1943

1943, the month when the first 15,000 people from the ghetto are deported. And no children, other than babies, arrive in Majdanek after the final deportation of the rest of the ghetto Jews in August of 1943. So it must be in the extermination camp of Treblinka that my pupils meet their death, along with most of the Bialystok Jews. Or so I believe...

I visit the museum of Theresienstadt in November of 1994 and learn that a large transport of children from Bialystok arrived there in 1943. After some time, these children were sent to the gas chambers of Auschwitz. Swallowing my tears, I study the children's drawings that cover the walls of the museum. I anxiously study the names that appear on those drawings, but not one of the names of my pupils come back to my mind. I search and search for the imaginary drawings of my little pupil whose angelic face I will always remember, but I do not know which, if any, of the imaginary drawings at Theresienstadt are his. Fifty years of life simply expunge the recollection of the style of my pupil's drawings and erases his name from my memory.

Years later I read the poem "The Butterfly," written at the ghetto of Therezienstadt by a Czech-Jewish boy called Pavel Friedman. And suddenly I recall the name of the Polish-Jewish boy called Pawelek Friedman, my imaginative pupil in the ghetto of Bialystok. I tell the story of searching for the drawings of Pawelek Friedman to a group of 7th graders at our local synagogue, and one of them tells me that I must go to Theresienstadt again and find the drawings of my pupil.

The following paraphrased excerpt is from April 2000 in the #362 issue of the Bialystoker Shtimme: "At the end of August 1943, at the time of the annihilation of the ghetto of Bialystok, 1,200 children ages 6-12 were transferred to Theresienstadt and placed in a special camp called Crete. The children who had infectious diseases were murdered in the small fortress of Theresienstadt. On the night of October 5, 1943, the Bialystok children disappeared. The only thing that remained was a list of the 1,196 children and 53 accompanying adults, listed as special transport number DN/a, to Auschwitz. Only after the war did it become known that the children were brought to Auschwitz and sent straight to the gas chambers. The children from the ghetto of Bialystok were among the last surviving Jewish children of Eastern Europe."

I read the List of Children, Yad Vashem Archive No. 064/318 Abtransport DN/a 5.10.43 published by the same issue of the Bialystoker Shtimme and do not find the name of Pawelek Friedman on that list...

"UNITED AND READY,
THE YOUNG OF THE UNDERGROUND,
WE'RE WAITING TO HAVE OUR DAY…"

"There appear at times writings of people who question why we, the Jews of Europe, did not stand up to the Germans, why we did not resist when they set out to annihilate us. We in turn ask those who question our impotence: Have there been many episodes of armed resistance by prisoners of war, by slaves, by enslaved people unskilled in the use of arms? Have there been many uprisings amidst civilians of ethnic minorities held in bondage within the evil empires?

Yet we—the most wretched of slaves, we who were dehumanized by the unrelenting brutality of the most malignant state in human history, we came up with a share of armed events that could match those of other desperate peoples of history's showcase. We staged uprisings in the camps and in the ghettos, with Vilno, Bialystok and Warsaw among many others…

And when they executed all who exercised leadership in our communities, all who could bear arms, all who could inspire insurrection, our youths provided the leadership and the hands to shoot the guns on the barricades of the burning ghettos and in the hideouts of their partisans, and we sang "Am Israel Chai! (Long live the nation of Israel)"

Above are excerpts of the speech I delivered during the Holocaust Remembrance Day at the school where I taught. In that speech, I emphasized the significant amount of passive resistance with which we Jews met the Germans' attempts to dehumanize us—a passive resistance that was, in several cases, coupled with an armed resistance. The ghetto of Bialystok is a shining example of both a passive and an armed resistance, and posterity has rated its August 1943 uprising as second only to the ghetto of Warsaw in historic significance.

Although I participated in the Bialystok's uprising only marginally, I was involved with the forces that shaped the course of both the fight in the ghetto itself, and of the partisan activities outside the ghetto. And if anyone were to ask me how and why I got involved, I could only say that I became involved when I had to and because I had to...

The early fall of 1942 is relatively mild so that our meager supplies of wood may hopefully last through the colder late fall and winter. Here and there, I meet my former classmates in the streets of the ghetto. Among these are Cyra Kreszes, Nesia Kaczalska, and my friend Ewa. But my relationship with Dasa proves to be very disappointing. I guess she has never forgiven me for my derogatory remarks about the slipshod performance of the Red Army in this war. At least, that is what I have sensed during my last visit with her and her boyfriend.

But lo and behold, Dasa has not forgotten my expressed interest in getting a contact with the resistance organization, if there indeed is such an organization in the ghetto. A few days after my visit at Dasa's home, Julek Mintz and his pal, nicknamed "Mycka," intercept me in front of my house and tell me that Dasa has asked them to talk with me. I immediately realize what they are referring to and feel quite ready to talk to them. The three of us take a walk up the country-like Czysta Street and Julek tells me, right off the bat, "Since your father works for the police, some people question the dependability of your participation in covert activities."

"Nonsense," I say to Julek. "You grew up in Grudziadz with me so you know that I do not have a very good relationship with my father."

"But what if your father's police pals come to your house, for one reason or another, and find weapons in it?" asks Mycka.

"Nonsense," I reply. "It is precisely because it is my father's home that they would never think of searching it!"

We go on exploring all the probabilities of either the Jewish police or the Gestapo searching my house, as well as the probabilities of a "slip of

172 | REVISITING THE SHADOWS

the tongue" on my part in my father's presence. Finally, my current political views undergo grilling and I am told to wait for the organization's decision.

A few days later, Julek comes to my house alone and the two of us go for a walk along Czysta again. Now it is my turn to ask questions. I ask for the identification of those who might place weapons in my care, and I learn a whole lot about the underground of Bialystok!

It appears that as early as October of 1941, an anti-fascist organization formed whose members initially undertook to aid, in various secret ways, the Soviet POWs and other foes of the Nazis who had been imprisoned in or near Bialystok. At first, this anti-fascist organization represented the various left-wing factions in the ghetto, but by April of 1942 they named themselves the Anti-Fascist Resistance Bloc. Loosely consolidated within the Bloc were the Communists, the Bund, and the Zionist groupings, from Hashomer Hatzair to the right-wing Beitar.

Initially, the Bialystok Judenrat, which supported the goals of the Bloc, channeled important information to its leaders and gave them financial support. But at this point, says Julek, the Block is a disunited grouping of men and women of so many varying ideological backgrounds that it is impossible for all of them to agree on the nature and the extent of their anticipated common resistance. Most of the younger members aim at the goal of forming partisan units to fight alongside other national partisan units in the Belorussian forests, while their older and more authoritarian counterparts advocate various forms of passive resistance, sabotage, and finally, an active uprising in the ghetto itself. Unfortunately, by the end of the summer of 1942, the Judenrat and the Germans become aware of the ongoing sabotage in some of the ghetto factories, as well as the other forms of passive resistance (sick-outs, for example, where people do not show up for work). Now both the Judenrat and the Jewish police are pressured to go after the underground.

I begin to understand why Julek and Mycka are urged to be careful about allowing a daughter of a police officer to join the ghetto's illicit organization. But to my surprise, the leadership of the Anti-Fascist Resistance Block (I assume) sides with me in viewing my home as a safe place to hide whatever needs to be hidden. Thus, I join the "progressive" (left-wing) faction of the Anti-Fascist Resistance Bloc—or so I think. I soon will be sleeping on top of a pistol hidden in the stuffing of my mattress, a pistol that was either stolen from the Germans or bought from outside the ghetto from suppliers of old Soviet weapons.

My contact with the underground is facilitated by discovering that both Julek's mom and my mom are eager to help a British woman, who gives English lessons, to earn money for extra food for her and her teen-aged daughter. So Julek and I share weekly lessons in English at my home whereby we also gain, before or after the lessons, some unchaperoned time. Thus I learn that the underground has just acquired a new leader, a guy from Warsaw, who has undertaken to coordinate our disparate political groups. No names are ever mentioned during my contacts either with Julek or with my later liaison with the underground, but I eventually learn that it is one of the former Vilno Resistance leaders, Mordechai Tennenbaum (Tamaroff), who was sent to us by the Warsaw Jewish Fighting Organization.

In due time, Julek quits our English lessons and "Berl-the-Shoemaker" becomes my liaison with the underground. In November of 1942, Berl informs me that our left-wing faction of the underground will be sending people to form a partisan unit in the local forests, and there is a chance for me to go along. I go through the torture of fear and indecision until I read one of the leaflets hidden under my mattress. The leaflets foretell a pending deportation of Bialystok's Jews to Treblinka and include a description of the gruesome gas chamber routines as described by a local Polish farmer. The leaflet helps me decide to go into the forest, and following Berl's instructions, I prepare my mom by telling her a cock'n bull story of my love for an enigmatic suitor (Berl!) who will soon take the proper steps to live outside the ghetto with me. My mom is resigned but my dad is anguished by the prospect of "losing his girl again," apparently referring to my escapade to the East in the spring of 1941.

Since the beginning of the fall of 1942 I have been holding classes for young children at my home. Late November of 1942 is exceptionally cold, and this morning is quite cold indeed. I finish the last class of the day and tell the children that I will not be able to hold classes during the next two days. Berl let me know yesterday that I must get ready to leave the ghetto and that he will pick me up today around noon.

My parents won't be home until later in the afternoon, so I can freely pack my knapsack and meet Berl at the corner of Czysta. He and I go toward the end of Fabryczna, we enter a house, and I follow Berl to a freezing-cold basement storage room. Berl disappears and I stay in this cold dark basement for a very long time. In the evening, a man finally shows up and tells me, in Yiddish, that the *Haverim* (comrades) have decided not to take me along at this time with the outgoing group. Apparently there are only enough weapons for those who are well-trained in their use, which means mainly men with military training, and not the likes of me.

I try to argue, but without success. "With my Aryan face and experience trading with the farmers I could be a great procurer of food for the comrades."

"Loaded guns will be a better procurer of food during this first foray into the forest. But perhaps you can go with the later groups, if and when amicable relationships with the farmers are established. In the meantime, go home and tell no one of this meeting, of this cache, or of anything else you know about our plans...By the way, word has reached the cell that you compose songs. Is this true?" I nod yes. "Well, then, why don't you go home and compose a partisan song while you wait to join one of the groups that will go out later on?"

Perhaps I feel a bit chided and surely a bit disappointed, but I don't show it. Neither do I admit to myself that I feel relieved and that maybe I am not yet ready at this point to leave the deceptively safe haven of the ghetto. So, with my toes nearly frost-bitten by the bitter cold of this unheated storage room, I go back home to tell my parents that my "lover" left the ghetto without me.

Soon after my unsuccessful escapade, I learn from Berl that the newly formed partisan group has had encounters with the Germans and has escaped deeper into the woods, nearly unscathed. My contacts with Berl remain alive and, during one of our Czysta meetings, I am given an old Russian pistol to hide in the stuffing of the mattress of my cot. Ironically, I now not only sleep on my cot where the gun is hidden, I also sit on it when I read or knit near the window or when I socialize there with my friends. This change takes place when, to accommodate my pupils, my cot is moved toward the window, opposite my parents' bed, and the table and chairs are moved to the slightly more spacious front area of the "school room."

The levying of a large tax on the rich of the ghetto by the Judenrat is a bad omen: The Gestapo's Friedel is restless, say the pessimistic naysayers of the ghetto, and they predict an *Aktion* sometime this winter. The happenings in other ghettos seem to show that the Nazis are in full swing of the "Final Solution." It is partially in response to these happenings that the late November group of underground members has gone out to form the partisan outpost in which I hope to be included someday.

We also learn at this time about the bad events boding for the Jews of the Sub-Carpathian Poland, ominous news that has to do with my own family. My cousin Wolfus shows up one day at his parents' room on the floor above ours. He has come from my Aunt Rachela's home in Boryslaw where both he and my sister lived since June of l941. Wolfus had finished his first year of engineering at Lwow University at that time and, when the war broke out, he somehow managed to get to my aunts' home in Boryslaw some 150 miles south of Lwow. After vividly describing to us the bloody pogroms of Jews that were carried out by the local Ukrainians, he relates that Aunt Rachela, her technician Eidikus, Aunt Giza, and both he and my sister had to hide at the home of a known anti-Semite, a man who turned out to be a decent human being after all. Aunt Rachela later found a Polish guide to take the bleached-blond Wolfus to Bialystok by train.

Soon after Wolfus's arrival in the ghetto, my sister's former piano teacher brings us a letter from Boryslaw. My sister writes that she is homesick and misses us terribly but that Aunt Rachela will not allow a girl of her age to travel to Bialystok, not even with a reliable guide. Aunt Rachela also believes that all ghettos, including that of Bialystok, are to be liquidated very soon. As for Wolfus, my sister writes that he had behaved so unreliably in the hideout that, for his safety and the safety of all the others, they sent him back to his folks.

The late fall and winter of 1942-43 remain fiercely cold and hunger is beginning to show among the indigent of Bialystok. Once a day, the soup kitchens provide the poor with a watery soup, and there is a place for them to sleep in the *kolkhozy* (communes) in the buildings of former schools and factories. Yet despite these efforts, there now appears in the streets a multitude of emaciated beggars, men and women with bedraggled children at their side. The sad Yiddish ghetto songs sung in the streets by the hungry vocalists bring a new kind of Yiddish folklore into Bialystok. Some of these songs may date back to the prewar days, but all of them are relevant to our current situation. Such is the prewar song *"S'brent Briderlakh, s'brent, our ohreme Shtetl takeh brent* (It's burning, brothers, it's burning, our poor little town is burning)." Other Yiddish folk songs are of a more recent origin, and I especially like one of the newer songs that describes, with wry humor, the deplorable housing conditions of the ghetto: *"Hitler hot gemakht in Bialystok a ghetto, Ay, yay yay yay! Yederem gegeben drei meter in netto, Ay, yay yay yay!* (Hitler made a ghetto in Bialystok, ay yay yay, and he gave everyone a net of three square meters of space, ay, yay yay!)"

On Kupiecka Street, near the knitting shop to which I bring my daily quota of socks, there stands a youngish woman with a small girl, and these two sing Yiddish songs that I have never heard before. I often bring some change with me and give it to the young girl, which gives me an excuse to linger by these street singers and listen to their songs. My Yiddish is so terribly inadequate that I finally decide to ask the woman in Polish about the origin of one of her songs, a very moving one. The woman starts to cry and it takes her some time to tell me that the song was composed by her invalid mother who just died in one of the shelters for the homeless refugees. As I apologize to the woman for having upset her and prepare to leave for home, she grabs me by my arm and stops me from going away. She wants me to hear her mother's song again…

I listen to the song again and I commit it to memory. I know that I will remember this song forever after.

> Vail in Bialystoker ghetto, a gevalt un geshrai,
> Vail in Bialystoker ghetto, yeder hartz tut er vei.
> Mir zitsen un mir klern, vos vet mit uns vern,
> Mir veesn nit vos vet mit uns zayn.

> In the ghetto of Bialystok, there's lamenting and crying,
> In the ghetto of Bialystok, there is pain in every heart.
> We sit and we wonder: what will happen to us?
> We just don't know what our fate will be…*
> (*Author's translation from Yiddish.)

Yes, it appears to us that the temporarily peaceful ghetto is in for bad times. We have been alerted to the fact that Lithuanian and Ukrainian SS guards were recently brought in to tighten the security of the fences of the ghetto. We later learn that an *Aktion* was supposed to have taken place on December 16, but the Judenrat managed to "buy us out" of the situation, at least for the time being. Apparently, the local German interests in our productive factories have, after all, prevailed over the authorities in Koenigsberg and Berlin and persuaded Dr. Brix, the Deputy of Governor Erich Koch, to cancel the order for the trains to Auschwitz. Yet my dad feels that something is in the air, that something is bound to happen to us, either now in December or at the beginning of next year. He provides ID cards of "Police-Dependents" for Mom and me and persuades the knitting shop to let me do some of my knitting there, for safety.

Largely because of the panicky atmosphere in the ghetto, my little "school" suffers a gradual attrition in the numbers of students, and I consolidate my remaining pupils into a single morning class. This leaves me free to work the afternoon shift at the knitting shop. In the evenings, I keep busy composing songs and I also join the painting group at Hanka's house once again. This time I set out to do a large oil painting titled "The Partisans." The painting has a catacomb-like setting and a group of partisans seated on the ground. There is a girl in this painting; she stands in front of the group and appears to be appealing to them for something. Hanka has set up eerie lighting around her brother and his friend Abrasha who are the models for my partisans, and it creates the somber mood of my painting. This is the first time that I paint people instead of the usual still life, but I guess I need to get the unsuccessful partisan venture out of my system.

There is a lull in Berl's contacts with me and I surmise that he is involved with the organizational activities of my cell, and perhaps also with the send-off of other groups into the forest. But now that I am back at my artistic endeavors, I spend some time composing and writing the Russian lyrics to the "Partisans' Song" requested of me during the ill-fated rendezvous at the basement hideout of the underground.

Both my painting and my songwriting will soon be curtailed by matters of the heart. But before these matters come about, I hand the music and lyrics of the freshly composed *March of the Bialystok Partisans* to Berl and hope that my song will inspire my comrades to action.

I will never know if my song was appreciated. Did it ever find its way into the hands of the fighters of the Bialystok uprising, or of the Bialystok partisan outpost in the forest? Did anyone translate my Russian lyrics into Yiddish? At least I myself will cherish that song and it will stay with me throughout the hell of the concentration camps. And it will reach the Statue of Liberty with me...

March of the Bialystok Partisans

The war rages on, far away and around us,
in blood of the righteous and brave.
We children of freedom, of hopeful tomorrows,
today we've been brutally enslaved.
Cut off in the ghetto, walled-in from humanity
and downed by the brute fascist might,
No matter how dismal the life is today,
we must trust that tomorrow will be bright.
United and ready, the young of the underground,
we're waiting to have our day!
For murder of children for blood of the helpless,
we'll give the Nazis their pay !
Ye partisan cadres, reach out from your hideout den,
let's plan common action for all!
When guns of the Soviets are heard around the ghetto,
we will break down the ghetto wall!
Oh, winds blow you fast to the battlegrounds, east and west
And carry our desperate plea...
And tell the brave soldiers of brotherly armies:
We're waiting to have them set us free.*

Ghetto of Bialystok, December 1942
(*Author's translation of her Russian lyrics of the song.)

IZIO PUPKO (1923-1943)

HANDle With Care.

Your father's hands, big and strong,
Steadied your bicycle as you learned to ride.

Your father's hands, big and strong,
Decided my family's fate with the flick of a wrist.

Your father's hands, big and strong,
Bounced you on his knees amidst glees of laughter.

Your father's hands, big and strong,
Tore babies from their mothers' suckling breasts.

Today your hands, tender and tenuous,
Tremulously reach out to touch one another.
(Deborah Shelkan Remis, February 1996)

I met with Helga Mueller at a dinner held in Boston for the members of a group called "One-By-One." This is an organization that pairs up children of the former Nazis with the children of the Holocaust survivors, including my son. The dinner was given by the United States contingent of this organization, and my son invited me to come along with him. This was the first time since 1993 that I met descendants of the Nazis who participated in dialogue sessions with children of the Jewish Holocaust survivors. These dialogue sessions have taken place both in the United States and in Germany. In the course of the dinner, I discovered that we few Holocaust survivors were a novelty for most of the German guests. They appeared to look at us timidly and with awe. I felt completely relaxed, however, and even enjoyed positive feelings toward these young breakaways from their Nazi heritage. Perhaps my positive attitude was the result of my former Marxist indoctrination with their truisms, of which one preached that "children are not guilty of the sins of their parents." Or perhaps I just had a positive view of the new generation of Germans because I had met some of these youngsters during my travels, and noted that many of them seemed to show a genuine remorse about the misdeeds of the Third Reich. I was also impressed with the young Germans who volunteered their services to the State of Israel.

Seated next to me was Helga Mueller, a quiet and somewhat sad young person with whom I talked in my broken German, about growing up within an ethnic German minority in the town of Grudziadz. I told Helga about the many years of Dad's work with Grudziadz's German community, and she could surely sense that the Germans of my childhood differed from the uniformed "Heil Hitler" oppressors of my wartime years. Helga was kind enough to volunteer to help search for Plischke, my dad's favorite German student. We continued our conversations by email via my German-speaking friend Gerda, and I invited Helga to visit with us in Florida.

But Helga didn't fare well at all. Through my son, I discovered that she suffered bouts of severe clinical depression that required repeated hospitalization. My son told me that Helga's depression stemmed from her childhood with a father who surely was an abusively psychotic SS man. I felt for Helga's suffering—I felt drawn to her and wanted to remain her friend. Yet I soon unearthed personal reasons that made me hate even the thought of her father...

I read the story about Helga's father's atrocities against the Jews in one of the earlier One-By-One Newsletters. In the late fall of 1942, her father ordered, and personally participated in, the slaughter of the 40,000 men, women, and children of Lida, a town in the environs of both Vilno and

*Bialystok. A counted few escaped this slaughter, and those who did sought
shelter in our then relatively peaceful ghetto of Bialystok. Izio Pupko was
one of these few.*

Early one evening in early December of 1942, my former classmate
and friend Ewa appears at my home accompanied by a tall, light-haired
young man from Lida whom I haven't met before. The young man's name
is Izio Pupko and Ewa asks if I could perhaps help him establish contact
with the resistance movement. "After all," says Ewa, "you are one of the
classmates who would be most likely to know something about it." To gain
time, I deny that I have personal knowledge of the underground. But if Izio
could wait a day or two, I could inquire of certain people at the knitting
factory, people who may have the proper contacts. Izio agrees to meet with
me at the factory in two days but doesn't show up. Instead of Izio, I spot
Berl who is waiting for me across the street from the factory, and I quickly
follow him towards our Czysta Street rendezvous spot. First he reassures
me that there is no reason to panic about the dreaded *Aktions* because one is
not likely to take place anytime soon. He then advises me to hold off the
induction of Izio Pupko into the underground until the circumstances under which he managed to escape the slaughter of the Lida Jews can be
investigated.

A few days later Izio pays me a visit, and despite my evasive answers
about the underground, he continues to call on me nearly every evening.
He soon starts to talk about himself and I learn that he finished his first year
of pedagogy at the Bialystok College of Education. He apparently knows
that my father taught music there during the 1940-41 school year. Before
the war, Izio's father owned a leather works' factory in Lida and was made
a manager of the factory when the Soviet State nationalized it. Izio's mother, who was one of Lida's leading socialites, used to spend much of her
time with Izio and his younger brother during their growing up years. The
Pupkos had a large extended family in Lida and in Bialystok, and now Izio
came to stay here with the family of his Uncle Rabin, whose daughter has
always been his favorite cousin.

Izio has a raspy, smoked-out voice, but I like to listen to his Litvak, slightly Russified Polish, and he has a true gift as a storyteller. He tells me about his mathematics-smart boyish girlfriend with whom he did all his college work and who managed to compete successfully with the male students in many subjects and even sports. At this point, I don't probe the more personal aspects of this relationship with his girlfriend, and since I don't aspire to it, I hope that Izio is not interested in me as a prospective girlfriend. We enjoy each other's company and may soon share a connection with the underground, and that seems to be enough for both of us.

Since I learn that the Pupkos have property in Palestine, I tell Izio about my past affiliation with Hashomer Hatzair, hoping to learn if he and his family were Zionists. He says that his parents weren't Zionists and that he has never belonged to a Zionist organization. I next probe his feelings about the Soviet Union and on that score his family had no leftist leanings, and he wasn't allowed to, nor did he want to, join the Komsomol. Although he sounds like a liberal when we discuss politics, I do not detect any of the standard Marxist expressions in his speech. I finally take a chance and proceed to tell Izio all about myself: about my former aspirations to join the Komsomol, the tales of my unsuccessful journey toward the Soviet interior, about my Student Organization activities in the Soviet high school, and more. Within two weeks, Izio knows a lot about me and I know a lot about him and his family, but I still don't know what drove him to search for contacts with the underground.

Izio spends New Year's Eve with the Rabin family, and I spend it with Hanka and her artistic friends. I feel kind of disappointed and lonely, but I certainly would not admit to myself that I might be missing Izio. As arranged, I meet with Berl on Czysta on New Year's Day, and he tells me that nothing could be learned about Izio's escaping the horrible slaughter in Lida. Izio's relatives, the Rabins, are known to be a respected family here, and the Pupko clan in Lida is known to have made many contributions to the welfare of Lida's people, but that is all that could be found out. I am now given more time to get to know Izio and to "pump" him about his miraculous escape from Lida's killing fields.

I sing my songs for Izio, I tell him about Bolek and Hanka, Rozia and Musia, and he tells me about his forays to the world outside of the ghetto, where he has business contacts with people who sell him cigarettes, sugar, and medicines for money or for valuables. Now I realize that I am dealing with a fearless smuggler who recklessly scales the fence and defies the possibility of being shot or apprehended by the SS guards. I have never known a young man like Izio and I am intrigued by him. He does not resemble the pampered Druskin boys and, since my experience with young men is so very limited, I cannot compare him with anyone else.

Izio finally surprises me one day and tells me that he is beginning to like me. This confession comes as part of the story of his meeting with Ewa. Izio met Ewa through his cousin who works at the hospital with Ewa's mom. He probably divulged to Ewa his interest in the underground. That is why she suggested that he meet me, a girl whom he probably won't like, but one who will surely know about the underground. Now Izio teases me that he is getting used to my ways and that he finds me to be likable, after all. To which I answer, "And you are OK, too."

In January of 1943, my mom stays in bed for more than two weeks with quite a severe bronchitis. Since I have to work the afternoon shift, my dad takes some time off from his clerical work at the precinct and comes home to tend to Mom. When I come home from work, I take care of Mom and I prepare our evening meal. I fry the daily batch of potato pancakes and "doctor-up" the precinct kitchen soup with grains, vegetables, and potatoes. I also have to do most of the cleaning up of our room now and, if it is my family's turn, the washing up of the bathroom. Izio often meets me at my factory and comes to help with the chores and have supper with us. Dad is smoking again and thanks to Izio, gets to smoke real cigarettes at times instead of the Russian *makhorka* (cheap tobacco) that is little more than rolled up tobacco in bits of newspaper. Now we also have real sugar sometimes and a bit of real fruit jam with our herbal tea. I notice that my parents' are beginning to like my friend, but neither I nor they dare ask about what happened in Lida, and Izio doesn't open up to us either.

Mom goes back to work during the last week of January and now Izio and I have more time to take a walk after my work and to talk with one another before Mom and Dad show up for the evening meal. On one occasion Oska, the Revisionist brother of my neighbor Cyla, drops into our room while Izio and I are alone, and blatantly hints of his involvement with the underground. Of course, both Izio and I deign indifference to Oska's hints, but I take advantage of the situation and touch upon the topic of the underground as soon as Oska leaves. I admit to Izio that I know about the absence of common direction and the disparate political groupings within the underground. Izio interjects that he would like to join the progressive groupings of the organization if I could only help him make a contact with these groupings. As before, I promise to keep on searching for a contact with the underground, but I make up my mind to probe Izio's recent experiences in Lida on my own, without Berl.

There are several preliminary chores I must do as soon as I come home from work, but on this particular day I do these chores early in the morning. I diligently grate a batch of potatoes for the evening's potato pancakes, I splinter the wood for the stove, peel the vegetables, and presoak the grains for the enrichment of our daily soup. This evening, Izio and I light up the stove, put the enriched soup on it for a slow simmer, and sit down on my cot and talk. First, I ask about the fate of Izio's family and I learn that his father was killed at his factory when it was hit by a German bomb. Only his heart could be found and only his heart was buried. Izio's mother and the two sons then moved in with their grandmother who lived in the Jewish section of Lida. As has been true of all other Jewish communities, the Germans carried out sporadic pogroms in Lida. About a month before Izio's coming to Bialystok, however, the Germans suddenly killed off the remainder of Lida's 40,000 Jews. Without warning, Jews were rounded up by the German SS and their Lithuanian underlings and taken by trucks into the depths of a densely forested area. Screamed at, kicked and beaten, Jewish men were separated from the women and children. Eventually, everyone was ordered to undress. Groups of the huddling, naked victims were prodded to march in the direction of the freshly dug ditches, clearly visible in the woodland's clearing. Those who waited for their turn could hear the cries and the prayers of the victims, accompanied by the staccato of the machine guns. "Women and children were the first ones to be killed," says Izio, and then his face, covered by his hands, comes down onto my knees. I feel his bitter sobbing and I begin to cry, too. He saw his mother undress, he saw the boots of a drunken SS man kick her, and then the same SS man whipping her as she ran to where she met her death. He saw his younger brother run to his place of execution. He saw him run with the shivering cold, naked children, terrified children who were crying for their mothers, children who begged their tormentors for mercy. He stood numb as he listened to the rattling of the machine guns, and he was completely resigned to die.

Suddenly a soldier wearing the black uniform of the Lithuanian Auxiliaries yanked him out of the line up screaming, "What the hell are you doing here with these lousy Jews? Are you playing a saint or something? Beat it, you idiot Polack!" The soldier was Izio's high school friend and a member of his school soccer team. Before Izio came to his senses, the Lithuanian had ripped the yellow Star of David off his coat, kicked him out of the area, and prodded him to go on. Then, when they were out of earshot of his mates, the Lithuanian friend quietly told Izio to immediately get going out of Lida.

I would like to hug and comfort Izio when he sits up again but I don't dare do it, so I just lend him my handkerchief and I whisper that I am sorry, so sorry. He says that he will be OK. If he gets the chance to join the underground and the chance to fight this dog, Mueller, he will be OK! I ask who "this dog Mueller" is, and I finally get the full answer as to how and why Izio came into the ghetto of Bialystok—and why he so badly wants to join the underground.

Mueller was one of the organizers and perpetrators of the massacre of the nearly 40,000 Jews of Lida. But he also became involved with the Bialystok Gestapo and it was he, rather than the higher-ups from Berlin or Koenigsberg, who instigated the aborted December deportation of Bialystok Jews. Izio maintains that the threat of future deportation of Bialystok Jews still exists and that Mueller will surely be involved with the future *Aktions* here. But in this big ghetto, the underground can take a meaningful stand against the Germans, and Izio wants to be part of it.

As to Izio's travel to Bialystok, he located his father's supplier of hides in the suburbs of Lida, a man who had remained a friend of the family during both the Soviet and German occupations. Izio stayed at his friend's home and before leaving for Bialystok, buried on his property a metal trunk containing his mother's mink coat, his father's fur-lined overcoat, and some heirloom jewelry. It was this trusted Gentile friend who drove all the way to Bialystok with Izio hidden in the straw under the covers of his horse-drawn wagon. Jumping over the ghetto's fence at night was a cinch for my daring friend.

Now I feel free to explain to Izio why it has taken so long to forge a contact between him and the underground. Next day, Julek Mintz helps us contact Berl who soon gets permission to be the liaison between the underground and the two of us, myself and my boyfriend Izio Pupko.

Later in January of 1943, we are offered the opportunity to join a group going to our partisan outpost. I am very anxious to make up for my earlier aborted partisan venture, but Izio talks me out of joining the partisans at this time. He strongly believes that now that the underground is under the leadership of the famed "Vilno-Warsaw-Tamaroff," we surely will organize resistance activities when the Germans start an *Aktion* in the ghetto.

Yet no directives for resistance activities come from our leadership when an *Aktion* actually takes place the following month in February 1943. Unfortunately, this *Aktion* takes place during the time of the underground's lack of coordination of activities, absence of common direction, and scarcity of weapons. My dad learns at the police headquarters that on February 5th of this year, the Germans will start deporting people to the "work" camp of Treblinka. He sets in motion plans to protect his family. He tells us that starting on the evening of February 4th, we will have to stay at the Judenrat, and that we must take along some food, clothing, and blankets. Once again, the Germans promise to deport only those who are "unemployable" in either the ghetto factories or outside the ghetto. I fear for Izio's safety because he is one of the "unemployables," and since he is not a member of the Jewish police or of the Judenrat families, he will not be offered refuge in the Judenrat building.

On February 3rd, Izio and I walk home from work and we hide our anxieties by talking about inconsequential things. Tomorrow night, Izio will move into his friend's hideout while Mom and I will join other police families crowded into an office room of the Judenrat. Tonight is our last evening together. We hold hands as we walk towards my home, and we kiss at the upstairs door to our apartment. We say goodbye and we don't tell each other that we've grown to care for one another, but we both know it.

Starting on February 4th, Mom and I spend six nights in the stuffy and noisy room at the Judenrat. Mostly women and children are there with us. We soon finish what little food we brought in, and the rest of the time we have to live on dry bread and tea brought in by the Jewish policemen. Outside our windows, we can hear the anguished cries of the Jews and the humiliating curses of the Germans who drag these poor people out of their homes and shelters. And we can also hear rifle and machine gun shots. As he emerges from his equally crowded Judenrat office room, my uncle commiserates with us and shares the news that Friedel is personally conducting this bestial *Aktion*. There are also reports of some resistance by ordinary men and women, and reports that several policemen took off their caps and armbands and joined the deportees.

I lie curled up on the table and watch through the window. The German and Lithuanian SS men poke about basement doors, obviously looking for hidden Jews. Sometimes, I daydream about an escape from the ghetto, sometimes I compose a new melody, and most of the time I worry about Izio. I worry if he will come out of this nightmare safe and sound. This time I am sure that I care for him.

Four days later, my father comes to tell us that the roundup is finished and that the police and Judenrat families are to go home and stay behind closed doors for 24 hours to allow for the cleanup of the "bloody mess." Next morning, my dad and a young policeman who is my former classmate walk us home. Mom and I, along with Aunt Pepka and her son Wolfus, keep our eyes cast down as we pass the SS guards along the empty streets. But my peripheral vision picks up the view of dead bodies in some of the empty backyards! As the others head for our upstairs apartments, my classmate stops me in the doorway to tell me what he has heard about Izio. Apparently, Izio's long legs were poorly hidden from the SS men who peered through the sidewalk grating into his hideout, a basement storage bin full of assorted junk. The Germans ordered the Jewish police to get the people out of this hideout, but the Jews refused to budge until they heard the Germans threaten to throw a hand grenade into the basement. Only then did they finally get out and the Jewish policemen were ordered to take them to the deportation site. All of them were marched off except for Izio, who refused to get out. Most probably, he was killed on the spot. I leave the young policeman without saying anything, and I go upstairs and cry.

The twenty-four hours of our confinement at home are painfully trying for all three of us. My dad was ordered to carry the bodies of men, women, and children who were beaten or shot to death, to the cemetery on Zabia. Dad's grief-stricken face tells of the suffering inflicted on him and his fellow-policemen by this gruesome assignment. Among the dead were the brutalized bodies of Itzhak Malmed and the Kurianski sisters. "There have been innumerable examples of resistance among the Jews who were rounded up for the transport to Treblinka," Dad continues slowly. "Although the resistance was neither inspired nor directed by the underground, the Jewish police believe that members of the underground put up resistance to the Germans on their own. We heard that Itzhak Malmed splashed concentrated hydrochloric acid into the faces of the Germans climbing the staircase of his home on Kupiecka 29, then single-handedly fought them off the stairs. The three Kurianski sisters defended themselves by breaking chairs over the heads of the Germans, but of course, eventually the Germans overwhelmed and vengefully killed them. All these deaths have served to spur the onlookers to put up a fierce resistance to the Germans, and quite a few Germans were left wounded or dead. But in retribution, some 2,000 Jewish men, women, and children have been brutally murdered."

Raszka, Cyla, and even Wolfus and Oska come in to share the news about the deportation of many of our friends and to commiserate with me about the death of my boyfriend. But I go alone to look for his body. As soon as the curfew is lifted, I go to the cemetery on Zabia Street and there I face a gigantic pile of bodies, one on top of the other. In the pile, there are infants, their heads cracked open, lying on top of their mothers, and bloodied bodies of older children lying on top of one another. There are many people at the cemetery, a large crowd of wailing, crying, and praying people who came to search for the bodies of their loved ones. I join them and search for the body of Izio but I can't find it. I look for the light curly-haired head, I look for the familiar long black boots, I look for the long-fingered right hand bearing Izio's mother's ring, but I cannot find anything that could be part of Izio's dead body.

Izio's relatives are at home when I call on them a day or two later. They also heard about Izio's death and they think that perhaps the Germans had him buried in the same backyard where they killed him. Next day, I go to the police headquarters and ask about their earlier burials of some of the victims. Sure enough, during the first days of the *Aktion*, the police were ordered to bury quite a few of the murdered Jews right on the spot of their execution. The police eventually exhume these bodies and bury them at the cemetery.

With my hopes dashed of ever seeing Izio again, dead or alive, I drag myself home and am greeted at the door by the smiling face of my mom, who points to Izio standing behind her! In disbelief, I look at Izio's "black-eyes," the deep bruise on his forehead, his bandaged hands, and I don't feel embarrassed to hug and kiss my boyfriend in my mom's presence.

Izio tells his story at suppertime and we are in awe of both his bravery and his luck. The story told by my policeman-friend was partially true in that Izio indeed refused to budge from the hideout while the others were marched off to where the trucks were loading the deportees. Luckily, he wasn't apprehended by psychopathic Lithuanians but instead by German soldiers. They were satisfied with just dragging Izio out of the storage bin, pummeling him with their rifle-butts, and then marching him off to be deported to "work." With all the others, he was loaded into trucks and then into trains bound for "work" camps. But my boyfriend knew where he was going when he passed towns that were on the route leading to the extermination camp of Treblinka, and he jumped out of an open window of the cattle-wagon into the snowed-in ditch at the track. He bruised his forehead and the palms of his hands in the fall, but he immediately picked himself up and ran toward the nearby woods, zigzagging to dodge the bullets of the Lithuanian SS men perched on the roof of his cattle-wagon.

Izio's luck was with him from the beginning of his escapade to its very end: the very first farmer's house that he entered proved to be the home of a courageous and a righteous Gentile who bandaged Izio's bleeding hands and face and let him eat and sleep with his family. Seeing my photograph, the farmer remarked that if Izio were to bring me with him, both of us could safely stay and work at his farm without anyone suspecting that we were Jews. With that, the farmer offered to take my boyfriend by horse and wagon along the country roads, part of the way to Bialystok, and then let him cover the remaining 15 to 20 miles on foot. The farmer's cap on Izio's blondish hair, and the farmer's wife's basket of buttered slices of bread and a can of milk, complemented the black boots and the lean gentile looks of my boyfriend. He easily passed for a young countryman "on his way to his grandma's house."

During his deportation, Izio didn't spot among the Jewish policemen anyone he knew, and that explains why we couldn't have learned about his escape.

Thanks to my dad's recommendation, Izio gets a job at the furniture factory so that he now has a legitimate work permit, the much-coveted *Arbeit Bescheinigung*. During the one free afternoon allowed the Jewish slave-laborers, Izio still manages to scale the fence and smuggle in cigarettes, sugar, and medicaments. The smuggled goods buy food, and we and the Rabins get a bit of that food, too. Mom is horrified by his adventurism, so Izio gives her his word that he will stop it. Of course, he doesn't keep his promise, but she likes him anyway and so does my father.

Berl soon contacts me and confirms that there has been no involvement of the underground in the spontaneous resistance of Bialystok Jews during the February *Aktion*. But the leadership of the underground is pleased with the Polish underground press report that relates many cases of spontaneous armed resistance and also of the widespread passive resistance of the ghetto's population who have either refused to assemble for deportation or who have physically refused to be moved from their homes and shelters.

It is estimated that at least 15,000 people were taken to Treblinka, possibly also to Auschwitz, and when life resumes in the ghetto after the February tragedy, I discover that I have lost many of my acquaintances and friends. The Vilno family is no longer staying behind our room divider—I assume they may have been deported. Tychocinski, the first principal of our Soviet high school, was made to chase chickens around someone's backyard and then machine-gunned down; his lovely wife now lowers her teary eyes whenever we greet her in the street. I don't see any of my pupils in the streets of the ghetto anymore, and I assume that some of them must have been deported along with their families. Of my former classmates, Mina Bialostocka, Cyra Kreshes, Hela, and Nesia are but a few that I discover to be missing. The saddest of all is the fate of the family of Bergman, our teacher of Latin and ancient history. After many years of waiting, a baby was born to them in the ghetto. When the baby cried in the crowded hideout, however, they had to smother it. I sometimes meet Bergman, but I don't talk with this now prematurely-aged teacher because I don't know how to express my sympathy for him.

But life must go on and Izio and I now acquire a group of new friends. Among them is the fine singer Yetta, my old pal Mirka with her new boyfriend Chmielnik, the violinist of my trio at the Soviet School of Music, and a few others. We meet during our free afternoons, we often hold political discussions, and at times, Yetta sings and Chmielnik plays his violin for us. But I refuse to share with these new friends my new pop song titled *A Rainy Afternoon*, a song whose lyrics express Izio's tender feelings for me.

My friendship with Izio is somewhat stifled by the gloom that now permeates our home and the ghetto. But on March 26, 1943, on the day of my mom's birthday, Izio surprises everyone at our supper table: he hands me his mother's ring and tells my parents that he is serious about me. Mom cries and Dad has tears in his eyes, but his are not the tears of joy. All of us well know that we may never have the chance to be married and to raise a family. Yet Dad feels that he now ought to, at least, extend the police-family protection to include his daughter's "intended." He inquires at the police headquarters if that could be arranged, and is assured that it will be taken care of.

Early in April, Izio and I transfer to the late shift of our respective factories so that we can work at the police vegetable field in the mornings. Although there is no pay for this additional work, there are other advantages to it. We are allowed to take home a few vegetables when they are in season; at work we can nibble on radishes and sweet peas, gherkins and tomatoes, which we have not tasted for nearly two years! And we have more privacy at work in the field than at home to talk and to steal an occasional kiss while the other workers are busy in their own part of the vegetable field.

Once or twice a week we spend an evening at Izio's home with his Uncle Rabin's family. While there, I learn about Izio's boyhood in Lida and about his extended family. As the summer progresses, we begin to freely take advantage of the curtained-off passage to our balcony now that the Vilno family is no longer with us. On balmy evenings, Izio and I love to sit on the balcony, and my mom also enjoys going out there with me. Sometimes, my mom confides in me about her earlier life with my dad, but most of the time she talks about herself when she was my age. I sense her anxiety about my relationship with Izio, a relationship so badly warped by circumstances. And I sense her doubts about our future.

Since the uprising and the subsequent fall of the Warsaw Ghetto in April of this year, I have had the same doubts about our future. These doubts become even stronger when I read the letter that my grandmother somehow managed to send to Bialystok from Brzezany. The letter says that most of the towns in their area have already been made *Judenrein* (cleared of Jews) by pogroms coupled with deportations to the extermination camp at Belzec. The same fate is expected to shortly befall Brzezany.

In June, another group of our underground people leaves the ghetto for the partisan outpost and I am asked to give up the pistol buried in my mattress. Once again, Izio and I are ambiguous about the matter of going with the group and we fail to make up our minds about it. We vow to ourselves that we will go out the next time around. Since there now exists within the underground a legitimate faction called "Forward" or "Forois" (a faction whose aim is to keep on sending people to the partisans), we may have another chance to go. But our expectations are about to fade away.

Late in the afternoon of August 15, 1943, Berl appears in Izio's factory and calls him out "to attend to an emergency at home." The two of them get me out of my factory and we all go toward my home. We learn that a "friend" in the Gestapo informed our people that the Germans' Ukrainian auxiliaries are in the process of encircling the ghetto and that the final and total deportation of all of us will begin tomorrow morning. Berl hands me a homemade hand explosive that I am to throw at a German tank as soon as it enters through the fence on Jurowiecka Street. Izio gets an assignment to meet Berl somewhere at the end of Fabryczna Street. As soon as Berl leaves, we dash over to the precinct and find everybody there ready to go to an emergency meeting at the police headquarters. But my dad is first going to get mom at her factory and then take her to the policemen's meeting. Izio and I decide to go back to my house and wait there for my parents and for the latest news.

We sit on the balcony's cement floor and watch the daylight fade above the familiar houses across the street. I point out to Izio the house in whose backyard, only two years ago, Rachelka and I studied for our finals. He points out to me the distant fence on Czysta which he used to scale in the pursuit of his illicit smuggling of food items and other scarce goods. I tell Izio that I wish we could have, before we die, the intimacy that people who love each other usually have, but he tells me that it is best to remain free of the burden of a past love should only one of us remain alive. I tell Izio that I will cherish the song that we have written together and that I will think of him whenever I sing that song. And he tells me to just live for the future and to forget the past, if I alone survive. This is our last private time together and we don't dare to lose ourselves in the tragedy of this evening.

I AM ONE OF THE FEW HUNDRED SURVIVORS OF THE 60,000 JEWS OF BIALYSTOK

There used to be a ghetto's cemetery on Zabia Street in Bialystok. An obelisk was recently erected there and it had these words inscribed on its face:

BROTHERLY GRAVE
OF THE FIGHTERS OF THE GHETTO OF BIALYSTOK
WHO DIED
IN THE HEROIC FIGHT
AGAINST THE GERMAN BARBARIANS,
THE FIGHT FOR FREEDOM AND HONOR
OF THE JEWISH NATION
16-25 VIII 1943

The following report appeared in the Bialystok Press of August 17th, 1998:

Yesterday was the 55th anniversary of the beginning of the uprising in the Jewish ghetto of Bialystok. Regional representatives, city officials, representatives of Jewish organizations of several countries and citizens of Bialystok met yesterday at the Zabia Street's obelisk erected there in the memory of those who perished during the August 16-25 1943 uprising of the ghetto of Bialystok. Participants of the commemorative ceremony listened to official speeches and to a personal account of memories of a survivor of the uprising. Israel's Ambassador to Poland, Mr. Yigal Antebi, spoke about the rich heritage in philosophy, literature, the arts, and industry which the perished Jewish Community of Bialystok bequeathed to Israel and the world. He said that the history of the uprising and the courage and sacrifice of the fighters of the ghetto of Bialystok have become part of the heritage of Israel, and that the names of the leaders of the uprising are indelibly inscribed into the memory of the Israelis. The speech by Sam Solasz, the president of the New York organization of the Jewish Immigrants from Bialystok, was especially moving. He told of his escape from the Treblinka-bound train and of his eventual refuge in the home of a Polish-Christian family...Felicja Nowak, the author of a memoir "My Star," urged survivors of the Holocaust to speak about this greatest of tragedies that befell the Jewish Nation...

The ceremony ended with a prayer by Rabbi Yonah Bookstein and with the laying of wreaths at the obelisk...

"A bloody pogrom took place when Germans occupied Bialystok on June 27, 1941. Besides the burning of two Jewish areas of the town and the killing of the Jews of these areas, the Germans set afire Bialystok's Great Synagogue with 2,000 Jews within its walls...At the end of July of 1941, the remaining Jews were walled inside the ghetto from which they were taken to their death...in 1943. The uprising was undertaken in response to the start of the final annihilation of the ghetto on August 16th of 1943; it lasted till August 25th...

"There are only a few hundred survivors of the 60,000 Jews of Bialystok...

"In regard to its significance, historians rate the uprising of the ghetto of Bialystok as second to the uprising of the ghetto of Warsaw..."*

(*Author's translation from Polish)

With Berl as our liaison with the underground, we are now in the know of its current undertakings. More members of its "Forward" or "Forois"

faction join the partisan outpost in March and June of 1943. Under the leadership of Tennenbaum-Tamaroff and his deputy Daniel Moskowicz, the movement regroups and steps up its activities in the ghetto. They now acquire more weapons, train the members in the use of these weapons and apparently also use these weapons. According to the reports of the Jewish police, an armed confrontation between the underground and the Germans has taken place somewhere at the fence of the ghetto. The skirmish happened on the night of May 24-25 and it was a miraculous one—when it was over, the Jews managed to escape with impunity. After this show of force, there comes into being, early in June of 1943, a unified "Armed Self-Defense of the Ghetto." Its leaflets call on the Jews to join its ranks and to prepare to stand up to the Germans in the future *Aktions*. The underground's "punitive commando" puts to death all those who, like the Judkowski brothers, served the Germans as informers and collaborators before and during the *First Aktion*.

Tennenbaum trains his Armed Self-Defense Unit to stage an attack on the Germans if and when they invade the ghetto for another deportation roundup. He trains people in the various ways of escaping from the ghetto and maps out the routes to our outpost in the forest for them. He intends to have our members persuade as many people as possible to get out of their homes when the police start their house-search during the *Aktion* days, and to follow our contact men to the forests. But the goals of all these long-range preparations are never realized once the surprise siege of the ghetto at dawn of August 16, 1943, actually takes place. There isn't enough time to set our plans in motion even though the leadership learns about the pending *Aktion* from our "sympatico" at the Gestapo as early as the late afternoon of August 15. We are apprised at that time that the Germans know about our plans for resistance! We also learn at that time that the Ukrainians, who are surrounding the ghetto, are a well-trained unit of Lublin's "Special Commando for the Final Solution," under the command of the infamous Olilo Globocnik

When I leave home in the early morning of August 16, 1943, I mull over Berl's prediction that our fighting forces of some 300 men and women will have to face a force of 3,000 German Wehrmacht soldiers supported by tanks; I pray that this prediction proves to be exaggerated. My dad has been released from his police chores and he and Mom tend to their packing. This deportation does not follow the routines of the first *Aktion* in that there is no house-to-house search. People are simply ordered, under threat of death, to line up at the end of Kupiecka Street from where they will be transported to the deportation trains. Dad tells us that only a few Jewish policemen have been assigned to patrol the assembly area and that German Wehrmacht soldiers will be there.

I leave my home early in the morning of August 16 and tell my parents that Izio and I will join them in the lineup later on. On my way, I pass Hanka's house and bid my friend and her family goodbye. Hanka's family has made up their minds to stay put and to die in their own home rather than go to their death in the gas chambers of Majdanek or Treblinka. The hand explosive bulging out of my skirt pocket reminds me of the imminence of my dangerous assignment and I feel scared and apprehensive as I head down Kupiecka toward Fabryczna Street. Pesia (Musia and Rozia's

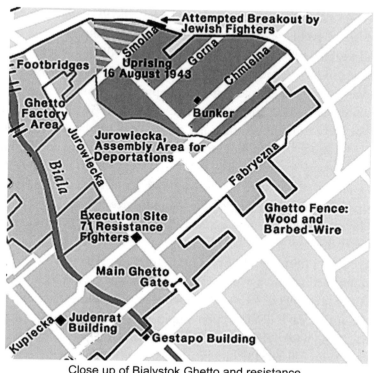

Close up of Bialystok Ghetto and resistance.

cousin) and her husband are heading my way. They no longer observe our orders of secrecy and tell me that they are going to the Fabryczna Street assembly point to join one of the fighting units there. I am speechless when I notice Pesia's blank face because I know that she has recently given birth to a baby daughter. Blandly, Pesia informs me that they have drugged the baby and left her to die in her crib. Heartbroken, I rush to meet Izio at the corner of Jurowiecka and Fabryczna Streets but he is nowhere to be seen. Then I do what I was told to do: I station myself inside one of the doorways on Jurowiecka Street, rather far away from the corner of Kupiecka but quite close to the fence through which the German tank is supposed to enter.

People are streaming from Jurowiecka and from Fabryczna, just as I've seen them stream from other streets of the ghetto, all going towards the assembly area on Kupiecka Street. All are carrying bundles and backpacks, all are sweaty under the layers of clothing which they hope to put to good use in the camps, and all are weary on this warm August morning. An occasional soldier of the Wehrmacht and a few Jewish policemen circulate around the assembly area and along the adjacent stretches of Jurowiecka and Fabryczna Streets. Pretty soon, shots are heard somewhere in the upper reaches of Fabryczna and I know that the uprising must have started.

I touch the "hand grenade" inside my pocket, I walk toward the fence that cuts off the Jewish part of Jurowiecka from its Gentile section, and I crouch at one of the houses near the fence. With my back to the passing people, I examine the odd-looking contraption in my hand and find that it does not have any movable parts. What am I supposed to remove from this "hand grenade" to activate it, the way I've seen it done in the movies? Anyway, there has been no sign of any appearance of a tank and I have no idea how to operate my pipe explosive, so I just let it lie in the mottled weeds near the house.

Suddenly, I hear a click. Across the street from me there stands, with his pistol aimed at me, a Wehrmacht soldier about as old as my dad. He says, "*Lass das liegen, du dumes Maedchen, lass das liegen und staeht langsam auf!* (Leave it alone, you stupid girl, leave it alone and slowly stand up)." I do what I am told and leave the hand explosive in the weeds at the house. With my heart wildly beating, I slowly stand up and stay there, some 60 feet away from the German and his pistol. I feel that I am losing control over my bladder. The German casts an eye at the Jewish families that are passing in wide circles away from him, and he puts his gun into its holster. I now realize that, luckily, I have been stationed far away from the resistance activities, that I have a backpack and layers of clothing on and look just like the passing Jews, and that I look younger than I really am. The old soldier just doesn't make the connection between me and the fighters on Fabryczna. He probably believes that I just stumbled upon the explosive that was hidden in the grass and crouched down to see what it was.

It is amazing how well I can understand the old soldier's German, considering the fact that I am scared to death. In a daze, I answer yes to his question about my parents being in the assembly line. And in a daze, I hear him tell another soldier where to pick up the crude pipe explosive which "this stupid girl nearly blew herself up into smithereens with." I follow the German toward the corner of Fabryczna and peek across the street and notice a group of men who are standing there with their hands raised high. I don't see anyone I know among them. We find my parents in the lineup and the soldier lets me go. My parents stand there forlorn and old-looking, so I don't even explain where I have been and why the German soldier brought me over to them, and they don't ask any questions.

About an hour later, Izio and Golda Lipkies (whom I had met at Hashomer Hatzair two years earlier), dash into the lineup. Izio tells me that they have just left a cellar on Fabryczna where they waited in vain for their directives from the underground. On their way, they saw men being led by the Germans toward Jurowiecka Street. They heard one of the men yell "*Als is forloren, Brieder!* (all is lost, brothers!),*" and decided, on the spur of the moment, to join the deportees. Izio intimates to me that Golda has given him the name of the woods where our partisans are and the train station which should serve as the jumping off point for it.

The Germans finally line us up, family after family, facing Jurowiecka Street. They send mothers with babies, the old and the disabled toward the ghetto's hospital. The rest of us are to form rows of five and march to the wide-open western fence of Jurowiecka. There, three Gestapo men once again select the older men and women with children and have them form separate columns. My family, including Izio, and my uncle's family "pass" the selection: we are included in the column of those who are *Arbeit-Taechtig* (able-bodied). I haven't seen members of the Lipkies family at the assembly area; Golda is walking behind us, alone, and I arrive at the sad conclusion that she will have to face the hell all alone…

The fence of Fabryczna has been opened and the Germans march us out of the ghetto into streets full of Gentile people of Bialystok who have come out to peer at us. Some have smirks on their faces, but most look at us with compassion and tears in their eyes and I wish I could ask them to hide us somewhere. Behind me, I hear Golda's sonorous Yiddish: "*Zey veinen, die Peilen take veinen far uns!* (They are crying, the Poles are really crying for us!)" Hot and thirsty, with the guards on the sides of the columns, we march along the road leading to the Bialostoczek Heights' freight train station, to the trains supposedly waiting there for us. There are no shade trees on the Heights and it is beastly hot and dusty. Mercifully, total strangers share with us and with others whatever water or tea they have brought with them. We spend a sleepless and restless night sitting or lying in the trampled grass of the Heights; Izio and I quietly talk about our previous commitments to one another. We swear to each other that the one who survives will feel free to love and marry, without any ties to our youthful romance in the ghetto of Bialystok.

Early in the morning of August 17, horse-drawn wagons arrive with mothers and their babies and the old and the disabled, all of them coming from the ghetto's hospital where they have overnighted. Among these, I can see the three generations of the Szabrynski clan clustered around the old grandfather in his wheelchair, all of them ready to go to their death together. Thus starts the second day of the final disposition of the remaining 43,000 Jewish people of the ghetto of Bialystok.

Five special trains have been dispatched on August 15, 1943, to deport the Jews of Bialystok to Treblinka and Majdanek. On August 17, one of these long freight trains waits for us on the sidetracks of Bialostoczek Heights. Along with the rest of the people assembled on the Heights, my family and I are ushered into the cattle cars of the waiting trains. Those who did not "pass" the selection, including mothers with children, the old and the not so old, the disabled and the rest of the "unfit to work," are placed into the cattle cars in the rear of the train. The rest go into the cars in front, and my family ends up in the same cattle car as Dasa and Golda Lipkies, Mirka and her family, and, as I will soon learn, two or three other escapees from the battle lines of the uprising.

The Germans crowd 50-60 people into one cattle car. High above the floor of each of these cattle cars are two small windows, one at each end of the car, and two "outhouse" barrels, one at each corner of the car. As soon as our wagon is loaded and its doors are bolted shut, Ukrainian SS men position themselves on the roof to guard us from above, and the train is then moved from the sidetrack into the freight depot.

The day is terribly hot and a merciful railroad worker fills and refills a pitcher of water for us. The guards on the roof allow those near the window to have a drink from that pitcher, and the people in the car begin to fight wildly for a space at the window. I don't get a drink but Izio manages to get some water for my mom who is as pale as a ghost. As the train begins to move, the horrible heat lessens a bit but not enough to feel comfortable in the overcrowded cattle car. Mom complains that she can't breathe so Izio helps her to squeeze in by the window, but she soon faints and slumps down to the floor. My dad doesn't budge, so I crawl over to him and yell at him to get up and help Mom, but he just sits there and doesn't respond. Golda, or someone else, hands me a handkerchief soaked with cologne. I rub Mom's face with it and she comes to. Someone else gives her a drink from his canteen and she just says, "Oh, why didn't you let me die." In the rear of the car, well-dressed men and women with their heads covered pray in a monotonous singsong. The train keeps on moving, slowing down a bit only at the stations we pass.

Shots are heard from above and several of us go over to the window and see a man lying in the ditch next to the railroad track. Another man is running out into the fields and is brought down, his body riddled with bullets. Mirka's boyfriend identifies the fallen man as the jazz musician, the idol of the ghetto's teenagers. Now Izio, Golda Lipkies, and I crouch next to some young people who are talking about the uprising and about the feasibility of jumping from the train. They say that Czyzew is the last station before Malkinia, that there is a road leading from Malkinia to the forest hideout of Soviet partisans and that, unlike the Poles, these partisans will take us in. They think the guys may have to be pushed out, but the women could easily fit through the windows. Each one of us must have some dollars, gold coins or jewelry before we venture the escape. We have some of it, but we decide to ask "the religious rich" for more. A young man who is fluent in Yiddish becomes our spokesman and we hear him making the case for helping to save the nation by saving its young, and that means us. The praying men answer that they need their money to pay for their own welfare in the work camps.

We prepare to jump from the train anyway. Golda, who has a pair of scissors, cuts our skirts open, top to bottom; the guys who are not wearing long boots tie their trousers around their ankles. We practice lifting one another to the window and wait for the slowdown at Czyzew. But as soon as the road signs show that we are at Czyzew, there rises a tumult in the car. People scream at us, yelling that we shouldn't endanger them, that the Ukrainians will machine-gun our car and kill innocent people as soon as one of us jumps out. And when the train starts slowing down, some men surround us and threaten to use force if we attempt to jump out. We pass the

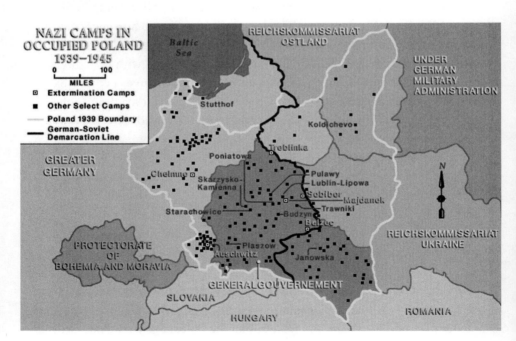

station of Czyzew, the train picks up speed and we crouch on the floor, disheartened and dejected.

Then someone provocatively starts the INTERNATIONALE and we join in with an equally spiteful furor. But instead of provoking the people in our car, the sounds of the hated Communist anthem provoke the Ukrainians on the roof of our car. A machine-gun volley sprays our car and two people sitting beside me begin to scream with pain. Neither my mom nor any of my friends appear wounded, and my dad continues to sit in his catatonic position, undisturbed. Along with other people in the car, I get up from the floor to help those who were wounded, fortunately only slightly. It is only then that I begin to feel pain and notice blood on the inside of my thighs. Before hitting the floor, a bullet must have passed between my thighs, grazing them, and there isn't much I can do for myself at this time.

Some miles after Malkinia, the train slows down as it crosses fields covered with whitish ashes and bits of bones. It stops at a desolate depot, and we sense that this is Treblinka. The door is unbolted, a Ukrainian guard looks at our deadly silent human cargo and orders us to stand up, one and all. After he looks us over, he bolts our door without a word. But we take a good look through the door before they close it and we notice people in striped uniforms coming out of a small group of buildings facing the railroad tracks. The striped-uniformed people run toward the end of our train. There is a commotion with a lot of shouting there, followed by a jolt—signifying to us that the rear cars have been detached from our train. In our car, some pray, some hug one another, some just peer into nothingness and wait. Golda Lipkies stands under the window with me and whispers: "They are going into the gas chambers right away, we will go later, but maybe there is a chance for us?" Finally, the train starts moving again and we all liven up—we made it through Treblinka! Another field covered by human fertilizer of white ashes and crushed bone confirms that indeed, we have passed the extermination camp of Treblinka without being unloaded there. Is it possible that we are going to a work camp, after all?

The train, now much lighter, speeds through the countryside of Poland, where rye and wheat are already harvested and tied into neat bundles. We are greeted by farmers whose ominous facial expressions do not support our hopes for a work camp ahead of us. Nevertheless, my father comes somewhat to life, Mom begins to fix her hair, and I try my best to hold a folded handkerchief with petroleum jelly on it between my thighs. Relatives of the two lightly wounded passengers bandage the hand of one and the knee of the other one using strips of cotton torn from their own shirts. A lighter mood overtakes our car so that even the stench of the overflowing outhouse barrels stops bothering us.

It is in this lighter frame of mind that the train brings us to the great big train station bearing the sign "Zugplatze-Lublin." But our mood is shattered by the brisk opening of our bolted doors accompanied by vicious shouts of *"Raus!! Alle raus! Mach schnell! Raus verfluchte Juden, Raus!* (Out! Out with all of you! Move fast! Out accursed Jews, out with you!)" The screaming SS officers with the skull-and-crossbones insignia on their hats are scurrying all over the platform. They come at us with whips, letting their dogs strain at their leashes and snarl at us ferociously. And they kick us, screaming *"Raus !"* and *"Mach shnell!"* as they prod us on and on, away from the platform and onto the dusty clearing enclosed by a few long barracks. We leave our backpacks in the hands of prisoners in striped uniforms who take them on pushcarts "to be deloused." Now other prisoners circulate among us and sell us drinking water in exchange for jewels and money, saying: "You are not going to need your riches where you are going!" Soon after we detrain, a loudspeaker orders us to form rows of five and face the pathway where German officers will be collecting our money, precious metal, and jewelry. It also warns us that possessing any of these precious things in camp is punishable by death.

Izio and I walk around for awhile and look for people we know. Here and there is a familiar face of a person with whom we may exchange a few questions and get a few guesses about our situation. We also notice that there are people who are lying on the ground, some of them nearly dead and others moaning with pain. Among them are Dasa's dad and the parents of Mirka, who tell us that they have taken poison, as have most of the other people who are now dying here. Then the loud speaker barks out an order for the men to separate from the women and to follow the SS officers who will take them to another area. When a few men refuse to leave, the SS make them kneel down in the dirt, shoot them in the back of their heads, and leave their bodies lying where they have shot them. Golda Lipkies uses her persuasive Yiddish to make sure that all the men around us follow orders and separate from us. I part with Dad and Izio without a clue that the SS are separating us for good.

Over the loudspeaker comes a request for young women to volunteer for fieldwork, and many do. In tears, Mirka and Dasa leave their dying parents and join a group of other fieldworkers wearing kerchiefs on their heads. I hug Mirka, she bursts out crying, and these are her last words to me: "Oh, what is the point of living...I lost my boyfriend, my mom and my dad...let me go to wherever they want to kill me." Dasa just looks at me and her eyes plead that I find the Komsomol booklet hidden under a tree in Walily, as if she wanted to say, "If I don't survive, let that booklet remind you of me."

In a short time, the vans that take our young women away come back empty and take more women "to work in the fields." None of these women will ever be seen again.

Although the men's assembly area is pretty far away from us, we can see that our men are subjected to a "selection" of those who are thought to be "able-bodied" and of those who are not. Thereafter, small groups of these men are marched off toward a group of long barracks. Women strain their eyes to see if their men will walk out of these barracks, and their faces light up with joy when they do. But many women are waiting in vain and it breaks my heart to hear their wailing. My dad, Izio, Wolfus and my uncle, all come out clad in assorted cotton trousers and shirts. I see my dad lift his hands towards the heavens, with a mute prayer of thanks, and I see Izio bend his head toward me, with a mute goodbye.

Thus I catch my final glimpse of Izio when he is marched off, along with my dad, to the concentration camp of Majdanek, where all of the Bialystok Jews are executed on November 3, 1943. With them die my dad, my Uncle Munio, cousin Wolfus, and my twenty-year-old Izio Pupko...

The women are also taken from the original dusty assembly square and seated inside the backyard of what looks like a cement hangar. The windows have been replaced with concrete slabs. My mom, my aunt, and I are seated right in front of this cement structure, so I stand up to survey the sea of women sitting behind us. I find Golda seated in the back. What surprises me is the fact that there are some women with babies among us, and I wonder how these women managed to pass the original "selection" at the exit from the ghetto. Then, unexpectedly, several black-uniformed Ukrainians come out of the hangar and proceed to crisscross our ranks and yank the infants from the arms of their screaming mothers. I hear the dastard Ukrainians tell the anguished women that since they are going to a work camp, their babies must be cared for in children's crèches, but those who wish to go with their babies may do so. In back of me, Golda and a woman wearing glasses both rise and yell at the top of their lungs: "Let your children go, women! You are young, you must stay alive and have more babies! Don't go to where they are taking your babies!" The Ukrainians indifferently allow one or two women to follow their babies and leave the others to wail in pain and woe.

Since I am seated in the front row, I can see some metal canisters piled up with other junk in front of the hangar into which the babies were taken. I can see some of the labels on these canisters, labels that clearly read: · ZYKLON B. I hear a woman whisper in back of me that the vans that took the young women to work in the fields dumped such canisters when they returned without their cargo.

It is nearly dusk when the SS line us up in groups and, one by one, march the groups away. We are marched along the paved road that leads away from what may have been a cargo railway station on the outskirts of Lublin. There are no city buildings along this road, just a few peasant huts among the harvested fields. SS men with dogs walk on either side of each marching column, and we know that there is no escape from this march. I try hard to draw solace from the peaceful sights of the countryside and hope that a work camp, not an extermination camp, awaits us within this beautiful setting. It is dark when the SS prod us into the receiving field of a camp. But the brightly lit-up barbed wire fences with their watchtowers, along with the pervasive acrid smell of burning flesh, do not suggest we have arrived in a work camp.

The arrival area itself is lit up by blinding floodlights. It has numerous watchtowers and armed guards walking up and down the entire length of its barbed wire fence. The fence bears signs on many of its posts saying, "Danger! High Voltage!" The two long windowless barracks abutting our area spell doom. I feel panic-stricken. I want to save my life. I want to escape from this enclosure. I run along the fences looking for an escape, but I can find no escape. Oblivious to the cries and prayers of others, I run about this human cage and rehearse in my feverish mind various scenarios for saving my life and that of my mom's. Mom, who sits on the ground in utter resignation, pulls me down beside her and says in Yiddish, "Oh my daughter, your grief and fear have darkened your bright face...why has God forsaken us?"

A view of the watchtowers and the electrified fences
surrounding the extermination camp of Majdanek at Lublin, Poland,
as seen in the summer of 1965.

Now I tear myself from my mom and decide to act out my plan for saving our lives. Using my most amiable Russian, I start a conversation with the most pleasant looking Ukrainian guard who, just as amiably, responds in Polish. I tell the guard that I am an illegitimate child of Marianna Soltysiak, a peasant servant-girl of a Polish woman married to a Jew, and that this couple had adopted me. With tears in my eyes, I tell of my devotion to my adoptive parents. I tell of the undying love of my Polish mother towards her Jewish husband, all of which brought us into a Jewish ghetto and finally into this deathtrap. I implore the guard to show mercy toward the two condemned Christian souls and let us out of here, before it is too late. The guard listens with sympathy and assures me that an escape is not at all necessary, since the Germans have already prepared placement for all of us in one of the women's work camps here in Majdanek. "The two *Saune*-barracks before you," says the guard, "are already heating water for your morning bath, and you can see for yourself that there is smoke coming out of the chimneys in front of you."

Just at that moment, the faint dawn begins to highlight the barracks. I can see the smoke coming from the direction of the two barracks and a rush of adrenalin starts to dissipate my despair. As if I have become obsessed, I dash here and there, calling out at the top of my lungs: "We are not going to die! These here are *Saune*-barracks! They are heating water for our bath! They are taking us to work! We are going to live!" The slouching women look at me as if I am crazy, but as I continue to yell and yell and the early light of the dawn clearly shows the smoke—a sure sign of water heaters at work—the crowd begins to liven up. The women award me with their approving smiles when the Germans begin to line us up in front of the two Saune-barracks. Our cheerful mood soon vanishes, however, because they make us go through another "selection." When my turn arrives to go through the selection, I attempt to hide the bow-legged gait of my bullet-bruised legs; my mom pinches her cheeks to make them appear rosy before her turn comes.

It is the usual German *"rechts"* and *"links"* (to the right and to the left) that make us soberly notice that only the chimney of the left *Saune*-barrack blows smoke. Those selected to go right will go to the other barrack. Although Golda, as usual, remains cheerful, my Aunt Pepka and the two of us enter the left barrack no longer convinced that it isn't a gas chamber. We each get a piece of soap, but that does not reassure us at all. To boot, we are told to undress in the presence of the staring German soldiers who derisively laugh when I try to shield my nakedness. I remove the snapshots of my sister and my boyfriend from behind my brassiere and hide them behind the two-by-four beam of the dressing room, just in case I do return here alive. We apprehensively enter the shower room and, when the doors close, each one of us anxiously looks into the showerhead above. Every person sighs with relief when water, and not poison gas, comes out to shower our bodies. I had hoped to return to the dressing room after the shower and retrieve my photographs, but we go into a storeroom instead. They give us here ragged, ill-fitting clothing, and when we go outside the sauna and look at each other we burst out laughing at our attire. But we soon stop laughing. We realize that the doors to our neighboring *Saune*-barrack remain closed, and that those who entered that door did not come out.

Barefooted and scared, we walk into the women's camp and are registered there by a Polish *Schreiberin* (scribe) in a striped uniform who asks, in a shrill voice, for the name and the date of birth. I stand before her shivering in my ragged dress. "Your name Rena is just a bastardized Jewish form of the name of Saint Irena—there has never been a St. Rena! Polish Jews have always used Polish surnames, so why shouldn't you use the names of Polish saints for your given names as well? From now on you will be known as Irena Hass!"I meekly acquiesce to her stern verdict and name change. My mom whispers, "Let it be…who knows, maybe that name will come in handy…maybe you can pass for a Gentile and help us both in this camp." Thus I lose my name Rena and from this point on my name will be Irena Hass.

The women's camp has parallel rows of barracks. We are brought into a barrack in one of the rear rows. The *Block Aelteste* (the Head of the barrack) assigns one top or one bottom bunk to three women. She orders us to choose a *Schtubedienst* (barrack orderly), and I am elected. I have to distribute the daily rations, see to it that our straw mattresses are straightened out, and make sure that we promptly line up for the twice-daily *Zaehl Appels* (prisoner counts). I have many other house chores and special assignments as well.

Soon after our arrival, we go for a medical examination at the camp's *lazaret* (field hospital). To my dismay, this turns out to be a brutal gynecological and rectal examination that adds to the discomfort of my lacerated thighs. When it is over, one of the old-timers at the clinic quietly confides to us that the purpose of this "medical examination" is to find hidden jewels.

A stench of burning flesh permeates the air above our camp and seems to emanate from the dug-outs outside the wire fences of the camp. The stench becomes unbearable when we work in the outside fields.

The abrasions of my thighs are now festering and I find it difficult to walk, so I overcome my distrust of the camp's *lazaret* (hospital) and have its nurse bandage my thighs. The nurse warns me not to show up in this *lazaret* again, or to even indicate, for that matter, that I ever feel ill again. Her warning prompts me to question the nature of this camp and the nurse confirms my worst fears. "Although Majdanek is not a typical extermination camp like Treblinka," she tells me, "it is a work camp where Jews are generally killed gradually. Large-scale gassing and mass executions are routinely used when large numbers of Jews are deported here. When too many people are killed at one time, cadavers have to be burned both in the crematoria and in the ditches outside the camp; thus the ever-present foul smell."

I will have to let the others know that we are in an extermination camp after all.

Crematorium complex and its chimney. Extermination camp of Majdanek. Photo taken summer, 1965.

On the last day of our fieldwork we come back to camp quite late and find the *Zaehl Appel* counting in progress. We normally line up next to the rear barracks, but since we are late this time, we line up at the empty front barracks and are the first ones to be counted. Apparently, Majdanek has received an order for slave-laborers, and the camp's SS *Aufseherin* (supervisor) settles for selecting laborers from those who are in front, and that means us! When the SS woman requests a show of hands by those who are experienced seamstresses, most of us raise our hands; I am sure that we would claim experience in any skill that could get us out of this extermination camp!

From those that raise their hands, the SS woman selects only young inmates who look like Gentiles and directs them to step aside. My mom is not selected, but as soon as I'm picked and the *Aufseherin* passes me, I grab Mom and pull her aside to go with me. When the selected women are counted again, I stand tall to shield my mom's face from view. She "passes" the final count, and the 150 Bialystok women march back to the Lublin *Zugplatze* where we are loaded into a train.

The train departs, but only after they load a contingent of 300 Bialystok men on board. Neither Dad, Izio, my uncle or Wolfus are among these men. I spot at the depot a former policeman who tells me that Dad has been chosen to play in Majdanek's band. No one knows if this position is a lifesaving one in Majdanek, but—there is always the chance that our men will be transported out of Majdanek to a better work camp…

The train takes the 150 Bialystok women and the 300 Bialystok men towards Radom and the nearby camp Blizyn, a small slave-labor camp for Jews skilled in machine-knitting and sewing.

After August 17, 1943, it takes Friedel and his henchmen at least five more days to finish the final disposition of the remaining Jews of Bialystok. Most of the staff of the police and of the Judenrat, the Chief Rabbi Rozenman, and the Head of the Judenrat, Barash, are among the last ones to go. On August 20, Friedel shoots most of the patients in the hospital and evacuates the rest, along with the staff, into the trains in Bialostoczek. Using specially

trained dogs, the Ukrainian and German SS men continue to search for Jews hidden in their dugouts, bunkers, hideouts, or for those who simply remained in their homes. They load the final Jews into the trains, executing those who refuse to go. Before her escape to the partisans, Ewa hides in the attic of a house on Kupiecka. Years later she tells me that she saw the torture and mercilessly painful killing inflicted by Ukrainian SS man on many of the hidden Jews. She also tells me that she saw Jewish babies killed by the SS bashing them against the wall till their little heads split open...

The sporadic outbursts of fighting by the underground will go on until August 25, and at the very end of the uprising, Mordechai Tennenbaum-Tamaroff and his adjutant, Daniel Moszkowicz, commit suicide. Most of the others either die in battle or are apprehended and executed. Some manage to hide in their bunkers for a while, but sooner or later they will be routed out and killed. Only a counted few break out of their bunkers and hideouts in the deserted buildings and get to the partisans. One of these counted few hears the words screamed by a routed-out comrade, words that accuse my liaison Berl of betrayal. Berl apparently informed the Germans of the location of a bunker of some 70 fighters, including their leaders. Although the Germans let Berl go and he manages to get to the partisan outpost, he is imprisoned for his betrayal after the war.

Those of us who end up in the work camp of Blizyn know nothing about the fate of the rest of the Jews of Bialystok. We assume that those who did not die in the uprising or in Treblinka will join those deported to Majdanek. And we hope that the Germans will eventually transfer our brethren from Majdanek to a work camp like Blizyn. But sometime during this winter of 1943 there arrives in Blizyn a cargo of wood bearing a message written on one of the logs in Hebrew. It tells of the November 3rd massacre of all of the Bialystok Jews who were in Majdanek. We internalize this awful message and tell each other that if we survive, we will be all alone in the world.

Of the 60,000 Jews of the Bialystok Ghetto, we alone, the 150 women and the 300 men who were sent to Blizyn, will remain alive—if we can manage to survive Blizyn and the concentration camps after that.

Part Four

UP AND DOWN
THE GUARDS ARE PACING

Up and down the guards are pacing,
No one, no one can get through...
Flight would mean a sure death facing,
Guns and barbed wire greet our view.*

*The opening words of a song of political prisoners of Börgermoor
Concentration Camp (located in northwest Germany).

WORK CAMP OF BLIZYN

My husband and I lived and raised our children in an apartment in the northeastern part of the Bronx. It was there, across the street on Gun Hill Road, that I once saw a woman that appeared vaguely familiar. The woman did not show a sign of having recognized me and I could not place her either. Some time later, I saw the woman again, and this time I quickly crossed the street and looked into her face. Yes, I knew her and now I hesitantly called out her name: "Yetta?" For a while, she looked as if she couldn't place me but she chanced a guess: "A Bialystoker?" She couldn't make a connection with Rena Hass from the Bialystok Ghetto, but when I mentioned Blizyn, something rang a bell and she exclaimed: "Irke mit die Mame! (Irke, the one with the mother!)" She did remember Irene, the girl who had what was most precious in a camp, a mother! Thus started my friendship with Yetta. Through her I met Buba, Franka, Bela, and Liska, all of whom had been in Blizyn with me. In due time, I discovered in Israel the Bialystok girls Musia Tapicer, Rachelka, and Haneczka who were in Blizyn with the rest of us. More recently, I established a contact with my Blizyn and ghetto friend Musia Offenbach who emigrated to Paris after the war.

Each February, services commemorating the annihilation of the Bialystok Jewish community were held at the New York Bialystoker Center. Later on these services were held in Miami, Florida. I recognized a few faces at these memorial services because I used to see these faces at the work camp of Blizyn.

The men and women who were with me in Blizyn were the only ones left alive after the final destruction of the Ghetto of Bialystok. Luck was with us when we were taken out of the extermination camp of Majdanek and sent to the work camp of Blizyn.

In Blizyn, we escaped the "selections" for the gas chambers and crematoria. But we did not escape hunger, disease, hard work, or the wretchedness of life characteristic of all German concentration camps...

The work camp of Blizyn lies somewhere between Lublin and Radom. It is not far from two other work camps for Jews, Plaszow and Starachow- ice. As is true of all camps for Jews, this work camp is in essence just another German concentration camp—it is completely isolated from the outside world, there is no mail (or packages) from anyone anywhere, and there is no freedom for the prisoners. The Ukrainian guards, the watchtow- ers and the wire fences that surround camp Blizyn are very much like those at Majdanek. Here too, men and women live in separate barracks. But un- like Majdanek, they can meet after working hours, outside and even inside each others' barracks. There are no gas chambers or crematoria here and the hospital is staffed by compassionate Jewish physicians and nurses. The *Saune* is just a bathhouse, nothing more sinister than that. The internal discipline in the camp is maintained by Jewish police recruited from among the old-timers of Blizyn. These old-timers come from the nearby Radom- Czestochowa region, as do Sroka and Minc, who head the police and who don't mind using the switch to enforce the discipline.

The old-timers have their own clothing; they even have their own bed- ding, and their *prichas* (bunks) have pull-curtains that give them some privacy. A greater privacy exists in the barracks of the "higher-ups" such as the head doctor Weinappel, the other physicians, the nurses, and also the policemen. These barracks are actually boarded-off into cozy upper and lower cubby-spaces, well hidden from view by heavy drapes or plywood doors.

Our Bialystok contingent arrives in Blizyn in the late afternoon and we are immediately deloused, bathed, and sprayed against scabies. They give us fairly decent clothing and shoes that are certainly better than what we got at Majdanek's *Saune*-baths, but here we must wear the abominable overcoats with a yellow cross painted on the back. They've erected a central row of upper and lower *prichas* (bunks) in each of the two women's barracks and we pick up straw-filled jute mattresses and coarse blankets for these bunks. These *prichas* are simply rows of upper and lower platforms, with ladders attached to the upper platforms. They run from one end of the barrack almost to its exit door at the other end. Mom and I sleep next to Golda Lipkies at the end of the top platform. Aunt Pepka lies on one side of us, a sullen pharmacist's wife and her daughter (both of whom come to Blizyn a bit later) on the other side. Not far from us dwell two sisters from the *Hanajki*, the "lower depths" of the old Bialystok, who treat us to a daily show of sisterly quarrels.

We are given a day to settle down and to register for work. The enterprising ones find jobs for themselves in the kitchen, in the hospital, at the gypsum quarry outside the camp, and at the *ciuchy* (old clothing) shack where clothes and shoes of the deported Jews are sorted for export to Germany. A few chosen ones will even get to clean the SS men's lodgings. Each one of these highly sought after positions promises extra food—food that is priceless in a concentration camp!

The rest of us end up working at either the *Strickerei* (knitting workshop), where army socks are knitted by machines and the worn ones are patched by hand, or in the *Schneiderei* (sewing shop), where army uniforms are sewn by machines and their details finished by hand. They wake us up at dawn, serve us black *ersatz* (roasted grain) coffee, let us wash our hands and faces at the sink in the outhouse, and send us off to work. At the factories, we get a mid-day serving of a grain and vegetable soup that, a few times a week, has shreds of horse meat in it. Late in the evening, when we come back from work, we get our evening meal of 300 grams of bread with margarine—and sometimes jam.

The day after my arrival in Blizyn, I become ill. I have chills and diarrhea and spend the day dozing off on my *pricha* or running to the outhouse, bowlegged. The abrasions on the insides of my thighs are awfully inflamed and that surely adds to my malaise. My mom is upset because she doesn't know how to hustle up jobs with "fringe benefits" for the two of us, but I feel so sick that I couldn't care less about that. Later that day, Mom holds me up when I register with the overseer of the knitting workshop. She then registers herself at the sewing shop and it looks like we will have to be satisfied with these jobs. I am not destined to get a good rest on this day, after all: I discover that my mattress is infested with fleas and I have flea bites all over my body. Mom dashes off to get some insect spray at the *lazaret* and comes back empty handed. We are told that the only way you can kill fleas in this camp is to air the mattresses and blankets in the sun. In the afternoon, all of the straw mattresses and blankets begin to sprout out in the grass around the barracks. Fleas can be seen leaving the sunlit mattresses for the shady spots in the grass. Deprived of my mattress and blanket, I lay down on a bare platform, feverish and exhausted by the runs, and I daydream that my dad and Izio join us here in Blizyn.

It takes more than one day to get rid of the fleas, so the sunning of the mattresses becomes a routine on the sunny Sunday afternoons we are off from work. In the meanwhile, Mom discovers that there is a *felczer* (medic) who takes care of first aid problems. But I loathe to go to the hospital alone to have a male medic examine the insides of my thighs, so my mom takes me there. The medic applies some antiseptic salve to my abrasions and bandages my thighs with strips of duck cloth. Thereafter, before Mom and I go to see the lustful *felczer*, I wash and dry my coarse cloth bandages and both of us keep our fingers crossed that my sores heal. In due time, both my sores and my pride do heal.

Within a few days, some newcomers arrive at camp. Among them are several families taken out of their well-supplied bunkers in the Bialystok Ghetto. These include the well-known Dr. Treiwisz and his wife, two other physicians, a pharmacist with his wife and daughter, and other medical professionals. We learn that they were all kept in one of Lublin's *Zugplatze* depot buildings and then sent to Blizyn. All of these medical professionals work at the hospital and also serve as the stand-by medical personnel for the SS, should an epidemic break out in our camp. While they were in Lublin, a few "strays" joined their group: three Dutch girls with shaven heads and several girls from the February round-up of Jews at the ghetto of Bialystok. Along with some other February deportees from Bialystok, these girls have been interned in Auschwitz-Birkenau. But they alone have miraculously escaped the fate of the others and have ended up in Lublin where they joined the Treiwisz group going to Blizyn. Perhaps, after we left Majdanek, its SS received a request from Blizyn for more workers, and that is why the new group came here. Unfortunately, the new group did not include any of our own men whom we left in Majdanek.

The camp of Blizyn includes an enclave of Polish prisoners whose barrack stands in a separate fenced-in backyard right next to the women's camp. On Sunday afternoons I chat with these men and discover that they are mainly petty offenders who have been incarcerated mostly for the illegal sale of meat or for the trading in goods subject to rationing. The Poles go to work on the roads and in the fields outside the camp and, unlike us, they do receive letters and packages from home. One of them takes a liking to me and promises to get me out of this camp and to have me join him when he finishes serving his time. He promises to get "Aryan" (Gentile) documents and a coat without the yellow cross for me, and he claims that one of the Ukrainian guards is his friend, a friend who will get me out of the camp. There would be plenty of work for me on his farm, he says, and looking at me and talking with me, nobody would suspect that I am Jewish. Although I don't believe a word of what he is saying, I thank the Pole for his good intentions and tell him that I must stay in this camp to watch over my ailing mother.

I wonder if he and the Polish farmers who plow their fields right outside our camp comprehend the enormity of the assault the Germans are inflicting on the Jewish people. Do they comprehend the difference between the often bestially harsh treatment of the Poles and the premeditated, well planned genocide of the Jewish people? Or, do they perhaps applaud the annihilation of the Jews of Poland?

There are several rows of knitting machines in the *Strickerei*. Under the windows stand several long tables for those of us who patch up the worn military socks. Yetta, Buba, Franka, and Bela sit next to each other and the rest of us sit further up and down the table. The patches are machine-knitted and we attach them to the worn parts by a special type of needle-stitching. There are thousands of these worn socks and we work on them all day long, without a rest. In addition to the worn socks, we stitch-together the open ends of the machine-knitted socks, once again using a special stitching that does not show in the finished sock. Our overseer is a demanding man so that all work must be meticulously done. This work strains our hands and eyes, and it feels good to relax now and then, and to chat for a few minutes.

But the luxury of taking it easy is fraught with the danger of being caught by the lurking *Hauptscharfuehrer* (SS equivalent of the rank of a captain) who is in the habit of unexpectedly coming in. A blow from his elegant switch usually accompanies his loud reprimand in the coarse German of a front-line soldier. Rumor has it that the *Hauptscharfuehrer* lost his foot in battle and that the artificial foot that makes him limp has turned him into an ogre. Our Bialystok girls devise a system of watching out for the approaching SS man: At the risk of not being able to complete their quota of socks, the two girls who sit at the window end of our table are designated to be the watch girls. They are to yell "*Sechs, sechs!* (Six, six!)" when they notice the German limping along the roadway to the factory. Somehow the Yiddish word *sechs* (the number six) stands for the word "Alert," and though it found its way into the vocabulary of the Jewish slave-laborers, nobody knows now why the number six was chosen to call for an alert. But the alert system isn't perfect and an occasional surprise visit ends in blows for one of us, after all.

Coming back from her *Schneiderei*, Mom complains that she has to struggle with the coarse military fabric when she tries to make perfectly even buttonholes in it, a job that is probably done by machines in the outside world. But she is thankful that she does not have to sew this heavy military woolen cloth on one of the vintage, manually-operated sewing machines.

October of 1943 is unusually warm and we are allowed to swim in the water hole next to the Polish camp during our Sunday afternoons off. On one of these warm October Sundays I go for a swim, but quite against my will. On this particular day, some of the men strip down to their boxer shorts and go for a swim, while several others stand on the high embankment and watch. A few Germans join us on the embankment and poke fun at the clumsily swimming Jewish men. Suddenly, one of the Germans pushes an older Jewish man off the embankment and into the deeper water at the center of the water hole. The Jew obviously does not know how to swim and begins to go under. Forgetting for a moment about my bandaged thighs, I take off my shoes and dive into the water hole. Holding the man's head up, I pull him to shore and then anxiously try to climb out of the water hole and head for my barrack.

I am blocked by one of the officers, however, the one who hasn't been laughing at all. He orders me to swim around the water hole till he tells me to stop. All dressed, and with my undone bandages flipping around, I swim around and around the water hole, terribly scared. The Germans are hilariously laughing, all of them except the lieutenant who has ordered me to swim. I sense that he wants to see me start going under before he allows me to stop swimming. I close my eyes for a moment, conjure up the image of the Brzezany pond, and see myself swimming there back-and-forth, without stopping, and I gain confidence that I can do it here, too. Most of the camp inmates are gone, perhaps afraid to watch me drown. The Germans aren't laughing anymore—they remain standing on the embankment and watch me swim on and on, without stopping for a rest.

At least an hour has passed since I started swimming for the lieutenant. He comes over to the lower bank and motions me to stop swimming and to walk over to him. Clumsily, I tie the ends of my bandages around my legs and walk over to the German who says, now in a softer tone, *"Du bist doch ein Mischling, nicht wahr?* (You are surely of mixed blood, isn't it so?)" I hear my trembling lips timidly answer the lieutenant, *"Nein, Herr Unterscharfuehrer, ich bin eine tolle Juedin* (No, lieutenant, I am a Jewess of pure blood, sir)." The German shakes his head as if in disbelief and walks off, leaving me there, a dripping wet and exhausted, but triumphant, *Niedrige Rasse* (lower race) Jewish girl.

Winter is coming and it is cold in the factory, in the barracks and outside the barracks. The counting of inmates twice a day during the *Zaehl Appels* leaves us numb—Mom's shoes are badly leaking and our thin coats don't protect us from the winds that blow from the barren fields around the camp. Luckily, the girls working at the sorting shed find lots of scraps of knitting wool for me. In the early hours of the night, I knit colorful swatches from these scraps and then combine the swatches to make two warm sweaters, one for me and one for my Mom. The sweaters are such a success that I begin to get orders for swatch-sweaters and go into business for myself.

At the sorting shed, I diligently scrounge for torn, hand-knitted wool sweaters among the worn clothing. I rip them up and use their wool to knit new sweaters. The German money I earn for this work does not amount to very much, but I do buy with it soap, onions and carrots, and even the coveted salve against the scabies.

Golda often keeps me company on our *pricha* when I sit there till late at night and knit my sweaters. She helps me fight sleep and the threatening company of rats that are as large as tomcats. These animals are totally unafraid of light and of the snoring women, but Golda and I manage to scare them away, at least for a while. These enormous rats climb up onto the top platforms of the bunk beds and wait for an opportune time to get at our bread rations that lie hidden under the "pillows" of our folded clothing. As if in a science fiction movie, I sit mesmerized by the high pitch of the rats' squeaks and by their phosphorescent little eyes. I watch the rats that are seated at the ledge of my bunk bed platform and those that brazenly climb up the poles supporting the roof, all of them waiting for their opportunity to get at our food when the lights are switched off. And as soon as the lights go off, there begins the nightly routine of banging shoes against the platform to chase the rats away, which works only for a while. At times, the animals outsmart the fitfully sleeping women and get at the hidden food. And at times, you can hear the screams of those whose nose or ears are bitten by a rat. On arising, we bemoan the rat bites of earlobes and bread rations alike.

The early winter brings another scourge: scabies and head-lice. The scabies mites may have come with the clothing given to us at Majdanek and then may have been passed around by the shared scissors and knitting needles. The mites initially dwell in itching blisters between the fingers but, since we scratch ourselves, these blisters spread all over our bodies. The dreadful *Kretze* (scabies, in German) become so widespread that the Germans begin to periodically fumigate our clothing and spray our bodies with disinfectants. To help matters, people purchase from the Ukrainians sulfur salve that further contains the infection; which I can eventually afford to buy thanks to my knitting.

The head lice must have also been imported by one of us and passed around by contacts with one another. Like a bunch of baboons, we sit on our bunk beds and kill each other's lice and nits and, because of the feared weekly inspection by the good nurse Vita, our grooming ritual goes on throughout our stay in Blizyn. If the nurse finds more than an occasional nit, she mercilessly mandates the shaving of our hair, which soon becomes a badge of dishonor. My poor mom never forgives me for the time my nit-picking wasn't diligent enough to save her hair, especially since her crew cut is quite grey. Even the multi-color babushka (head kerchief) that I knit for her doesn't ease her hurt pride and I will feel guilty about it for the rest of my life.

We get Christmas day off and the Germans treat us to a special Christmas dinner: a dense soup with lots of meat and potatoes. The festive mood of this day is also evidenced by the profusion of couples that can be seen on the camp's grounds. All along I have envied Golda Lipkies's friendship with Abrashka, who has visited her almost every day. Now during our day off, the two of them join the other couples that walk, arm in arm, in front of the barracks. My mom must have sensed my feelings of loneliness because she grabs my arm and drags me to meet a man, a barber by profession, who works with her. I end up walking with him and listening to his barbershop jokes. Not the best way of spending a Christmas day, I think to myself, but I don't yet know that the days that come after this Christmas will be much worse.

In January, a new commanding crew of SS officers come to our camp and change our lives for the worse. The new camp commandant and his lieutenants personally oversee the daily morning and evening line ups at *Zaehl Appels*. They delight in beating up stragglers, kicking men in the groin, and slapping women's faces, all for as small a provocation as sneezing or coughing or talking in the line up. The failure to remove one's hat or lower one's eyes in the presence of an SS man inevitably results in a beating. My poor mother becomes a victim of a deformed SS lieutenant who passes her on the camp road; for days she broods over a hurtful slap in the face by this psychopath. Hardly a *Zaehl Appel* passes without at least one man getting tens of lashes on his bare back for some petty offense.

Socializing is forbidden, privacy curtains are eliminated, and just a minimum of spare clothing is left to the old-timers whose "riches" we used to envy. Before the night curfew, women are no longer seen exiting the cubby-spaces of the police and doctors' quarters. No longer do we enjoy the Sunday afternoons off. Sadly, the two or three children that used to stand in the count-off lines are no longer seen and no one knows where these children were taken. There is only one of us who still remains cheerful, and that one is my pal Golda Lipkies. Time and time again I hear her tell someone, "Don't give up, you can't give up, you must live and tell the world what they have done to us!"

The food is now horrible, there are fewer and fewer chunks of potatoes or turnips floating in the midday soup, and the sawdust and milled seeds from the horse chestnut tree in our bread makes it taste awful. But there is one improvement that the new management brings to our camp: their use of bait loaded with an extremely effective poison exterminates the rats in our barracks. As we soon learn, the new staff is bound to excel in the exterminating skills since they have all come from the "downsized" concentration camp of Majdanek.

On one of the early winter evenings of 1944, my mom and I sit lingering with other women from Bialystok in the dressing room of the sauna when we suddenly hear someone crying in the boiler room. Nurse Vita hurries into the boiler room and comes back with horror written all over her face. She tells us that a fresh supply of firewood has just come to us from Majdanek and that one of the logs bears a description, in Hebrew, of the "downsizing" action at Majdanek. The Hebrew inscription says that on November 3, 1943, as the loud speakers played military marches, the nearly 18,000 Jews from Bialystok who were left alive in Majdanek were gunned down and buried in huge mass graves. The Germans justified the massacre by claiming that weapons were brought into Majdanek for a "rebellion" by the Bialystok Jews.

My mom and I don't quite believe the story we've just heard. Mom speculates that if the story is true, then the camp's band with my dad in it was made to play the military marches that were beamed over the loudspeakers, and that Dad was thus forced to witness all the horrors before he himself was murdered…Oh no, God would not have allowed this to happen! We both go on speculating that if it did happen, then, who knows, maybe all the young and healthy men like my boyfriend Izio and my cousin Wolfus were sent out to work camps before the massacre? Or else, maybe some of our men were left alone—surely they could not have killed all of the Jewish inmates in a camp with no massive gas chambers or crematoria?

After a sleepless night, my mother accepts the possibility that what we have heard may be true. "If I survive the war without my husband," my mom muses, "I will have to find someone else to care for me." I don't know how to react to Mom's musing, and besides that, I just don't believe, at least not yet, that our men were killed.

(In later years, I will learn from the published accounts of the Christian inmates of Majdanek the details of the massacre. From the peep-holes in the doors of their locked barracks, the Christian inmates saw the marathon of men and women forced to run between two lines of SS men who beat them as they passed. When the victims reached the open-ended barracks, they were made to undress. Prodded by whips and clubs, the naked martyrs were forced to run one last time—through the opened rear-walls of the barracks to the freshly dug graves outside these barracks. They were told to lie down in the graves before being killed by a volley of bullets. The Germans included the remnants of Jews from around Lublin in this massacre of the 18,000 Jews of Bialystok, and Majdanek became Judenrein—cleared of Jews. According to Gilbert in his book, *The Holocaust*, in a few days a total of 50,000 Jews were shot in ditches behind the gas chambers at Majdanek.)

So many worn military socks come to our knitting factory during the winter that Blizyn is forced to import workers from the camp at Plaszow. We now go on a double shift and I end up working the night shift. It is during one of these night shifts that a tall, heavy girl from Plaszow begins to complain of terrible stomach cramps and goes outside the factory to relieve herself. We notice that the girl is holding up her bloated belly as she paces back and forth around the piles of coals behind the factory. When time passes and the girl doesn't come back, one of my friends goes out to look for her. After a long while, she comes back alone and reports that she had to take the young woman to the hospital because she was bleeding. Luckily, the *"sechs"* alert isn't called for this evening and the girls around our table are free to share with one another the tale of the Plaszow girl who, as we learn, has just delivered her stillborn baby behind a pile of coals. We marvel at the girl's ability to hide her pregnancy as well as her stoicism in bearing her labor pains in silence. And we can't get over her delivering the baby without anyone's help, alone and in the dark behind the coal pile, within a few hundred yards of the Ukrainian guards. How was she able to do it? Was this truly a stillborn baby or was it simply a miscarriage? Or did she, a deeply religious Orthodox Jewish woman, kill her newborn infant? A woman goes outside to find and dispose of the fetus or dead infant and I am aching to go along, but the overseer lets the stove-stoker go to help the woman, and another man to keep watch.

When the three come back, the overseer makes a simple clear statement in Yiddish: "You have seen nothing, nobody has been out tonight, nothing has happened tonight, and outside there is nothing to look for." Within two days, the much more slender and pale young woman comes back to work, and no one says a word to her—at least, not in the factory.

Early in March of 1944, an epidemic of typhus breaks out in camp. There are body lice—the carriers of typhus—in the worn socks and torn uniforms that we repair. It is almost impossible to guard against lice when you are handling infested socks and uniforms. A typhus epidemic is inevitable and one by one, we come down with the deadly disease. My mother is one of the first ones to become infected and she stays in the hospital for more than two weeks. She runs a very high fever, she mumbles to herself words that make no sense and, at times, doesn't recognize me. On some days, an empathetic kitchen worker brings me some vegetables so I can cook up soup on the barrack's heating stove. Mom can be coaxed into eating some of that soup but she won't drink water, and that has me worried because of the dangers of dehydration.

Delirium, a side effect of typhus, is a common sight at the hospital. I often see delirious women who scream, break loose from the restraining arms of the nurses and attempt to run out. Typhus is a dangerous disease and several people die during the most acute stage of it. Those who eventually survive this stage, my mom among them, take a long time to come back to health. We are not granted the luxury of convalescence, not even for one day; I see convalescents who faint in the factory and others who are unable to stand upright during the *Zaehl Appels* unless someone supports them. Golda Lipkies is the one who usually finds a spot for herself next to those who may need her support in the line up…

Every cargo of military socks and uniforms is now steamed and disinfected before it is delivered to us, and that seems to decimate the body lice in our workshops. Fewer people come down with the typhus and in April the epidemic subsides. Just when there are no more new cases of typhus, I come down with it. During one of my night shifts at the factory I become feverish and finally pass out. Fortunately, the *Hauptscharfuehrer* doesn't put in an appearance at the factory that night so I can be safely escorted to the hospital. There are hardly any typhus patients here and the doctor on duty finds it hard to diagnose what ails me. In the morning, he calls on the other Jewish physicians to come to my bedside, and they look puzzled as well. They do find the telltale symptoms of typhus—the red blotches on my body and the swollen spleen—but only a moderately high fever and few signs of general malaise. The next day, a German military physician shows up; apparently the Germans want to make sure that there indeed is a new case of typhus after the epidemic has ended. It is surprising to see an SS physician climb up the steps to where I lay, palpate my Jewish abdomen, and even admonish me: "*Maedchen, du musst doch trinken sehr viel Wasser*! (You must drink a lot of water, girl!)"

My hospital stay is shorter than was the stay of the others. My fever is not as high as theirs had been, and since I am not that sick, hardly anybody pays much attention to me. My mom visits me everyday, though. The hospital is well supplied with food so I ask Mom not to bring me anything to eat, especially since I have no appetite at all. But I do have an appetite for daydreaming and, when you have fever, you can do some great daydreaming. I go through several fascinating post-war scenarios before I get out of the hospital. But even though I have had a relatively easy time with the typhus, I find it difficult to stand during lineups; and as expected, Golda comes to my aid. Back on the night shift at the factory, my friends finish the quota of socks for me and allow me to take it easy.

By May, I recuperate enough to enjoy the sounds of the Russian artillery reaching us from the east. The camp is bustling with all kinds of hope-filled gossip: "The front is nearing Radom, the Russians are coming to liberate the camp." Or, "The Germans will sneak out at night and we will be free to get out!" Or, this: "The Germans will fatten us up and fix up the camp to show the Russians that life in the camps hasn't been bad at all."

But our hopes are dashed when we are told that we will be transferred to a camp farther west. At this time, my mom is hospitalized with pleurisy, which needs to have fluids periodically drained, and the pending "relocation" comes too soon for my comfort.

But as always, we have no choice. Once again we are loaded into cattle-cars and shipped into the new camp farther west. My mother is riding in the car for the hospital patients, the policemen, and the medical personnel. Oddly enough, this train ride "farther west" does not take long at all. In a few hours, we arrive at the new camp's long red brick building, and our train enters through a wide gate beneath its central tower. One of the girls who came to Blizyn after a stay at a few other camps recognizes the gateway as Birkenau, the satellite camp of Auschwitz. Auschwitz's main function is the extermination of Jews in Europe.

The gate opens to let the train go through. Some 200 yards farther, the train stops and the cattle-car doors open to let us out onto the platform of Birkenau-Auschwitz...

Sometimes, I count the names of the Bialystok survivors of the camp of Blizyn and I wonder why the tally does not add up to what might be expected. Of the 60, 000 Bialystok Jews, some 450 of us were taken out of Majdanek before the rest were massacred. I wonder if many of these 450 died in the relatively benign working camp of Blizyn. I knew of several women who died of typhus there, but did many Bialystok men succumb to typhus? Eventually, Dr. Weinappel finds his way to the United States and practices medicine in Ellenville, New York. I have a chance to meet with the old physician and discuss the matters of health and survivorship of the Jewish inmates of Blizyn. He tells me that not many women, but quite a few men died of malnutrition and many kinds of diseases there, including typhus.

I ponder about the trainload of Blizyn's Jewish men and women that arrived in Auschwitz-Birkenau and wonder how many of the 450 survivors from Bialystok were still there? And why did so few of our people on that trainload actually survive?

"ARBEIT MACHT FREI!"
(WORK WILL SET YOU FREE!)

On April 12, 1991, Yom Hashoa services were held at our local synagogue, the Tremont Temple. The services were followed by a commemoration of the greatest tragedy that befell the Jewish nation—the Holocaust. My grandson Jeremy and his parents invited me to attend the ceremony with them. At the age of twelve, Jeremy was a tall "he-man" whose successes in baseball and other sports I've shared with his parents and at whose birthday and school parties I was privileged to play the role of "the Grandma." That was about all that the role of a grandmother of an American pre-teenage boy could entail. But during this Yom Hashoa (Holocaust commemoration), my grandson surprised me with an unusual attentiveness; I found him at my side both during the services and during the ceremony. When the rabbi said that our people must forever bear the loss of the 6,000,000 souls, Jeremy looked at me with unusual intensity and warmth. He remained at my side when I signed the commemorative book, when we both discovered that the names of the extermination camps of Treblinka, Auschwitz, Belzec, and Sobibor were engraved on the tombstone outside the Temple, and when I told him that all my aunts, uncles and cousins were gassed at Belzec. Then he looked at me as if he disbelieved that his own grandma could have been in one of these extermination camps. I pointed to the name of Auschwitz and hesitating, I nodded my head…

The time that I really owned up to having been in Auschwitz happened in April of 1996 when my daughter visited there with me. My family and I had seen the camps of both Auschwitz proper and of Birkenau twice before, but I acted like an uninvolved guide on these occasions: here and there I pointed to the various structures and told everybody what I knew about them, as if I were narrating scenes from the life of another person, not mine. I guess that a reawakening of buried feelings was needed before I could place myself back into these horrid places. That reawakening happened in the 80s, when Holocaust survivorship finally came out of its seclusion—a seclusion imposed by humanity that willed this tragedy to go away from its consciousness.

So, in the spring of 1996 I was ready to go back, and I took my daughter there with me. Many of the wooden barracks had rotted away by that time, but I recreated for my daughter the activities at the railroad ramp, the whereabouts of the block (camp barrack) for me and my mom, and the route of our entry into the camp via the crematorium complex in the poplar grove. In the freezing cold of this early spring, my daughter was patient enough to roam with me, back and forth, across the former encampment of the yellow brick barracks. This is where there stood the "Block of the Doomed" of my painting, the block that became a Home for the Older Women in which I left my mother, never to see her again. That day with my daughter was the time that I really went back to Auschwitz-Birkenau, and I needed her to help me go through it.

Oswiecim, the Polish name of Auschwitz, is quite familiar to most people, but not so *Brzezinka*, the Polish name of Birkenau that implies a grove of poplars. As the doors of my cattle car open in May 1944, I indeed see in the distance tall poplars, and hidden behind these poplars are buildings with five threateningly tall smokestacks. We quickly respond to the *Raus!* and *Mach shnell!* of the SS men on the platform and get out of the train. Mom joins us and we all line up for the expected selection, but there is no selection! Instead, inmates in striped uniforms circulate among us and demand that we promptly surrender, "under the penalty of death," all monies and valuables. Although I am told that German money has no value here, I decide to keep the money that I've earned knitting sweaters in Blizyn, anyway.

The entry to the main camp of Auschwitz

Next, they tell us to march, the men separately from the women, toward the ominous poplar grove. Strangely enough, most of the SS men remain on the platform and only a few guards go with us. We enter a large antechamber of a large *Saune* barrack. The *Schreiberins* (scribes) register us here and they dexterously tattoo camp numbers on the insides of our left forearms. I now become the nameless prisoner #A15467 and my mother becomes prisoner #A15468. We assume that the tattoo implies a temporary "warehousing" of our group and a reprieve from the imminent journey into the gas chambers. We also learn that because they shortened, but did not shave our hair, is a sign that we eventually will be shipped out to work camps in Germany. But, are we all here, or are there some who are missing? How well did the men fare in this enclave of the sinister buildings with their tall chimneys? Perhaps we will never find out.

After a shower and a stinging disinfectant spray, they dress us in assorted ill-fitting hand-me-downs collected from Auschwitz's transports, and we enter the women's Camp B. (Concentration camps are subdivided into many fields which are referred to as Camps, i.e. Camp A, B, and so on.) We promptly line up in front of the two barracks overlooking the railway ramp where we left our train just a while ago. We are about to get the first taste of crazy Sally, our *Block Aelteste* (barrack elder), and her adjutant, the *Stubendienst* (barrack orderly) Mela.

Sally is a toothless Polish-Jewish blonde who screams at us in garbled German and who kicks and hits us more often than she screams. With each reprimand, she points to the distant smokestacks and foretells that we will all go there if we don't change the nonchalant ways in which we obey the rules of this camp. From this day on, we no longer walk out but, instead, we run out of the barrack at the time of the *Zaehl Appels*; and then we stand absolutely still and straight during the many hours of the line ups. And we never go over to the soup barrel for seconds, unless we happen to be the lucky ones who get picked by the adjutant Mela.

At all times, the counting of prisoners is done by the barrack elders and their orderlies, and it is double-checked by the SS women. Each tally is then picked up by a *Lauferin* (a courier), who reports the tallies to the SS men in charge of the individual fields, who then add up the block tallies and let the couriers bring these counts to the central Birkenau office for the final count. When the counts in the various blocks and in the various fields (Camps A, B, C, D and so on) do not add up to the expected number of prisoners, the line ups last for long hours. At such times, all barracks, outhouses, and official buildings are searched. The couriers run back and forth between the various buildings and fields, and the SS men holler and curse at their Jewish underlings. In the meanwhile, emaciated starving prisoners stand lined up in twos or threes in each row, stand for long hours, huddled together for warmth and supporting one another so that no one falls. The prisoner who falls stands a chance to be carried away to the *lazaret*, and the *lazaret* is a dangerous place; it gets periodically emptied of patients who inevitably end up in the gas chambers.

Mela is Sally's friend and confidante and knows Sally quite well. She confides to us that Sally has been in Birkenau-Auschwitz during the last winter and spring when, besides the gassing, thousands were starved and beaten to death, thousands died from malaria and from exposure to the freezing cold, snow and rain. Apparently Sally used to stand with her mother in the lineups for long hours, knee-deep in mud mixed with snow, and wasn't allowed to help her mother or to pick her up when she saw her fall.

Finally, one day Sally had to leave her mother lie in deep mud mixed with snow for hours on end, and her mother died in front of Sally's eyes. That is how Sally has become "crazy," says Mela. Now Sally hollers and beats us up because she wants us to harden, as she puts it, so that we don't die the way her mother did.

Periodically, we are sent to "work." We are made to carry rocks from one place to another, line them up neatly, and on the next day, take the same rocks to another place. A day or two later, we bring our rocks back to where they came from in the beginning. At times, we perform real work: for instance, after they gassed the Gypsies, they made us clean up the Gypsy Camp. Gypsy families and their children had been allowed to stay together and had littered their camp with all kinds of odds and ends. My heart breaks when I pick up a baby's pacifier or a raggedy doll of a little Roma girl who is no longer here to grow up into a woman.

One sunny day, they send us to clean up the site where the unforgivable crimes of the German nation are being committed: an old and inactive gas chamber. By the way of the grapevine from the Jewish *Sonderkommando* (the special detail working in the extermination area known as "Canada") we learn that an efficient new set of gas chambers has been constructed in the basement of the extermination complex. What we are cleaning is an old, above-ground gas chamber that may be used as a spare in times of high activity. The bottom of the structure's concrete walls shows flows of yellowish-blue hue interspersed by dark bluish blotches. The concrete floor bears encrustations of a nondescript matter that comes off when we scrub it with soapy wet rags. We are told to scrub the walls as well, but the stains don't come off. My eyes wander towards the opening at the side of the concrete ceiling and I imagine seeing the ZYKLON B pellets pour down onto its grating and release poison vapors on the tangled bodies of the condemned. And I feel that unless I immediately come out of this chamber, I too will be asphyxiated. Luckily, there always are pails of soapy water to be poured out and refilled and I volunteer to take the pails out as soon as the water turns slightly dirty.

Most of the time, my mom and the other women just hang around the sunny side of the barrack and talk about the good old times, which is not enough to fill my days here. Unfortunately, there aren't many work assignments for the women of Camp B, so to kill time and to forget about the constantly gnawing hunger, I wander about the camp in search of contacts with inmates from other cities and countries. The first friendly soul I bump into is Colette, a Parisian girl I meet during an extraordinary event in the camp. On this particular Sunday afternoon, the Germans let the camp's band perform for us and we are allowed to gather on the camp's green. Notwithstanding her shaved head, Colette is new to camp life and is still a full-bodied, lively girl who doesn't yet show the wear-and-tear of those of us who have already done time in camps. My high school French is not great but it picks up as days go by. Colette tells me that she has a contact with the *maquis* (French partisans). I learn about the French resistance efforts and about the exciting life in prewar Paris. And in Colette's company, I relearn to smile and to enjoy a contact with an interesting girl. Colette, on the other hand, is most eager to know about the life in Soviet Bialystok, about the ghetto, the underground, and our uprising.

Once we get to know each other a bit, Colette introduces me to a French old-timer inmate, a Communist who wears a red triangle on her striped uniform. The young woman invites me later to come to her barrack and I meet there two other French women. All these women are just as eager as Colette to learn about the Soviet life and the Bialystok resistance, as well as my political viewpoints. As for me, I get from them a real treat: two thick slices of bread with jam that I proudly carry to my mom. But since I've learned from Colette that the French Communists and their sympathizers are maintaining a cohesive illicit cell in the women's camp, I suspect that this gift is a down payment on a possible service that might be asked of me in the future.

Then, one day, Colette disappears along with all of her barrack mates. Her French friends, whom I occasionally meet, don't volunteer to tell me anything about Colette's whereabouts, and I know better than to ask about her...

I next meet Rozhi Glueck, a working girl from Moldavia—which is now part of Rumania. Ethnically, Rozhi is a Jewish Hungarian and she speaks German, Hungarian, Russian and also Rumanian. She has a Christian-Rumanian boyfriend, a Communist who has been deported to Auschwitz. Rozhi and I become good friends and spend many hours sharing the tales of our lives with one another. Rozhi touches my short hair, and with tears in her eyes, tells me about her beautiful blond braids that were cut off before her hair was shorn. I keep on touching her blond stubble and reassure her that her hair is already starting to grow back and that, anyway, she is beautiful and her crew cut becomes her. We finally decide to find Rozhi's boyfriend.

Women's Camp B is wedged between women's Camp C and the men's Camp A, which overlooks the entry to Birkenau. As is true of all the other camps in Auschwitz-Birkenau, electrified fences and watchtowers separate our three camps. There is a four to five feet wide walk between the fences of two adjacent camps and, at times when the current is cut off, there is a guard who paces up and down the walk. One day, Rozhi and I take a walk along the double fence between us and the men's camp and we locate the barracks of the newly arrived Hungarian Jews. The Hungarians are lingering in front of their barrack and Rozhi asks them about the whereabouts of the Moldavian Jews. We learn that most of the Jewish men, both Hungarians and Moldavians, have been gassed, and that the few who have escaped that fate have been placed with the "Rumanian deserters" in one of the distant blocks of men's Camp A. And that is where the two of us are now heading.

As we approach the distant *blocks*, we hear a chorus of men singing Hungarian and Russian songs, and songs that Rozhi knows to be Rumanian. The men in the chorus identify themselves as either Moldavians or as Rumanian "conscientious objectors" who refused to fight against the Soviet Union, alongside the German army. None of these men know anything about Rozhi's boyfriend but they suggest that he may be among the "Rumanian deserters" who are thought to be elsewhere in Auschwitz.

We come back to see these men again and again and finally learn that many of the Rumanian "refusenicks" have been sent to work on German farms and that, except for the Communists who have been executed, all other Rumanians are alive and working somewhere in Germany...

Rozhi and I don't have much of a chance to be together for any length of time. One day soon after her sad discovery, Rozhi doesn't show up at the spot where we usually meet and there is no one in her barrack to tell me what happened to all the Hungarian girls who had formerly occupied that barrack.

Conditions of life here at Auschwitz-Birkenau are infinitely harsher than were those in Blizyn. Bread rations are smaller, the bread has more wood dust in it, and the pat of margarine that goes with it is very tiny. Starvation is visible everywhere—women attack soup-barrel carriers and, mindless of the blows they receive, plunge their tin cans into the barrel and scoop up a bit of soup. After the *Block Aelteste* finishes dishing out the soup, her women crowd around the empty barrel and scrape out the remains of the soup with their bare hands. There are no rats in the barracks of this camp but bread rations must be guarded from human predators day and night. It is quite common to wake up to the wailing of an aggrieved woman whose ration was snatched from under her head while she was asleep.

Cruelty of punishment is in evidence everywhere and at all times. I commonly pass by some women who are forced to kneel in the dirt with their arms raised for hours, and I often see women who are whipped mercilessly by a raving SS man or an SS woman. Every *Capo* (Camp Policewoman) feels free to kick and punch her subservients, and so does every *block*-Elder or other camp official in a striped uniform. Since many of these officials in the women's camp happen to be Hungarian, we soon learn some of the Hungarian orders that are barked at us, such as "*Nem lekhet* (it isn't allowed),""*Kifele* (get out)" and "*Diorshan* (hurry up)." All these Hungarian phrases will remain with us for a long time.

With the onset of summer, my roaming about the camp is curtailed because we are now frequently subjected to a *Blocksperre* (curfew) for hours at a time. We soon realize that they confine us to barracks when they are conducting a major "selection" or when a fresh transport of victims arrives at the railroad ramp. Transports from all parts of Europe keep coming daily, all summer long. And since the ramp is right in front of our barrack, we can readily see these arrivals through our half open doors. The Jews who come in the summer of 1944 are mostly those who were recently rounded up in many of the European countries. These Jews are well dressed, they most often come with their entire families including their children, and they have no idea about the sinister nature of the camp. We watch the German "white glove" routines of coaxing the people out of their cattle-cars, of the fake concern with which they aid the victims to load their luggage onto carts and to memorize the numbers of their carts. These sophisticated newcomers are, for the most part, lined up with some degree of courtesy and are slowly walked off toward the poplar grove and its chimneys. Thousands are marched away from the trains, yet only a few dozen of the young women of each transport are actually bathed, shorn, and brought into our camp. This is exactly how it happened when Colette's and Rozhi's transports came to Birkenau.

The Birkenau chimneys belch their noxious smoke over the camp without stopping. Someone says that a train load of Jews just came from the Ghetto of Lodz, and I run around camp looking for women from this transport. I look for women from Lodz because I know there were several Jewish families from Lodz in Grudziadz, so maybe…? I finally locate some newcomers with freshly shaved heads from Lodz but their faces are unfamiliar. Disappointed, I take off for my own barrack when suddenly, I spot two pretty blonds with full heads of hair. One of them yells out, "Rena, Rena Hass!" and I yell back at them, "Hela! Mania!" We hug and cry and hurriedly tell each other about the misery that has brought us to this horrid place. And I learn that while I have been looking for them, or anyone else from Grudziadz, Hela has been looking in the Bialystok barrack, for me!

In essence, all three of us have looked for someone from Grudziadz, hoping to be with that someone for at least a while. But as destiny will have it, we barely manage to exchange the stories of our lives in Lodz and in Bialystok before we must part. Each of us is destined to go to another concentration camp, to perhaps survive there against all odds. Will we survive? Are there others from Grudziadz who will survive?

Throughout the day and night of the new transport, the five chimneys belch out black smoke. The smell of burning flesh envelops our camp. But the crematoria aren't idle even during the days when there are no victims who arrive by train. The Auschwitz-Birkenau population of Jews is continually trimmed down by "selections" of those whom the Germans don't find to be worth even a temporary stay in camp. In the case of the Gypsies, the Germans hardly bother to preserve the better specimens for whatever service these might render; the Roma people were marched off from their Gypsy Camp directly to the ovens. At times, some other fields are emptied out with but one or two barracks left to house those who are selected to stay alive. And we are privy to just such a happening in the neighboring Camp C. When we first arrived, we used to see many old-timers from Camp C in striped uniforms going out and coming back from their daily work details. But now, during one of our current *Blocksperres*, we witness, through cracks between our wallboards, a major "selection" in Camp C, one that ends in severely decimated numbers of its old-timers. What we witness is truly a sight to behold: we see the handsome Dr. Mengele and his assistant Dr.

Dr. Josef Mengele was given nicknames by the prisoners: "Angel of Death" and "Beautiful Devil." Because he planned selections on every Jewish holiday, they called him the "Jewish Calendar."

Klein probe and scrutinize the skinny bodies that pass before their eyes, we see the "to the left" and "to the right" flicks of Mengele's baton, and we see the assignment of the fittest to one side and of the rejects to another side. After this selection, Camp C will store batches of newcomers in its now empty blocks, just as our empty block stored us when we arrived. I look at my tattoo and recall what I no longer believe to be just one of Mela's jokes. After our arrival, Mela wished us to have better luck with the A-series of tattoo numbers than had the many batches of prisoners who wore the same series before us.

There are also small-scale selections in our own camp that are most often performed by SS women. Some of these selections are said to be aimed at resettling some of the women to other camps, be it for a questionable "work" or for the dubious "health" reasons. Both Colette and Rozhi have disappeared after such selections. We thus find out that indeed Auschwitz, in addition to its "in situ" exterminating functions, also serves as a hub for prisoners who will be "warehoused" for some time and then resettled to other camps. My Grudziadz friend Hela and her sister Mania who come from the liquidated Ghetto of Lodz, stay here for a while and then end up in another camp where they will survive the war. Our emotional reunion in Birkenau will eventually be replicated in New York.

The Bialystok girls with whom I've worked in Blizyn stay either in my barrack or in the one next to it. As of this time, we have not been subjected to selections and are still harboring the pipe dream that sometime soon, they will send us to a work camp much like Blizyn or Plaszow. But then I realize that not all of us are still fit enough to go to a work camp. Neither my aunt nor my friend and comrade Golda Lipkies stay in the same barrack with my mom and me. (I periodically inquire about these two.) My aunt is doing fine but I hear that Golda has been coughing a lot and that she may have TB. I am baffled when I discover that she has taken a chance and checked into the camp's *lazaret*, which is notorious for its periodic "clearings" of patients. I immediately go to the *lazaret* where the nurse tells me that Golda is very contagious (how do they know that?). I may neither come close to her nor visit her again. A few days after my visit, two of the Bialystok girls get hold of me in the morning and give me an account of their ill-fated visit in the *lazaret* earlier this morning. In tears, they tell me that Golda had failed Mengele's selection and had been placed in the upper level of the *lazaret*, the "export" wing for the crematoria. They were allowed to stand for a few minutes at the door of the upstairs room and Golda asked that they come back with me.

The *lazaret* has been readied for the export of its patients and is off-limits when we come back. The girls and I stand in front of one of the upper windows and call out to Golda. A shorn head and a drawn pale face shows up behind the iron bars of the window. This is not the face we know, the face of our dark-eyed and dark-haired beautiful Golda. But the voice is the same, the voice that calls out to us in Yiddish: "Don't forget the way they will have me die! Don't forget that we tried to stand up to them till the last moment! Don't forget what they are doing to us here! Don't forget! Swear to me that you will tell the world!"

The three of us look at each other with pain and sorrow. I raise my hand and give a silent promise to Golda. At night, I think that I can hear the motor of the black van taking patients to the gas chambers…and I cry my heart out for Golda.

The camp always seems to need repairs, and men from other fields come to our camp to do the needed work. I meet Russian POWs among these men and learn that there is a Russian underground organization aimed at getting as many POWs out of here as possible and into partisan hideouts. Just how these men could get to the partisans and where these partisans are remains unclear to me, but apparently the concentration camps remain the only source of commanding officers and army physicians needed and in great demand by the partisans. After I become quite friendly with a few Russians and earn their trust, they tell me that the men's *block* right across from my own barrack houses a few high-ranking Russian officers and army doctors. These mistreated and starved officers are marked for sure death unless they are soon spirited away. In the meantime, women of the French *Maquis* attempt to pass food through our fence to feed these starving men. I have been right to think that my French friends may call for my help some day—they ask me at times to stand a rear guard while their export of food goes on.

Sometimes, when I socialize with the Russians during their midday meal, they treat me to a tin can full of dense soup, which I promptly run over to my mom to share it with her. Poor Mom later confides in me that the women she usually passes time with in back of her barrack are "digging" her about the questionable source of this extra soup. Why do I get this soup? What have I done to earn it? The time finally comes for me to level with my mom about my past and present political interests. After hearing about my doings in Bialystok, Mom laments, "How could you have endangered us so? We could have all been shot because of you!" So, I omit telling Mom about the political implications of some of my doings here in Auschwitz. I just tell her that I hang around the Russians who work in our camp because I want to hear from them the news about the advancing Russian front—hence the occasional extra soup!

The Russian POW workers again reappear in our camp in the fall and I learn that a Russian physician and two high-ranking officers have gotten out and that the rest of the officers are now kept in Auschwitz proper.

My mom is again suffering with pleurisy. It is too dangerous to have her stay at the *lazaret* and have her pleura drained because the patients there have been recently subjected to daily selections for export to the crematoria. Yet there is another problem that brings Mom to the *lazaret* despite all the dangers. Lacking fibers in her food, my mom has continual problems with her intestines and becomes chronically constipated. She suffers an occasional impaction of her large bowel and the impaction has to be promptly removed. Life has become very difficult for mother; she has aged, and she finds it hard to walk or to stand in the lineups during the cold fall mornings. Plus, she had become terribly demoralized and depressed when a woman had been found hanging onto the electrified fence in front of our barrack. And both she and I have finally accepted the idea that Dad and Izio had been indeed executed in Majdanek and that the two of us will have to take care of ourselves, if we survive.

At the end of August 1944 something new is in the air and we don't know what to make of it. The stacks cease belching out their gigantic volumes of black smoke and one or two of the stacks seem to no longer function. Rumors circulate in our camp that an uprising of the *Sonderkommando* of the crematorium's complex has taken place, that most of the Jews and a few Germans have been killed, and that several gas chambers and crematorium ovens have become inactive. At the same time, few new transports arrive at our railroad ramp and rumor has it that the Allies have bombed the Buna factory at Auschwitz and that the Russian front is quite near us. What is totally unbelievable is the rumor that, somewhere in Birkenau, there is a "mock" convalescent home and supposedly a barrack for the older women. Then, one day, elegantly dressed civilians appear in our camp and we learn that they are members of the Swiss Red Cross who have come to inspect our camp facilities. Now we understand why the Germans have been giving the camp a softer image!

There are also other civilians who appear in Birkenau, apparently representatives of German industrial firms who have come to select slave-laborers from our camp. Most of these selections are taking place across the railroad tracks in a field with brick barracks, and that is where they take the Blizyn contingent of woman. We bid goodbye to Mela and Sally and they cheerfully tell us that, in this new camp, we will become a pool of workers for German industries. As we enter the new camp, we are lined up for a selection. This one is not a benevolent selection for work, however. Two SS women proceed to select out older and more emaciated women from our midst, and my mother is among them. Panic stricken, I scream…I attempt to run after her when the selectees are led away, and the SS women actually wave at me to come along. But those around me, knowing where my mother is being taken, hold me back. I guess the instinct for survival takes over and I stay in line.

We who "pass" the selection enter one of the brick barracks and I spend there a sleepless night full of remorse and sorrow. At dawn, one of our

Bialystok girls comes running into our barrack and calls for me in Yiddish: "*Vo iz Irke?* (Where is Irke)" Out of breath, she tells me that someone has seen where the Germans have led the older women, and she asks me to follow her. Mercifully, the *Block Aelteste* of our barrack doesn't put in an appearance and there is no one to stop us from going out, so I follow the girl to a large brick building surrounded by a wooden fence with a locked gate.

The building has only one exit door and, in addition to the ordinary windows, has two sky-lights. It is quite light now. My friend leaves and I sit at the wooden fence waiting for someone to open the gate. I sit there and despair at the thought that this may be the infamous "waiting" building where the condemned ones are left before they are taken to the crematoria. Just when I am about to give up hope that anyone will open the gate for me, a woman unlocks it, walks out through it, and without a word, nonchalantly leaves it open for me. I dash inside the gate and through an unlocked door into the building. I disbelieve my eyes. My mother is there with a bunch of older women, all of them at leisure on their bunkbeds, talking with one another! In the distance, the barrack elders blow their whistles calling the prisoners to line up for the morning *Zaehl Appel*. There is no call for a lineup here, however, since the women here are in no shape to move anywhere. I hug my mom and promise to come back right away. On the way to my own lineup, I debate with myself whether I should somehow get myself situated with my mom, or go with a transport to a work camp in Germany and leave Mom in her plush setup alone.

The atmosphere in this expansive encampment of yellow brick buildings to which they've transferred us definitely suggests a transit camp. The lineups are almost completely unsupervised and the tally is perfunctory. The explanation for that probably lies in the constantly changing numbers of inmates who are left in camp after the nearly daily transports to Germany. It is comforting to know that these transports must be for real since the slave-laborers are hand-picked by the emissaries of the various German industrialists, including Audi, Telefunken, Volkswagen and many others. We can only surmise that things are going badly for the German industrial might, now that the frontlines are getting closer and closer to the heart of Germany and the sources of non-Jewish laborers have dried up. And, since the sources of human fuel for the crematoria ovens have also dried up, the smoke stacks stand nearly completely idle. Furthermore, there may be some truth to the contention that the International Red Cross has been breathing down the neck of the ailing German beast and that small numbers of juvenile, elderly and ailing Jewish prisoners have actually been housed in special barracks to either become museum pieces for the post-war world or to serve as an alibi for the Nazi murderers. Based on all this, I make up my mind that I will escape the selections for work in Germany and become a helper at my mom's Home for the Older Women.

Ever since I discovered Mom's whereabouts, I have been spending all of my free time with her. The Home's elder consents to give my mother the responsibilities of a barrack orderly provided that I do the chores instead of her. That suits me fine. As soon as my morning lineup is over, I go to work in Mom's barrack for which the two of us get to share the orderlies' daily award of extra soup and bread. In the meantime, the nearly daily selections for the transports go on. Pretty soon my own barrack mates are gone and I have to attach myself to women from Blizyn in another barrack. That kind of maneuvering from one block to another goes on until finally most of the women from Blizyn are gone and I end up with a group of Hungarian, Czech, and Austrian women with nobody catching on to me!

Physical activities fail to mask the poor state of my digestive system, which shows up when I eat. As soon as I finish eating, I begin to suffer from an acid reflux powerful enough to make me throw up the food I've just eaten. In addition, I begin to experience abdominal cramps and diarrhea and can find nothing to help my condition. A Bialystok woman doctor who works at the camp manages to get some bicarbonate of soda for me but it doesn't do much good. The doctor fears that I may become severely dehydrated, lose electrolytes, and die. She hints that I ought to start thinking about leaving for Germany.

The doctor and I discuss my mom's situation here in Auschwitz, and we both have the feeling that once the Germans decide to get rid of older women, staying with my mother couldn't help her. Since "fitness to work" is the only passport for survival, we decide that Mom ought to go through another selection and, hopefully, be reclassified as an *Arbeitstuechtig* (fit to work) woman. With that in mind, the doctor suggests to her boss Dr.

Klein, the German physician in charge of the *lazaret*, to conduct a "positive" selection at the Home for the Older Women, a selection aimed at enlarging the pool of the candidates for work in Germany. Dr. Klein conducts the suggested selection and makes a short list of the eligible older *Arbeitstuechtig* women, which includes my mother.

It is late October 1944 and very cold. I manage to get warm hand-me-down clothing for my mom from those who are selected to go with a transport. (Inevitably, those who go with a transport shed their ragged clothing and get a higher grade of used clothing to wear in Germany.) Quite auspiciously, I bump into my aunt Pepka who is about to go with a transport and donates her warm overcoat to Mom. Now I tell my mom the truth about my digestive problem and my loss of weight, and we both decide that it is best for me to get out of here as soon as possible. There is a chance, we both feel, that my vomiting is caused by the fermented vegetables that form the base of our food here and that the food in Germany may be much better for me.

During the next few mornings, I stay with my barrack mates and wait for a selection. On one of these mornings, the Germans do come to my block and select most of us to go to Germany. This very evening we are to appear at the sauna for a bath and a change of clothing. Our departure is scheduled for the late night hours.

I spend my last day with my mom reassuring her that, as a barrack orderly, she will always get an extra portion of soup and bread and that her work needn't be too difficult for her. We both have discovered that all it takes to keep the floor clean is to wipe it with a broom wrapped in a wet rag. I reassure my mom that the donated extra clothing, including some of mine, will protect her from cold and that sooner or later, she will be taken to a work camp. I wish that I could tell my mom that she has been the essence of my survival and that caring for her has been worth living for, but I am incapable of telling her that. My mom tells me that she has always felt that I have been a good person, despite the rough edges I've inherited from my dad. Perhaps she wishes to tell me that she will miss me terribly—but she doesn't. She makes me promise, however, that I will do every thing possible to find my sister and to take care of her.

When she walks with me in the evening to the *Saune* and the time comes for us to part, I break down and beg her to take a chance, to get into the *Saune*-bath and pretend she is one of those picked for the transport. After all, we were successful in performing such a trick at Majdanek. Why not here? "Because here they will surely beat me up and I could no longer take a beating," says my mother. I am in tears when she holds me tightly and says, "I have lived a full life, you have not. It is your time to try and save your life. If I don't make it, you make it instead of me. Get married, have children and grandchildren and tell them for me that I loved them even before they were born." In a daze, I join the young women in the dressing room of the sauna and there in the window, I see, for the last time in my life, the dearest face of my mother. She waves her hand to me and I read the Polish blessing on her lips, "*Niech cie Bog prowadzi, moje dziecko* (May God guide you, my child)."

They walk us toward the ramp on which we arrived seven months ago and from where we watched thousands of people arrive to be gassed at Birkenau's crematoria. My heart is heavy with chagrin because I am deserting my mom. I can't appreciate the significance of leaving this ramp in the direction opposite to that of the poplar grove and its crematoria. I can't even appreciate the fact that I am leaving this camp of inhumanity and mass murder for good. It is completely dark as the train slowly inches its way past the buildings of Auschwitz proper and past its gate with the infamous sign, "ARBEIT MACHT FREI (Work Will Set You Free)." I think of Golda Lipkies, of Rozhi and Colette, of the young woman whose electrocuted body draped the electrified fence, and of all those other unknown Jewish souls who gained their "freedom" inside gas chambers and not at work. And I creep back into my guilt about leaving my mother in this Dante's Inferno, leaving her alone in this hell where no one will care for her...

Never will I forget this place, never will I forget Auschwitz-Birkenau. Through the years, I repeatedly make pilgrimages to Auschwitz-Birkenau and pay my respects to the shadows of the millions murdered there. I revisit the shadows around the skeletons of the gas-chamber complex whose cyanide infarcts can never be traced by scientific methods. I retrace the

death routines of the ramp along the railroad tracks and I revisit the shadows on the rotting bunk beds of the decaying barracks of Camp B. I wander among the yellow-brick barracks of my final days at Birkenau and pray for one little whisper from my dearest shadow there.

Time and time again I say my Kaddish (Jewish prayer for the Dead) at the piles of shoes and hats and combs; I say it at the piles of Jewish prayer books and ritual shawls and phylacteries in the museum at Auschwitz proper. And I will always grieve at the sign of the perfidious "ARBEIT MACHT FREI," grieve that the perpetrators of such enormous crimes against the Jewish people were never brought to justice.

Monument at Auschwitz

THE FREEDOM ROAD FROM LIPPSTADT TO KAUNITZ

In November of 1997, my husband and I took our long awaited trip to Italy. Although this was an organized tour, we were in Rome on our own. As we had done in Venice, we looked for the Jewish synagogue and spent some time viewing its phenomenal structure; we learned about both the Sephardic synagogue housed in the lower level of the building and about the Italian synagogue housed on the main floor. Somehow, the guide touched upon the topic of the German occupation of Rome and the deportation of Rome's Jews to Auschwitz where all of them perished, except for one woman who was sent from Auschwitz to work in Germany. Of the entire community of Rome's Jews, this woman was the sole survivor of the camps.

I had known a Jewish-Italian woman from Rome who was transported with me from Auschwitz-Birkenau to Lippstadt, Westphalia, a camp from which we both had been liberated by the American Army. I quietly told the guide about it. But there were other tourists in the synagogue and I didn't want to make a spectacle of myself, so I just swallowed hard and proceeded with the sightseeing.

Just as we were about to exit, the guide called me over and showed me a booklet in which the history of Rome's Jewish community was described. She told me that this history included the story of the one and only survivor of the deported Roman Jews who, she thought, may have been the woman with whom I worked in Lippstadt. When I offered to pay for the booklet, the guide refused to take my money.

After it leaves Auschwitz, the train continues to head northwest all through the night and throughout the next couple of days. But we lay asleep inside the warm, multilayered paper sleeping sacks, and during the night we are oblivious to the train's course. Everybody is asleep except me. When I am in distress, I stay awake and daydream of things that have not happened, but could have happened. So, there is my stowaway mom in a sleeping bag next to me, and there the two of us go to work in Germany where the food is abundant and healthful…Or, I am initially alone at the work camp in Germany, but my able-bodied mom soon comes into the work camp after the liquidation of Auschwitz-Birkenau…Or, the Russians launch a surprise attack on Auschwitz-Birkenau and liberate the camp with all its prisoners alive and well. Mom is offered a means of transportation to Boryslaw, she finds her sisters and her younger daughter there, and I come to stay with them once the war is over…

The journey is slow on this stop-and-go railway, with frequent switching of tracks. We get plenty of water to drink and enough bread and margarine to sustain us. We see a number of bombed-out buildings and many bomb craters along the railroad tracks, with trainloads of German soldiers passing us on their way east. After the two days of slow travel, we finally arrive in Lippstadt, Westphalia.

We enter a small camp whose SS commandant addresses us without the usual bark of the SS. The SS *Aufseherin* (supervisor) gets a kick out of our disheveled hair and clothing and sends us to wash up. I am assigned a top bunk bed to share with several Polish-Jewish women from Plaszow, but I am unable to collect myself, so I simply stay outside the barrack. A Hungarian woman notices my morose face, she strikes up a conversation with me and I pour my heart out to her, after which she invites me to share the bunk with her and her daughter. Both the mother and the daughter are wearing a cross on their necks and I hesitate to join them, but their warm coaxing helps me overcome my reluctance.

During the first two nights, I sleep cuddled between the two women in the Hungarian-Czech barrack and cry my heart out about the loss of my mom. But thereafter, I opt to go back to the Polish-Jewish barrack and meet

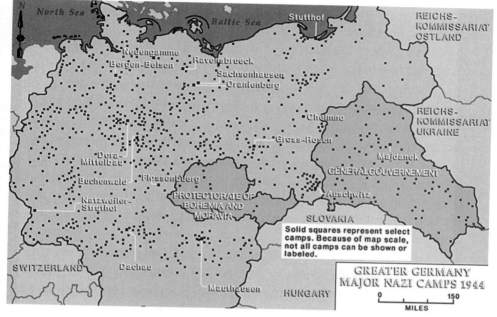

Major Nazi camps in Greater Germany, 1944

two women from Bialystok. One is Raya, who attempted a botched-up suicide by cutting her wrists in Majdanek. The second one is Luba, whose two daughters about my age were asphyxiated in the vans that had transported them to a "work" place. During our sharing of the top bunk, Luba becomes my substitute mother and I spend much time talking with her during the day. Luba never sheds a tear when she tells me about her daughters and her stoicism hardens my resolve to overcome my grief.

We start working a day after we settle down into the routines of this new camp. Ushered by our SS men, we enter early in the morning the Krupp's Munition Werke. Most of us are assigned to one particular detail in the construction of hand grenades. Each specific detail requires the use of a specific machine and they train us how to use these machines. Next to me sits Rosa Conti, a Jewish-Italian woman who does not speak a word of German. The overseer attempts to teach us how to operate a stamping machine that cuts the needed grooves in the shafts of the hand grenades. But since Rosa has a tough time understanding the overseer, he calls over an

Italian worker who speaks some German, and this man helps Rosa understand the directions.

We soon befriend the young Italian man and learn that he is one of the soldiers of the Italian battalion that refused to fight against the Soviet Union, and had therefore been deported to do compulsory labor in German factories. He translates for me the story of Rosa's life and, thanks to him, I learn that Rosa had been deported to Auschwitz along with the rest of the Jewish community of Rome and had left her little son with her Gentile husband in Rome. Rosa's eyes often fill with tears when she attempts to tell me about her *bambino* (baby), and all I can do to show my feelings is to go over and hug her shoulders. In the next few days, I learn a few Italian words and Rosa learns some German words, and the two of us manage to communicate with one another.

The Italian ex-soldiers often sing at work; their repertoire usually includes the pop song *"Mama, se tante felice"* sung intermittently with the Italian Communist anthem *"Avanti populo."* Rosa writes out the words of these songs for me so that I can sing them along with the others. I find it strange to work in a factory alongside Italian, Czech, Ukrainian, and Polish laborers because we are the only contingent of prisoners from a concentration camp and we alone are totally deprived of freedom. The others seem to walk out of the factory and go home on their own, they get some spending money and are allowed to go into the town of Lippstadt to buy things and go to the movies.

The German factory overseers of our area seldom yell at us but other women tell us of some brutality that they experience elsewhere in the factory. Quite unexpectedly, one of the older German employees in our area strikes a friendship of sorts with me and I learn from him that there are in Germany many civilians who abhor what the Nazis have done to us. This older man keeps on coming to my station during his lunch hour and leaves me, very unobtrusively, an apple or a pear and sometimes a tasty meat sandwich. Equally unobtrusively, pretending that he is examining my machine, he asks me about Auschwitz. He wants to know if the rumors that the civilian Germans are hearing about concentration camps are true. Is it true that we have been terribly mistreated and starved? Is it true that women have been raped? And so his questions continue. He is shocked when I tell him the bare truth about the gas chambers and the crematoria, about the millions of Jewish people of Europe who were gassed in Treblinka, Majdanek, and Auschwitz-Birkenau. One day, he says with obvious anguish, *"Oh, du Deutschland, das wird auf ewig eine Schande fuer dich sein!"* I would like to believe his words and repeat to myself the Polish translation of what he has said, "Oh, yes, Germany, what you've done to us will remain your people's shame forever!"

The conditions in this small outpost of concentration camps are quite benign. The commandant seems to be busier with his SS Aufseherin-mistress than he is with us. The guards of the camp are old German soldiers who very obviously enjoy talking with us across the non-electrified wire fences. One of the guards speaks Polish and, to my amazement, I discover that he is a Polish national and comes from Grudziadz! He tells me that he has been a known activist of the Polish Socialist Party and was first jailed and then sent to Auschwitz for his political activities. His ethnic-German wife and their children remain with his wife's relatives in Grudziadz. In Auschwitz, he and some of the other Socialists and Communists had been treated very badly, and when they had been offered the option of a home-front service in the German army, they had all taken the option, and that is how he has become our guard here. By profession, he is a trumpet and a bassoon player and had occasionally bumped into my dad in Grudziadz's German Community Center, which he and his ethnic-German wife had frequented. I find it hard to believe in this coincidence, but then again, any human contact becomes a true find in this hostile environment, so I buy his stories.

In December of 1944, our small camp is threatened by an epidemic of typhoid fever thought to have originated from the typhoid bacilli in the polluted water served to us during our train ride through Germany. Those with an onset of fever and diarrhea are immediately quarantined in the isolated "Typhus Barracke" located in the distant peripheries of the camp. I soon come down with the fever and go into the isolated barrack as well.

There are six typhoid-fever patients in the quarantine barrack, one patient with syphilis and one with tuberculosis. We have one nurse and one woman doctor to care for us. The typhoid fever patients, the nurse, and the doctor are all from our camp. The Ukrainian girl with tuberculosis comes from Stalino, a town somewhere in the steppes; the girl with syphilis is Polish and comes from around Poznan. As is the case with other foreign slave laborers, these two girls have either volunteered or have been "coaxed" to work in factories in Germany. They have been housed in a nearby un-guarded camp for foreign workers and now are staying in a small room in isolation from us. Of our Jewish girls, one is Dutch, two are Hungarians from Budapest, Simone is a Parisian and one woman has been, during her better days, a Viennese operatic singer. I am the only Jewish girl from Po-land. Both the nurse and the doctor are Viennese who, in 1937, had escaped to Czechoslovakia, from where they had been deported to Auschwitz last year. Health wise, the Dutch girl and I are doing quite well but, since our tests unequivocally show that we have typhoid fever, we will have to stay in the quarantine for seven weeks, along with all the others. The others are quite ill, especially Simone who in addition to having typhoid fever, suf-fers with a bronchial pneumonia, or worse.

Our physician is amazed that I am doing so well: I barely stay in bed, my fever is soon gone, and my appetite is great. The other patients don't eat much so that I have plenty of food and I soon begin to gain weight and, for the first time since my confinement in concentration camps, I begin to menstruate. Since we are both quite well, the Dutch girl and I serve as nurse's assistants and help with the feeding and washing of the other pa-tients. But more than anything else, we socialize with each other and with the girls who are more sick than we are.

The Dutch girl is a simple, fun-loving person. She keeps telling us about her favorite snack foods and her tales become so suggestive that when we munch on our dry bread, we actually taste the thick layer of butter mixed with raw sugar of her Dutch butter-bread snacks. At the other ex-treme, Simone and I have long talks about her elegant party life in Paris and in London where her father served as an attaché to the British consul. My French has become good enough so that I can relish the nuances of Simone's tales about her dress-up socials and youthful flirtations with the young men of the Parisian society.

It is also fun to hear about the life of the well-to-do Jewish community of Prague and Budapest. These tales of the Hungarian girls bring to me the heretofore unknown vignettes of life in private prep schools and of

Mediterranean vacationing, all of which my family could never afford. But it is the cute Viennese nurse who has become our source of entertainment and merriment! She often sings for us risqué Viennese songs and she charms us with the facial expressions and body movements of a Viennese cabaret performer. We keep pestering her to perform a particular song for us, one about the adventures of a local beauty who had her clothes stolen while she went skinny-dipping in the river. Soon, all of us memorize the verses and join in singing, *"Kaetchen ging nach Flusse baden, das kan nicht schaden, wen Man es tut* (Katie went for a swim in the river and it surely couldn't have hurt anyone)," and so on. But, of course, true concerts can be had only when our Viennese opera singer deigns to perform for us; and during the gala soirees we hold on the nights of Christmas and New Year, she does perform for us the elegant songs by Hayden, Schubert, Liszt, and Chopin.

Foolishly, I pay several visits to the two Gentile inmates in their separate room, one of them with TB, the other with syphilis, but I sit at a safe distance from their bedside. I hear them talk about their hometowns and about their family life; they talk in a way that makes me realize that these two young women are not facing the fact that they may never return home. Untreated, syphilis and tuberculosis are deadly diseases and I feel that it is hardly possible for these two to recuperate. But I pretend that I believe in their eventual return home and maybe that helps them sustain their hopes. Of course, I get a lecture on the dangers of what I have been doing when our physician catches me during one of the visits with these women, and I have to stop seeing them.

The friendly Polish guard has apparently discovered that I have been quarantined and comes to visit me here at the "Typhus Barracke." He is cautious enough to stand outside the barrack so that we can only communicate through a slightly opened door or a slightly cracked window, but he often brings me a fruit and, at Christmas, a piece of gingerbread cake. In January, he offers to write a letter to a friend who serves as a guard in Auschwitz to ask about the conditions that exist in Birkenau. The letter comes back, however. The camp is either already in Russian hands or is encircled and about to be liberated. He also verifies the fact that all Bialystok Jews were murdered in Majdanek in November of 1943. Apparently, before the Russians liberated the area, one of his fellow guards served in

Majdanek and had heard the story from the old-timers there. But the guard also heard of transports of some Jewish prisoners to other camps just before the massacre took place. This again gets me to daydream about my dad and Izio. And conditions for daydreaming in the solitude of the "Typhus Barracke" are ideal—we are in a snow-covered, peaceful German countryside, we have no *Zaehl Appels*, and no SS men to contend with during the seven weeks of our convalescence. Sometimes I feel as if I am no longer an inmate of a concentration camp.

I sit for hours at the window and look at the pristine flowerets of snowflakes falling on the windowsill and feel lonely for my boyfriend. Out of nowhere, there grows in my mind a melody of a love song, just like the ones I used to know in Poland. Then Polish lyrics about the snow spring up from within me, and I don't even have to write the song down. It stays in my memory—it will stay there forever—and it will retell the lonely quarantine times in the winter of 1944-1945.

Snieg za oknem pada monotonnie,
Tona w bieli oczy me.
Moze dzisiaj znowu przyjdziesz do mnie,
Moze sniezna dal wywabi cie..
Snieg za oknem pada, taki bialy,
Ciemna jest samotnosc ma,
Moze dzisiaj moj pokoik maly
Znow rozjasni biala szczescia skra?
Moze snieg wywabi cie z daleka
I rozproszy zapomnienia mgle?
Moze wspomnisz ze ktos ciagle czeka,
Ktos co wciaz tak bardzo kocha cie..
Snieg za oknem juz nie pada wcale,
Zmrok wieczorny ziemie skryl.
A ja wiem juz o tym doskonale
Ze nie wrocisz nigdy, nigdy, ty...

Outside my window, the snow keeps on, monotonously, falling down,
My eyes are drowning in the white distance.
Perhaps you will come today, come to be with me again.
Perhaps the snowy distance will beckon you to come.
The snow, so white, keeps on coming down,
Yet my loneliness is so dark.
Could it happen again? Will a spark of white happiness
Lighten my somber space?
Maybe the snow will bring you forth from afar,
Maybe it will lift the fog of forgetfulness,
Maybe you'll remember that someone is waiting for you,
someone who loves you so much…
Outside my window, the snow is no longer coming down,
The earth is hidden behind the evening dusk,
And I know it now so very well
That I will never, never see you again…*
(*Author's translation from Polish)

Early in February 1945, we return to our camp and to our factory. The guards notice my healthy looks and tease me saying, "How was it at the health spa?" Unfortunately, Simone is still ailing with bronchial pneumonia or perhaps even tuberculosis, and she ends up in the camp's *lazaret*. Rosa Conti greets me warmly at our factory post and she immediately calls over one of her Italian friends to give me the clandestinely obtained BBC news that children, as well as elderly and ailing men and women, were found alive in their special Auschwitz enclaves when the camp was liberated by the Russians. I immediately latch on to the scenario of my mother's reunion with her two sisters and her younger daughter in Boryslaw and I just hope for a speedy end of the war so that I, too, may return to Poland.

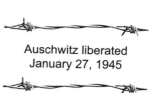

Auschwitz liberated
January 27, 1945

And all signs indicate that the war will soon end. For one, the Italians bring us the BBC news about the Allied armies advancing along the Western front and supposedly nearing Aachen in Holland, an area quite close to

Westphalia, where we are. Secondly, with the British staging air raids during the days and the Americans at night, we are now constantly going to the air raid shelter, and that is surely a sign of the war coming to an end. We hear that German overseers have become very polite and caring toward the Jewish women whom they had previously abused. But I wonder why the older German employee who used to visit me does not come to my post anymore. I finally bump into him during one of the air raid alerts and he whispers to me that he can't talk with me because he has been "watched." He also quickly adds, *"Das ist die Ende* (this is the end)." Well, maybe, but not so fast.

In March, we begin to work longer hours. The older women and women who are not too healthy are selected to go to Bergen-Belsen where, we are told, they will not have to work. Simone goes with this transport and so does my older Bialystok friend Luba. They also take away the Czech woman who mothered me during my grieving over the separation from my mom. I no longer believe that I should have forced my mother to sneak into our transport to Lippstadt; she would have been separated from me anyway! Since we are working very hard now and we don't yet fathom the horrors of Bergen-Belsen, we are not too concerned about the fate of the women who are taken there. And, soon we will have to leave this camp ourselves.

Toward the end of March 1945, we are told to get ready to leave this camp because the front is coming too close to Lippstadt. It is rumored that we are going to Buchenwald, an earlier concentration camp for political prisoners, gay people, priests, monks and Jews. Since Buchenwald is supposed to be primarily a men's camp, and since it is quite far to the east from us, we are beginning to doubt if Buchenwald is our true destination. It is only after our liberation that we discover that not Buchenwald but Bergen-Belsen had been the final destination for the Jews who remained in all the other camps, including ours. The camps' SS men had been ordered to shoot their prisoners if it looked to them as if they weren't going to reach Bergen-Belsen.

Early in the morning, the guards, the camp commandant, and his mistress, march us out of the camp and lead us along country roads and lanes, our destination unknown. We carry with us a supply of bread and our blankets, which serve as our overcoats during the cool last days of March. We sleep in barns, we drink well water, and we eat turnips that are found in the fields along the road. The German guards alternate with one another in getting their meals at roadside farmhouses and we are allowed to rest at these times. Surprisingly enough, they don't count us too carefully when we leave the barn or come back from the edge of the woods where we relieve ourselves. Escaping crosses my mind, but the sight of the many armed members of the Home Guard and Hitler *Jugend* (Hitler Youth) marching along these country roads makes me give up that thought.

We spend the last night of our travel sprawled in a meadow alongside a country road and wake up to the sound of a plane circling high above the meadow. The camp commandant, his mistress, and the guards hold a pow-wow, leaving us alone in the meadow. Then suddenly they return and holler at us to creep into the deep ditches behind the shrubs alongside the road and to lie there absolutely still, or else. Peeking through the branches of the shrubs between us and the road, we can see a military car approaching along the road from the right. Before the car passes, I notice a white star on its side. This car differs from the German military cars that I've seen before, but I know I may be shot if I stand up to take a good look, so I continue to lie still, as does everybody else. But why does a plane keep circling above our heads, I wonder…I wonder, too, about the villagers' homes across the meadow with white sheets and pillowcases hanging out of their windows—is this everybody's wash day? Or could it be something else?

After a while, I turn around and see our German keepers disappear, one by one, so that there remain now only three guards with us, and these three are crouched behind a large combine abandoned in the field. Yes, the commandant, his mistress, and the rest of the guards are gone! Yet we continue to cower in the ditches on both sides of the road. What else could we do? Then, from the right, a German youth comes along the road. He yells to us loudly with words that finally penetrate my consciousness: "Hey, you stupid girls, what are you waiting for? Get going, your English are in the village!" I get up first and hurry down the road and, one by one, everybody gets up and follows behind me—an army of young women wrapped in their blankets, all dashing toward the village square. We are followed by the three guards, whose uniforms no longer bear their military insignia.

In the village square stands a large tank with several soldiers on it, and, next to it, a military vehicle with two soldiers standing nearby. I have never seen such bowl-like helmets nor such olive-green khaki uniforms whose trousers are tucked into short brown boots. And I have never seen adults chew gum; but then I have never met the English, either. The soldiers look at us with obvious surprise and I feel taken aback by their staring and their occasional giggling, but as I look back at our blanket-clad motley crowd of girls, I could laugh at us myself. I quickly review in my mind the phrases that I've learned during my junior high school years and the later ghetto classes of English. "Who are you?" I ask. They promptly reply, "We are Americans." That answer befuddles me since I didn't think the Americans were actually fighting the Germans here in Europe, so I foolishly ask again, "Are you not English?" There are smiles up on the tank and they answer, "No…we ain't English, we are Yanks…we are Americans!" There is a joyous commotion as the girls behind me pick up on the word "American," so I feel that I must make sure these soldiers are not poking fun at us. "But how did you come across the ocean?" There is more laughter from the soldiers and one of them points to the tank, moves his arms to describe a gliding motion and says, "Oh…these go on water!" Now I know the soldiers surely are having fun with us.

One of the soldiers standing by the military vehicle is not laughing at all, but instead is looking at us intently. He approaches us, pulls out a cylindrical ornament hanging on his neck chain. He shows it to me and asks, "Do you know what this is?" There is a moment of silence among us, and then a tearful cry comes from behind me in Yiddish. *"Oy s'is a mezuze, a mezuze, er is a Yid!* (Oh, it is a mezuzah, a mezuzah, he is a Jew!)" Several of the women are crying and I am on the verge of tears myself as the soldier walks over to the tank

A *mezuzah* is a scroll of the Ten Commandments.

and explains to the other soldiers who we are. And there is no more laughter there.

Suddenly, the soldiers raise their guns and we see that our three guards, with their arms raised, are coming up from behind us to surrender. One of the Americans begins to rough up the guards searching for hidden weapons. I approach the tank and, using my best English, quickly intervene for my "friend" the Polish guard. They must understand a little of what I say about him because they lead him away separately from the others. I suddenly hope now that the Polish guard told me the truth about himself.

There is more traffic in the village square and we stand aside to let a multitude of military trucks pass by, trucks that seem to have picked up a great many refugees from the camps. The refugee men joyously shout in French, Polish, Yugoslav, and Italian, and I am happy to see my friend Rosa Conti chase after the Italians and chat with them. One of the trucks makes a stop in the village and its soldiers surround us with obvious joy and curiosity. Our Jewish soldier now explains to us, half in English and half in Yiddish, that yes, the Americans and the Canadians had invaded Europe last year and have fought alongside the British and the French armies. We are the first Jewish prisoners whom they have found alive since they have come into Germany.

The soldiers fill us in on how they found us. An American spotter plane had discovered us early this morning and the pilots immediately realized that we must be inmates from a concentration camp being led to Bergen-Belsen. The Americans also realized that, as has been the case with other Jewish death marches, the Germans were likely to shoot us if they saw the Allies attempt to surround our convoy, threatening to cut it off from the roads to Hanover and Bergen-Belsen. That is why the Americans had to rush their assault and surround the village quickly enough to prevent our execution. Our Jewish friend then calls over one of the soldiers and makes him show me his bandaged hands that were hurt when his platoon cut through the German obstacles.

Several other Jewish GI's, as they call themselves, come up to us, some in tears, some handing out their candy bars, some asking for our names and telling us that they will write home about us. Other GI's join in and tell us that since the Germans have abandoned the village, the United States army will help us "liberate" the German homes and their possessions for ourselves.

One after another we "invade" German homes and gorge ourselves on leftover foods. Cold potatoes and soup, bread, sour milk, boiled cool milk—we eat and drink it all until some of us begin to puke. We put into bowls food that we cannot eat and save it for later. Our GI protectors ransack the

Germans' clothes closets, expropriate their best shoes, coats, dresses, and even fabric and, towards the evening, help us settle down in the vacated village homes.

A bunch of Polish-Jewish girls invite me to stay with them in the upstairs apartment of a farm house. Some Hungarian girls settle in the downstairs apartment of that house, and all of us become "owners" of the cow in the barn. I settle down to sharing the upstairs apartment with Cesia, Dinka, Ewa, Dinah—all of them from Radom—and Gerda Rosenthal. Gerda is from Berlin and is about to become my best friend and my coworker in the army unit stationed here in Kaunitz.

Today is April 1, 1945, and it is my first day in this village of Kaunitz. This day is the most wonderful April Fool's Day in my life, a day when I am free at last, free after four years of slavery and humiliation, of deprivation and of constant fear of death. Today is April 1,1945, and I have come to the end of my freedom road from Lippstadt to the village of Kaunitz in Westphalia, Germany.

One day I travel through much of Africa, Asia, South America, and Europe, but I still find the thought of visiting Germany too painful to contemplate. Yet I always think that maybe I ought to retrace my freedom road from Lippstadt to Kaunitz. Maybe I ought to do that before it is too late for me…

Part Five

FREEDOM ROAD TO THE STATUE OF LIBERTY

When Israel was in Egypt's land
Let my people go,
Oppressed so hard they could not stand,
Let my people go.*

*Words from the song "Let My People Go (Go Down Moses)," an American slave spiritual (author unknown).

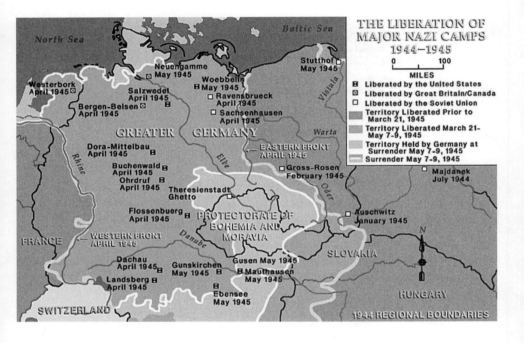

THE LIBERATION OF
MAJOR NAZI CAMPS
1944–1945

0   100
MILES

⊞   Liberated by the United States
⊠   Liberated by Great Britain/Canada
☐   Liberated by the Soviet Union
▩   Territory Liberated Prior to March 21, 1945
▨   Territory Liberated March 21–May 7–9, 1945
▧   Territory Held by Germany at Surrender May 7–9, 1945
—   Surrender May 7–9, 1945

North Sea

Baltic Sea

Stutthof
May 1945

Neuengamme
May 1945

Woebbelin
May 1945

Westerbork
April 1945

Salzwedel
April 1945

Ravensbrueck
April 1945

Bergen-Belsen
April 1945

Sachsenhausen
April 1945

GREATER GERMANY

Warta

Vistula

Dora-Mittelbau
April 1945

EASTERN FRONT
APRIL 1945

Majdanek
July 1944

Buchenwald
April 1945

Ohrdruf
April 1945

Gross-Rosen
February 1945

Theresienstadt
Ghetto

Oder

Flossenbuerg
April 1945

PROTECTORATE OF
BOHEMIA AND
MORAVIA

Auschwitz
January 1945

Rhine

Elbe

WESTERN FRONT
APRIL 1945

Danube

SLOVAKIA

N

FRANCE

Dachau
April 1945

Gunskirchen
May 1945

Gusen May 1945

Mauthausen
May 1945

Landsberg
April 1945

Ebensee
May 1945

HUNGARY

SWITZERLAND

1944 REGIONAL BOUNDARIES

FREE AT LAST, I AM FREE AT LAST!

In April of 1993, an inauguration ceremony for the opening of the Holocaust Memorial Museum was held in Washington, D.C. The commemorative proceedings held at the Memorial Rotunda of the Arlington Cemetery included the honoring of the units of the American, British and Soviet armed forces that had liberated the various concentration camps in Germany. As my husband and I sat in the Rotunda viewing the presentation of the flags by the contingents of the British, Russian, and American armies, my thoughts went back to the village of Kaunitz in Westphalia, Germany, and I relived April 1,1945, the day of my own liberation by the American army. I pondered the first days, weeks, and months of my freedom. How was it to be free again? Much of my newly won freedom was spent working, first with the American and then the British army units at Kaunitz, and the only persons who could tell me about myself as a newly liberated young woman in 1945 were the two captains who were my army superiors, Bill and Pat. Pat disappeared from my life without leaving me his address in Great Britain, or South Africa, where his family lived. But I did have the Bronx address as well as the army address of Bill and I wrote to him, once from Poland in the fall of 1945, and then in New York in 1946.

I met with Bill at my workplace in the East Bronx. He told me that the recently liberated girl in 1945 who worked for him in Kaunitz was an awkward Jewish girl who didn't act her age and lacked maturity, feminine appeal, and a sense of self-assuredness. I didn't learn much more about my newly liberated self from Bill, although his stories about Kaunitz helped me refresh my memory about my post-liberation life in Germany.

I wake up in a real bed with clean white bedding that includes a delightfully fluffy pillow and a real quilt, and I hear music coming from the radio in our sleep-in kitchenette. Everybody is up. Dinka is cooking porridge for our breakfast and I volunteer to milk the cow to get us some milk. Nobody really trusts my milking skills and two other girls come down to give me a hand. In the barn, the cow is mooing and mooing, standing in such a position as to suggest that I must milk her along her exposed side. No such luck. The cow kicks me on that side and continues to moo. I try the other side, squeezing and pulling the cow's udder, but to no avail. We call on the Hungarian girls who live on the first floor but there aren't any country girls there, either. Finally, two African-American GI's pass through the village square in front of our house and they stop by to help us. Now we're in luck. Not only do they milk the cow for us and fill their own canteen with fresh milk, but they also promise to come back in the evening and milk the cow again. We have never seen African-Americans in person before and we keep staring at them out of curiosity. The two GI's don't seem to be embarrassed by our stares, perhaps they have had previous encounters with Europeans curious about their dark skin. In the evening, the guys come back and again there is enough fresh milk for them and for us. Next morning, the German owners come to claim their cow but they promise to bring us some fresh milk every other day, which is fine with us.

We spend the next few days searching the abandoned German houses for clothing and food. We slowly become accustomed to eating just until we're full rather than gorging ourselves, as though it could be our last meal. We also begin to thaw out inside, inside our persons. We begin to reminisce and we begin to cry after those we've lost. Cesia is the only one of my roommates who not only believes that her husband is alive, but that he may be in one of the liberated camps in the nearby Hanover area. I, of course, remain sure that my mom is alive and is by now in Poland. As soon as the war ends, I will be able to travel there.

Our village becomes a Displaced Persons' Camp. With the help of the local mayor, the army provides food supplies for us to prepare our daily meals. The army also sets up a Registry Office in one of their buildings. While I'm registering I discover the army already has the list of our names and I wonder how this is possible. Perhaps our names had been received via telephone from Lippstadt or perhaps our German camp commandant had been captured and had turned in a list of our names, or else one of the captured guards had a duplicate list on him. At any rate, the new version of my name is already there, and I am assured that Irene, and not Rena, is a common name in the United States and elsewhere in the West. So I forego the change back to Rena and keep Irene, adding a middle name. In fact, this is the first time I hear about the use of middle names in the West, and my old middle name Ela becomes my new middle name of Elizabeth.

Passover falls early in April this year and the Jewish GI's and their chaplain hold a festive Passover *Seder* (Jewish ritual supper) with us, our first *Seder* in many years. The *Seder* supper isn't a lavish one, but there is some matzo, gefilte fish and chicken soup. As far as we are concerned, this is a Judaic feast. The GI's coax us to sing the Passover songs with them, though many of us can't help crying. One of our girls has composed a funny Yiddish song about her imaginary visit to "the other world," a song in which she compares *"die Velt un yener Velt* (this world and the other world)." And a GI plays the piano for us, performing the latest popular songs of the United States. "Alexander's Ragtime Band" immediately becomes our favorite. Then I perform some of my piano pieces and I am truly surprised that I still remember how to play after four years without practice.

I get an invitation to join a fireside chat with two soldiers who "liberated," as they put it, a German mansion. This indeed is a unique opportunity for me to listen to the American-English language. I find it challenging to fish for English words that are formulated in the depths of their throats, words that exit through the teeth that either chew gum or chew on a pipe. It is also quite an experience to listen to their talk about the life "back home" and to listen to their dispute about the Brooklyn Dodgers and the New York Yankee Bombers from a game called "baseball.". Yes, it feels great to pal around with these American Jewish young men who have lived in freedom all of their lives and whose world's riches are so inviting!

It appears that the fame of this displaced persons' (as we are now called) village of Jewish women has traveled far and wide, and a few days after the *Seder* several people from the newly liberated camp of Bergen-Belsen come to Kaunitz looking for relatives and friends. We all run out to meet them and sure enough, there are two women and a man from Bialystok among them. To my utter disbelief, they tell me that my mother is still in Bergen-Belsen. No one knows how she got there but she was recently seen walking in and out of the *lazaret* of this horrible camp. As soon as I hear about this I dash over to Army Headquarters and ask for the Jewish Chaplain. I beg him to take me to Bergen-Belsen. The chaplain gives in to my pleas and promises that we will go to Bergen-Belsen within the next few days. My roommates and I get an extra cot for our apartment, we prepare a trunk full of clothing and shoes for my mother, and my joy has no end!

It is a fairly short ride to the town of Celle and from there, through the desolate woods, to another displaced persons (DP) camp. After their typhus-ridden old camp had been burned by their British liberators, the inmates of Bergen-Belsen were transferred here. We immediately discover just what kind of camp Bergen-Belsen had been—an extermination camp for Hitler to complete his "Final Solution" with the remainder of the Jews of Europe. He carried out his genocidal scheme here by killing the Jews without gassing or executions; rather, they died from exposure to the elements, deprivation of food and water, and untreated disease.

The chaplain and I begin a fruitless daylong search among the dead, the half-dead and the living, but emaciated, inmates of the new camp. My mother is nowhere to be found! Because the inmates were transferred into the new camp just two or three days ago, the lists of the living are not yet completed, the lists of the dead are unreliable, and I cannot find people from Bialystok who can tell me where my mother might be. The chaplain gets permission to transmit Mom's name over the loudspeaker, and to ask in Yiddish, Polish, and German for anyone who knows about the fate of Ernestyna Hass to come to the British Military Police Office. No one shows up. I next go searching through the bodies in the morgue, the half-dead people sitting in the sun, through the barracks and the strolling groups of emaciated former inmates. I even carefully scan the death registers that have been kept by the Germans in the old camp, all to no avail!

A British physician tells us that the British found thousands of unidentified bodies when they liberated Bergen-Belsen and had the SS guards bury these dead in common graves. And the thousands who had subsequently died during the many chaotic days after the liberation were likewise buried, unnamed. The death registers of the old camp are totally unreliable because inmates were dying like flies for weeks before the liberation of the camp and records of these deaths were never kept. Therefore, there simply is no chance of knowing for sure about my mother's fate, or if indeed she had been in Bergen-Belsen at all. The chaplain implores me to keep my hopes up about my mother's whereabouts, and I return to Kaunitz with these hopes. Perhaps it wasn't my mom, after all, who was seen going in and out of the *lazaret*?

Our Hungarian neighbors are now wearing little Hungarian flags in their lapels, and the Czech girls are wearing their colors, basically to help identify them to their countrymen. The Polish-Jewish girls, however, decide against wearing the red and white flags of our anti-Semitic fatherland. I decide to place a little red flag in my lapel. After all, the Soviet Union was my latest homeland, my parents had Soviet passports, and I have considered myself a "lefty" to this day. No one in our village pays the slightest attention to my adornment except for an occasional GI who merrily yells out in my direction, "Hi, Russky!" But on the day of my visit to the mayor of Kaunitz, my little red flag does merit some coveted attention.

A modest leak in our frying pan becomes the *cause celebre* that initiates the course of events of that particular day. My roommates dispatch me to the mayor to get a new frying pan because the Americans have told us that the mayor's obligations towards us are those of a landlord. A jeep intercepts me on my way to the mayor's office and the officer in the jeep inquires about my little red flag. I proudly explain why I have decided to wear it. My explanation must have impressed him because he asks if I would like to work for the American Army. "Sure," I respond. The officer then invites me into the jeep, extends his hand and introduces himself. "I'm Bill, the captain in charge of the local army unit," he explains. "I could use a translator who knows Russian and a few other languages to help me with the various DP and POW camps in my jurisdiction."

We drive to the neighboring village of Verl. "Pick a house you'd like to work in," says Bill. I really don't care much for the looks of any of the houses so I tell him it would be nice to have a piano. With the frying pan still in my hands, I follow Bill into several houses in Verl until we finally find a two-story house with a well-tuned upright piano in living room. The captain goes into the kitchen, leaves my leaky frying pan there and gets the kitchen's best frying pan instead. He tells the owners of the house that he is requisitioning their dwelling on behalf of the American Army Corps and that they have twenty four hours to move out.

When we go back to Kaunitz, Bill asks me to show him where I live. My roommates are flabbergasted to see this American officer who not only hands them a fine frying pan but also says, "*Ikh bin a Yiddishe boychik fun der Bronx*" to let them know that he is a Jewish guy from the Bronx (which we assume is a Jewish town!). On our way back to the jeep, Bill stops to tell me that he is "progressive" (a left-winger)—that's why he chose a girl with a red flag to be his translator. Before leaving, he tells the driver to pick me up each morning and to bring me back home each evening after work.

From the last week of April until nearly the end of June in 1945, I leave Kaunitz early each day and go to the United States Army Outpost in Verl. My friend Gerda, the Berliner, goes there with me. Our job deals primarily with the welfare of the DP's (displaced persons) and of the Russian POW's (prisoners of war) in the American Occupation Zone of northwestern Germany. Almost every day, the two of us visit one of the camps with Bill to deal with the organization of social welfare, discipline, and the availability of medicaments and proper nutrition. We also help solve any emergency problems that may arise. The few languages I know certainly come in handy, but Gerda's proficiency in German proves to be more helpful when we deal with the non-Slavic inmates of the camps.

Emergencies do arise and, on occasion, we are summoned to visit camps outside of our normal schedule. One such time involved the kangaroo court of one of the Russian POW camps that had sentenced two soldiers to death for their cooperation with the Germans. It took a lot of persuasion on our part to prevent the camp from carrying out the verdict. We placed the suspects in the custody of the United States Military Police who assured the aggrieved Soviet soldiers that justice would be done, that the culprits would be held responsible for their misdeeds and would be appropriately punished. This emergency alerted the captain for the need of organizing a co-hesive social structure among the Soviet citizens in our care. It would have to be a familiar social structure to them, like the *Grazhdanskii Comitet* (Citizens' Committee), and would have to include cultural centers like the *Krasnyi Ugolok* (the Red Corner) back home. As a result of our organizing efforts, we were often invited to the camps' shows and concerts, at times held after our working hours.

My weekends are usually free, but I do get one weekend emergency call at one of the Soviet POW camps. This time it's a medical emergency. A dozen or so Soviet POW's have gotten drunk and violently ill from drink-ing a crude vodka (*samogonka)* distilled out of a commercial-grade alcohol used as an antifreeze. Fortunately, the Emergency Care of the hospital where we take them is successful in pumping their stomachs out so that none of the soldiers die.

At work, Gerda and I are treated daily to two meals, both of which are cooked and served by one of the Italian "refusenicks" liberated by the Americans. Much of the food is prepared from the military K, C, or other rations, but the cooks enhance it with spices and locally grown vegetables so that it truly acquires a good taste. Two lieutenants who work with Bill sit at our dining table each day, and I find it difficult to understand the English of the American South that these two lieutenants speak. But what surprises me most of all about the American officers is their easy-going rapport with one another and the lack of rank-rigidity in their rank-relationship with the enlisted men in their service.

I find Bill's manners hard to take at times. I can't get used to him sit-ting with his feet on the table. I become furious with him when he jokingly taps my buttocks with his foot to get me to hurry on. Furthermore, I don't know how to react to him calling me "Toots"—is he slighting me or is he, as he claims, using a term of endearment? What is the code of behavior of the Bronx men towards their women? Could American manners really be so grossly different from ours here in Europe?

But then, Bill is a tough guy, as you can tell from his encounter with a German countess in one of the princely mansions on his route through Germany. According to Bill, the countess had treated the Americans with disdain. When Bill reprimanded her for it and asked if she perhaps had been and was now a Nazi, she answered, "*Ich bin ein schtoltzer Nazi!* (I am a proud Nazi)" To which Bill slapped her face and said, "*Und ich binn ein schtoltzer Jude, du Nazi Schwein!* (And I am a proud Jew, you Nazi pig)" While I may generally approve of the bad manners and toughness that Bill exhibits towards the Nazis, I can't put up with his toughness in every instance.

One day, Kaunitz women apprehend a former German overseer from Lippstadt and bring him to us in Verl, an overseer who has terribly mistreated them at work. Bill first roughs up the overseer and then leaves him standing at attention for the rest of the afternoon. He next tries to get the military intelligence service on the phone, hoping that the German will be imprisoned and tried by the military, but he fails to get the military's cooperation. The women who apprehended the German implore me not to go easy on this evil man. But outside of our house stands his crying wife and her two little children. His wife takes hold of my hands and begs for her husband's release, and I feel torn between justice and mercy. My captain, who is now in his tough-on-the-Nazis mood, concocts a scheme for killing the German. He orders the GI standing guard to shoot the German if he so much as budges from his spot. The captain then moves to a position where the German prisoner can see him, but where he, the captain, is out of sight of the American soldier. The captain then motions the prisoner to come forward. I don't know why I couldn't whip up enough hate for this German to let him die. I just couldn't, so I scream at the GI at the top of my lungs, "NO! DON'T SHOOT!" Bill will never forgive me for, what he calls, my lack of conviction.

Captain Bill does show some softness when it comes to my need to find my mother, however, and he arranges for me to go to Bergen-Belsen once again. I decide to go on this second search because a girl from Bergen-Belsen greeted me saying, "Regards from your mother, who has been worrying about you ever since Auschwitz!" When I question the girl, she admits that she may have heard of my mother's worries not in Bergen-Belsen but at the Home for Older Women in Auschwitz-Birkenau. Yet she continues to maintain that she has subsequently seen my

April 15, 1945
The first British troops
enter Bergen-Belsen

mother in Bergen-Belsen shortly before the liberation of the camp. Based on this information, Bill advises me to go back there now that the new camp is better organized, to see if I can at least get some information about my mother.

There are better lists at the Bergen-Belsen camp's office this time around but I still don't find a trace of my mother. Again, she is not listed among the living or among the dead. I'm able to meet a few of the girls who were at Blizyn with my mom and me, but they claim they have not seen her here. In fact, they doubt if, at her age, she could have made the "death

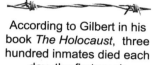

According to Gilbert in his book *The Holocaust*, three hundred inmates died each day the first week following the liberation of Bergen-Belsen.

march" from Auschwitz to Bergen-Belsen, alive. Once again, I return to Kaunitz without a clue as to my mother's whereabouts.

I settle down to my job but soon learn that the Americans will be transferring their Occupation Zone in Westphalia into the hands of the British. Indeed, a bit later in June, the British do take over. Bill parts with me, urging me to return to the Soviet Union since eastern parts of Poland where I may find my sister lie within the Soviet Union. He gives me his home and his military addresses and I promise to write to him. Meanwhile, I adjust to living under the British occupation forces, which promises to be good fun.

Since British soldiers are not allowed to fraternize with German women, their officers invite us to the afternoon dance parties organized for their men. On those occasions, a military lorry arrives in the village square and transports us to the Social Hall of the British military camp of Sennenlager. We are welcomed by one of the Staff Sergeants of the local British Army division, the 9th (Irish) Battery of the Royal Artillery, and we sit down with a few of our hosts to have tea and cucumber sandwiches. The band plays on, mostly slow foxtrots and waltzes, as well as some popular, jazzy American songs. The mostly Scottish and Irish soldiers stiffly dance for a couple of hours with us, and the lorry takes us back to Kaunitz when the dancing ends. Most of our girls don't speak English and their conversation with the soldiers is quite limited; as for me, it takes a few repetitions of the various phrases before I can understand this Gaelic variety of the English language.

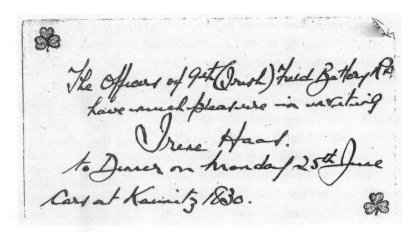

Irene's invitation to the dance

During the subsequent dance parties, a few officers also come to the dance hall along with their commanding officer, Major Lister, and several of his captains. The Staff Sergeant introduces me and the Hungarian girls who speak English to these officers, and although we find their dancing rather awkward, we can understand their "Oxford" English fairly well. I soon strike up a friendship with Pat, a jolly young South African captain of Boer-English parentage, who has taken over the responsibilities previously held by Bill and his American army unit. Both Gerda and I are asked to work with Major Lister's outfit with duties similar to those we had before.

Soon after I start working for the British, Blizyn's Jewish police officers, Minc and Sroka, come from Bergen-Belsen to Kaunitz accompanied by their girlfriends, Bala and Lola. My feelings toward Minc and Sroka are ambiguous but I accept Bala's invitation to visit them at their home. Once again, I hear that my mother must be somewhere in Bergen-Belsen. Bala

Anne Frank died in Bergen-Belsen in March 1945 with typhus. She was 15 years old.

assures me that my mother has quite recently spoken with her, perhaps just before or perhaps just after the camp's liberation. And, I am told again that my mother was walking in and out of the *lazaret* on her own. Furthermore, Bala has heard that early on, some of the liberated ailing inmates had been transported from the original camp of Bergen-Belsen to Sweden. She suggests that perhaps my mother's name could be found on the list of those who went to Sweden. The only thing I can do is to go to Bergen-Belsen one more time. Bill Miller, a talkative Scottish driver, takes me there by jeep and I am so busy trying to understand my driver that I forget my worries about my mom.

Bill Miller of the 9th (Irish) FBR. My best dancer at Sennenlager and my driver to Bergen-Belzen.

This time, I actually have the British camp supervisors let me see every list of inmates compiled in Bergen-Belsen but, once again, my mom's name is nowhere to be found. I meet my friend Hanka and she tells me that she has not heard of anyone from Blizyn going to either Sweden or any other country. At this point, I begin to disbelieve that my mother ever was in Bergen-Belsen, and I share with Hanka my conviction that my mom may have been liberated by the Russians in Auschwitz and that to find her, I will have to go to the Soviet Union. Hanka is aghast: "Go to the Soviet Union? You must be crazy!"

On my way back to Kaunitz, I once again review all the possibilities of the Bergen-Belsen enigma and decide that my mother either died there during the interregnums when no lists were compiled, or she had never come to Bergen-Belsen. In any case, there was no point in going there again.

I am free at last, but like most of the other survivors in the camps, I am alone in the world. I am free and I ought to start a new life, but life has little meaning for me now that my mom will not share it with me. I guess I must find my sister so that I have someone of my own, someone to take the place of Mom, someone to share my newly won freedom with me...

Years later, I meet my ghetto and Blizyn friend, Musia, in Paris. She tells me that she repeatedly visited my mother in the lazaret of Bergen-

Belsen; my mom lay there, starved and debilitated, until the day when Musia came and no longer found her in her bunk. The night before Musia's last visit, my mother died of starvation and exhaustion. My mother died in Bergen-Belsen about a month before the camp was liberated.

In 1993, I go to Bergen-Belsen and cry out my sorrows at one of the mass graves of the unknown victims who shared with my mother the cruelties of life and death at Bergen-Belsen. This was the camp where the last chapter of Hitler's Final Solution took place. I gather a bit of soil from around the mass graves of Bergen-Belsen, soil that will henceforth represent some of my mom's ashes...

SEARCHING FOR A CONNECTION

My Aunt Rachela, her husband Emil, and my younger Aunt Giza, left Poland in 1956 and settled in Israel. Through the years, I maintained a close and loving contact with them. When I finally came to see them in Haifa in 1965, however, Aunt Rachela wasn't alive anymore. Aunt Giza died a year later. I miss that connection very much.

My sister and I maintained a steady contact with one another and so did our respective families. We visited with them for the first time in 1965 and I have gone there nearly every other year, sometimes by myself, sometimes with my husband and with one of my children. Later on I even went with some of my grandchildren. My sister and her daughter visited us in New York in 1959, and my niece again visited us with her husband in later years. I cherished the connection with my sister and her family and cultivated it as best I could.

My sister and her family are Catholic and proud of their ethnic-Polish heritage. My family and I are Jewish and are proud of our Jewish heritage— but we are forced to hide our identity when we visit Poland.

My mom asked me to find my sister and to look after her; I kept my promise through the years and maintained a loving connection with my sister, regardless of its limiting circumstances...

In July 1945, Gerda and I receive a new responsibility. We become official liaison-interpreters for the British at conferences held by the three Occupation Armies of Northern Germany. The conferences are held at various places, often at Dortmouth and Kassel, and are intermittently hosted by the Russians, the Americans, or the British. Most of the time, the conferences deal with matters concerning the administration of POW and DP camps and plans for the ultimate disposition of the inmates of these camps. The debate about the repatriation of inmates drags on and often becomes quite heated. I feel squeamish translating some of the language of the Russians to my stiff-lipped British bosses. And there is another problem in meeting with the Russians, especially when they are the hosts of what they refer to as "the Russian tea." This entails many rounds of toasts and drinks of straight vodka, but no tea at all…Even though this drinking is always accompanied by eating an array of *zakuski* (sour and salty hors d'oeuvres), my British officers have a hard time holding their liquor, which means I usually have a hard time holding on to the jeep driven by one of them as we return back home.

After work, Pat usually drives us back home and often stops by to say hello to my roommates. He takes me by surprise one day when he suggests that he will teach me to drive so that perhaps I could drive home from the next "Russian tea." We drive out onto an open field and, sure enough, I lose control. I drive into the ditch and give myself a good-size cut right across my right eyebrow. The military First Aid station bandages my forehead and I swear to myself never to drive again. Once the eyebrow heals, however, I try driving again—more carefully this time.

Now that I am ready to become more positive about my driving lessons, I also begin to sense a change in Pat's attitude toward me. During the lessons, we drive less and talk more, and Pat begins to intimate that he would want me to be more than just his secretary-interpreter. His marriage is on the brink of breaking up and he feels free to start new relationships with women. He finds me to be a very interesting and enticing girl. This situation is nothing I could have anticipated or thought about, and my reaction is that of a frightened woman who does not feel like "an enticing girl." Doing my best, I try to explain to Pat that I need some time before I can feel womanly—that I have not yet "come to life." When Pat takes me back home, I implore him to let me be.

Without disclosing the real reasons for my action, I tell Major Lister that I might seek being an interpreter for the British Occupation officials at the nearby Guttersloh or perhaps at their HQ offices elsewhere. The major writes me a very nice letter of recommendation and Gerda and I set out by bus to Guttersloh for our first job interview. It ends with positive results, but soon afterwards, Pat urges me to continue to work with him. I gather that Major Lister questioned him about offending me in some way. To allay the Major's suspicions, I resolve to stay but Gerda decides to transfer to Guttersloh. My friendship with Pat becomes much cooler. He often visits our Hungarian neighbors, and I feel terribly hurt.

In September, the 9th Irish Battery leaves and another British army unit takes over. Our former British friends hold a very special dance reception for us and Pat comes over to me to say goodbye. He asks me to forgive him if he has hurt my feelings and tells me that he has cared for me all along but simply did not know how to handle my bruised soul. During the final round of the "Auld Lang Syne," Pat and I hold hands and promise to think of one another now and then.

The new British army unit concentrates on matters of repatriation for at least some of the displaced persons and Soviet prisoners of war. I am urged to dissuade the Soviet citizens from going home because rumor has it that many of them may become imprisoned as soon as they return to their homeland. Stalin apparently does not want to forgive his "children" for having "volunteered" for work in Germany. Nor does he want to accept the fact that his soldiers may have surrendered not because they were traitors or cowards but because they had no way out. During our final conference of the Occupation Armies' Coordinators of Repatriation, the Russians angrily demand that the British force all Russian citizens to go back home. In fact, their emissaries visit the camps under the Allied Forces' jurisdiction and are said to promise their people that "*rodina proshchayet vsio* (your fatherland forgives you for everything)." Most of the displaced persons from the Soviet Union proper do register for their return home, but those of the Baltic Republics and of the Western Ukraine do not. I feel torn. On the one hand, I believe that surely the best place to be is among one's own people and in one's own hometown. On the other hand, I feel it is my obligation to repeat to the refugees what the British have heard–that a punishment may await them back home.

Even for myself I am torn between what I should do and where I should go. I meet with the fatherly Soviet-Jewish colonel, Altshulev, whose exploits from Stalingrad all the way to Berlin awe me. He helps me decide what to do with myself and how to advise others. He tells me to return to my aunts' Boryslaw home in the Western Ukraine, and adamantly denies the rumors that those who return to the Soviet Union go to jail or to Siberia.

At the end of September and in the beginning of October, the British set out to organize the first transports for those who want to be repatriated to the Soviet Union. Dina and Ewa are the only two of my Kaunitz roommates that decide to try their luck in the Soviet Union, provided I go with them. Dina feels that with no one and nothing to tie her to Poland or any other country, she is free to go anywhere. Ewa has a legitimate reason to go to the Soviet Union—she has a nephew who is a physician in Moscow. I decide to go to Boryslaw but leave an open door for my return into the Allied Occupation zones of Germany should my search for my aunts and my sister prove fruitless. With that in mind, my current British boss prepares an imposing document for me stating that I am an employee of the British Occupation Forces who has been granted a leave of absence to search for my relatives in Eastern Europe, and that every help in that respect would be highly appreciated. Along with this document, I get a letter of recommendation which intimates that I have overcome the stressful years of confinement in concentration camps well enough to allow me to serve in the capacity of a multi-lingual translator both with the American and British Occupation Forces in Germany. To make sure I do not share the fate of the other refugees, whatever that fate might be, I am assigned to go with the transport not as a member but as its nurse.

The transport starts gathering members at one of the displaced persons' camps near a major train depot. Gerda decides to return to Berlin and joins Ewa, Dina, and myself. The four of us leave our Kaunitz home of six months for the transitional DP camp where we will start our journey across all of Europe. We leave behind our happy Cesia, whose husband returned from another camp just about two months ago, and Dinka, who hopes to find a husband from among the single men or among those who have lost their families. Our train gets an ample supply of canned and dried foods, potatoes, carrots, and other vegetables that we'll cook on the road using camp stoves fed by charcoal and bits of dry lumber.

I get a supply of first aid medicaments and bandages and, accompanied by a British sergeant, I go to meet my prospective patients in their clean but spartan third-class compartments. My friends and I and a few leaders of the transport are given the comfort of the second-class compartments, one for women and one for men.

The train ride will take several weeks! First of all, we encounter breaks in the railroad tracks. The train must back up and switch tracks, which of course takes some time. Secondly, most of our food is cooked around the sidetracks while we remain stationary, and that takes a lot of time. Finally, our daily wash ups and laundering also take time. All this is done at the train stations, where we draw the water and heat it on the charcoal embers that are left after our cooking.

When we get to East Germany, our train is unloaded by the officers of the NKVD (later the KGB), who then transport us by trucks to a transit camp. We are interviewed there and segregated according to the places we are traveling to. My job as a nurse is no longer in force and I am treated just like anybody else. Gerda is allowed to stay in East Berlin and is the first one to leave us. The NKVD men are quite impressed with my Auschwitz tattoo. They shake my hand and congratulate me on having survived the concentration camps. They confiscate my most recent letter of recommendation but I manage to hide the earlier one written by Major Lester. Also hidden is the imposing permit for a leave of absence from my last British Army post. These two documents will surely come in handy in the near future.

Two days later we again board the train and head for the Polish border, where the train stops and allows two Polish citizens to disembark. The NKVD agents inspect the train and keep asking if there are any Polish people among us. I notice the agents are carefully listening to our pronunciation of Russian words so as to spot a Polish accent, but my answers are without a trace of an accent and my Polish friends just keep mum. We pass the inspection and continue on to Poznan where they transfer different groups of people into various trucks. My truck goes through Warsaw, which is all in ruins. It is heartbreaking to see street after street of demolished houses in this formerly beautiful "Paris of the East." It is painful to see the valiant defenders of the city live in the basements of their ruined homes. Somewhere among these ruins, I think to myself, lie the demolished houses of the Jews who died a heroic death in the uprising of their ghetto in April of 1943.

The trucks enter Soviet Union proper at Brest-Litovsk and we are housed there for two days at Brest's dilapidated train station. The station is filled with men and women, most of them refugees, who are coming back from Germany. There is a military field-kitchen there and we are fed potato soup, Russian black bread, and tea. We sleep on our bundles of clothing right on the floor of the station. Once again, we must register for the places we want to travel to. I part company with Dina and Ewa, both of whom are going to Moscow. I am heading to Berdichev, a hub for the trains that will go to the various parts of the Ukraine. Now I am truly alone. It was hard to part with Gerda but is even harder to part with Ewa and Dina, the last two friendly souls with whom I shared my newly won freedom. As I board the train alone, I worry about the difficulties they will face without me, their Russian spokeswoman.

We reach the station of Berdichev and I recall with sorrow that Berdichev used to be the Russian-Jewish *shtetl* of renown. But after the German's occupation, surely nothing remains of Berdichev's Jewish community. As was true of Brest-Litovsk, there is some food for the refugees in Berdichev as well, and I eat before changing trains for the Western Ukraine. Now the train goes through familiar villages and fertile fields that I had known so very well in my childhood while traveling to Brzezany. We finally arrive at the train station where, with nostalgia, I read the Latin inscription I had committed to memory during my childhood: "*Leopolis Semper Fidelis* (the always faithful Lwow)." It is an emblem of historic distinction for this great city. How well I remember the many times when my family and I had come from Grudziadz to Lwow to catch the train for Brzezany!

Again, I sleep among the other refugees on the floor of the station's waiting room and, in the morning, I get some hot tea and bread before boarding the local train for Boryslaw. The train is packed with Ukrainian families, and on the way I learn about the sociopolitical upheaval that has taken place in the formerly eastern regions of Poland. Polish inhabitants of the formerly Polish Ukraine and Belorussia have been resettled to western Poland. Farms and homes vacated by these Poles are offered to Belorussians and Ukrainians of Poland. In view of these current facts, I begin to doubt, as the train enters Boryslaw, that my aunts are still here. I soon discover that, indeed, they have left for Poland.

Thanks to the fact that Aunt Rachela is well-known in Boryslaw, people here readily direct me to a home of her Polish friends. Her friends are also on their way to Poland and tell me the amazing story of my sister's and aunts' survival. My aunts Giza and Rachela, along with Eidikus, my aunt's dental assistant, were saved by living in hideouts in the homes of their Polish friends. My sister was placed with a caring Polish family in the western-Carpathian town of Sanok. As to my family's present whereabouts, their friends believe that my aunts have been resettled in the western territories of Poland that now include a thick slice of Germany. They also advise me to go to Krakow first because the Jewish Committee there maintains lists of all the Jews who were resettled from the east.

Back in Lwow's train station, I head for the NKVD office to get a permit for emigration to Poland. They listen to my story of roundabout travel from Germany to Poland via the Soviet Union and tell me that I don't have to go. If I like it in the Soviet Union, they say, my stay here could be arranged. I think of my American captain, Bill, and I feel sure that he would say to me, "Stay in the Soviet Union, stupid, not in Poland!" But, I am all alone. "*Mnie siemia nuzhna* (I need a family)," I say to the Russians. The NKVD officer looks at me with a bit of sympathy and gives me the needed permit, though he instructs me to keep my eyes open in Poland and to report anti-Soviet activities to the proper authorities.

The train to Krakow is a slow one. Time and time again I overhear the viciously anti-Semitic statements made by my co-passengers who obviously don't know I am Jewish. To add insult to injury, I see in several of the train stations police notices about executing perpetrators of murderous pogroms staged against the *zeturrung*—the Jewish Holocaust survivors. Oh, how hurtful it is to hear words of sympathy for the murderers, not for the Jews! So, that is my Poland!

In Krakow, I spot a Jewish-looking woman who leads me to the Jewish

Committee where I get my aunts' address in Walbrzych. Walbrzych lies in the eastern part of Lower Silesia, newly acquired from Germany. The Jewish Committee women also give me a voucher for my morning train ride to Walbrzych along with some Polish money. At the station I get a chance, for the first time in a very long while, to actually buy food. I treat myself to a sandwich and tea and, once again, I sleep on the station floor until I can board the early train to Walbrzych.

Walbrzych is a rather large German city severely damaged by bombs. I need to take a trolley-bus to get to my aunt's suburban house. When I enter, Aunt Giza, who is at home alone, greets me with a scream: "Rena, you are alone, Rena! Where is your mother?" I feel like crying—I survived, I am free, I found my family, but they don't want me here without my mom.

Aunt Rachela's suburban home does not include her dental offices and that is why I don't see her here. My younger aunt Giza introduces me to the young German landlady of the house who lives, with her Italian boyfriend, upstairs above my aunts' apartment. We take the trolley-bus downtown to Aunt Rachela's dental offices. I immediately read the disappointment in my older aunt's face and am not surprised that she, too, asks for my mother. My aching heart reads the reproach: Why did you let your mother die? People have seen you in Auschwitz with your mother, so why did you leave her there? Again, I feel unwanted, I feel that my survival, without my mother's survival, isn't worth much. Right there and then I decide that I will leave my aunts and go back to Germany with my sister. But in the meantime, I reconnect with my aunts. Both my aunts and Eidikus look much older than they did when I last saw them just seven years ago in Boryslaw. I readily understand why they have aged so much when I hear about the hardships they suffered during the Holocaust.

Initially, they had remained hidden inside their own attic hideout and watched the Ukrainian pogroms and merciless murder of their Jewish community from the little attic window. After the last pogrom, Aunt Rachela married Eidikus and the two of them sought refuge with their Gentile patients in a village near Boryslaw. They remained hidden there in a barn storage bin. Only late at night were they allowed to stretch, to eat and to walk a bit. During the day they had to keep absolutely still while the farm laborers walked in and out of the barn. Giza remained in a similar hideout hole under the floor of a pantry room at another Gentile friend's house. She also had to lie still during the day hours. It was hard to imagine how anyone, for some 17 months, could put up with such terrible conditions—let alone people in their fifties!

My sister's rescue was truly miraculous. A patient, wearing all black, burst into tears in my aunt's office, telling her of the death of her teenage daughter. After consoling the grieving mother, my aunt asked, "Would you like to save the life of a Jewish teenage girl in the memory of your daughter?" The woman willingly passed on her dead daughter's birth certificate to my sister. A hired guide took my sister to Sanok where she stayed with the dead girl's relatives. My aunt left enough money in the hands of her patient to pay for my sister's long-term upkeep. For safety, the caregivers were told that my sister's father, a high ranking Polish officer, had been executed by the Russians, and that her mother had died in Siberia. In this way, my sister's new family could not been implicated in hiding a Jewish child.

When my sister had learned a sufficient amount of Catholic doctrine and most of the Catholic prayers, the guide "Uncle Zygmund" boarded the train to Sanok with his "niece Irena." All would have been fine had it not been for an SS search for hidden Jews towards the end of their journey. One of the SS men came into their compartment and pointed at my sister, shouting, "*Du bist doch ein Juedin* (you surely are a Jewess)!" The guide showed the German the Christian birth certificate and convinced him that she was his niece. A bit later, during a short layover and a change of trains, my sister hid in a station outhouse and did not come out until the guide assured her that Germans were known to harass all dark-haired Polish people. "Your new documents will protect you," he said, "in case they ever try to intimidate you again."

The Polish family cared for my sister for nearly two years and had made her feel fairly comfortable in their home. She shared the house chores with the other members of the family, she went to church and celebrated Christian holidays with them, and she gradually became accustomed to being a Christian girl. Apparently, the Christian patients of my aunts had been able to receive and transmit news about my sister. That is how, late in the summer of 1943, we had learned in the ghetto of Bialystok that my sister was in hiding. That is why my mother implored me to find her.

It is not very easy to get my sister to come from Sanok to Walbrzych in the middle of her Gimnazjum fall term. At first, when my aunt writes to my sister about me, she says that she would come to Walbrzych right away if Mother were with me. At this point, I am nearly ready to leave Poland without seeing my sister, but my aunts urge me to meet her in Sanok first and then get her to come to Walbrzych. So I take the train to Sanok and intercept my sister and her gang of friends at the gate of their Gimnazjum. My sister looks at me for a long while as if she doesn't quite recognize me. Then she coolly tells me that she will pack her belongings and meet me at the next train to Walbrzych. She shows up at the train station accompanied by her current boyfriend, Staszek, who will come with us to Walbrzych.

My 16-year-old sister whom I found in Walbrzych, Poland, in late September of 1945

My sister is a beautiful brunette, 16 years old and slender. Staszek is a tall blond who is madly in love with this Gypsy-like beauty. Whenever I am with them, I feel like the proverbial "fifth wheel," so I resort to staying home and re-making my sister's dresses, of which she has but a few. I feel as if I am assuming my mother's role in caring for my sister, but very little is coming back from my sister Irena. As to our doubling up on the name Irene, we get away with it since everybody knows me as either Rena or Renia. Of course, Staszek does not know that the girl with whom he frequents the daily early morning mass is of Jewish origin.

My sister "drops a bomb" when she explains that she must daily pray for the sins of her Jewish parents. I guess I am too young to understand the factors underlying my sister's behavior, so I just walk around with a deep hurt in my Jewish soul. Finally, one day, my sister walks in on me as I lie on my cot with unhappiness written all over my face. She points to the portrait of St. Mary and tells me, "Once, when I was terribly afraid about my safety, I vowed to St. Mary: 'I don't know if you ever really existed or

not, but I promise you that if you save me, I will believe in you forever.'"
She keeps her word and I know now that I have a very valid reason for
wanting to go back to Germany. I decide to hang around a bit longer, just in
case there is a sign of change in my sister.

As I stay on in Poland, more threats begin to surface. A Russian Jew
moves in next door and prospects me to become his wife. Aunt Rachela has
a hard time keeping him away from me. His friend, the chief of the Polish
Secret Police, also lives nearby. The two of them barge in on us, both com-
peting for my attention. Once her boyfriend Staszek returns to Sanok, my
sister conspires with me to keep the suitors away—we claim that we need
to be alone to make up for the time we were separated from each other.

The truth, however, is that I fail to bridge the gap between my sister
and myself. Time and time again she tells me that without Mom and Dad,
the two of us are not a family. She gives me the same answer whenever I
ask her to go with me to the West: she is now a Catholic Pole and she
belongs in Poland. And she displays the old Polish chauvinism vis-à-vis
the Russians, the Ukrainians and, of course, the Jews.

As if that wasn't enough of a headache, Aunt Rachela keeps introduc-
ing available Jewish bachelors to me. She also arranges interviews for me
at the Krakow University Medical School. I begin to feel as if the air in
Poland is suffocating me, and I prepare to leave the country.

My plan is to use my two British documents as proof of my British
citizenship. I will conceal my Polish nationality so that I will not be turned
away from the Polish-East German border and sent back to Poland. I memorize enough Czech phrases from a Czechoslovakian textbook to carry on
a brief conversation with Polish border guards. I am also going to claim
that my mother is Czech, my father is British, and that he and his family
live in some small English town , a town whose name I found in Aunt
Rachela's world atlas. According to this scenario, I have been granted a
leave of absence from my British army unit to search for my mother and
my sister, both of whom have been stranded during the war in Czechoslovakia and have apparently perished in concentration camps. Now I must
return to my army post in Germany, which my impressively stamped British documents will verify. In reality, I am aiming to obtain a scholarship to
study medicine at a German University, preferably the Medical School at

Heidelberg. I am told that normal studies resumed there at the beginning of November of this year.

My aunts are appalled by my plans. "Our family has never had a conniver of your caliber and you will surely end up in jail," they tell me. "We live in a country that is but an adjunct to the USSR, and although the Soviet Union does invite the entry of communist-sympathizers from the Western world, it strictly prohibits an exit of its own people into that world." Surprisingly, my sister now begins to show an interest in my daring plans. She would, perhaps, consider joining me were it not for my aunts' refusal to let her go. And their intimidating predictions of the bleak fate that is sure to befall us at the German border prove to be truly frightening for my sister. Aunt Rachela finally eases up on her matchmaking schemes of finding me a husband and offers to support me through the Krakow Medical School, obviously hoping that I will give up my plans of attending the Heidelberg Medical School. My aunts challenge me time and time again, "Why would you chance being caught at the border? Why don't you want to stay with your family here in Poland." I offer few convincing reasons to my aunts. I know deep inside, however, that I do not belong in Poland with my aunts, that my sister and I are strangers to one another, and that I must go and create, on my own, a new life in a new world.

My sister spends most of the day with me before I depart from Walbrzych and the change in her softens my resolve to leave. She finally asks me questions about the ghetto of Bialystok and about my life there with our parents. She is anxious to know if we took her treasure box with us into the ghetto, if we talked about her, if we missed her, and if I will come to see her again in the future. I sense that she has become ambivalent about letting me go without her, and I promise that I will do everything possible to bring her to where I will finally settle down—if she will then wish to come to stay with me.

Late in the evening, my sister asks me to sing with her, as we have done in our childhood, the sweet "Berceuse Slave" to which I wrote Polish lyrics. We remember Dad playing this song on his violin accompanied by me on the piano and both of us cry as we sing:

"Zaszlo juz sloneczko, zaszlo za chmurami,
zegna ta ziemie, i zrasza ja lzami..
Zapadl juz wieczor, gwiazdy juz zalsnily,
szeleszcza drzewa w letni wieczor mily..."

The sun sets behind the clouds and sheds tears,
bidding the earth goodbye.
The evening sparkles with its stars
and wishes the summery rustle of the trees...*
*(Author's translation from Polish)

My sister then recites a Polish poem for me which I can't place, although its flavor is much like that of my lyrics to the "Berceuse Slave":

"Zapadla noc w ksiezyca poswiacie,
usiadla na globie w granatowej szacie
I cicho, cicho zasnal swiat.
Usnely wszystkie dziecinne sprawy, usnal motyli roj zwawy
I glowe schylil kwiat."

The night, clad in moonshine and a navy blue wrap,
sat upon the world
and quietly, oh so quietly, put it to sleep.
Children's matters and swarms of lively butterflies are also asleep;
and the flowers lower their heads.**
(**Author's translation from Polish)

On and on, the poem continues with tales about the sad fiddler whose fiddle cries in the night because it must share the life of a wanderer with its master. I am just about to ask my sister about the origin of this poem when she surprises me by saying: "This is your poem, Rena, I was a little tot when I memorized it, and I will remember it for ever and ever." Oh yes, now I remember that my career as a well-rounded family artist had begun with maudlin poetry and progressed to the painting of somber sunsets and the mellow colors of fall foliage. But now I also know that this sister, although she is estranged from me, is carrying in her memory song lyrics and poems of our childhood because she needs to stay connected with that childhood. And perhaps also because she has always loved me and still cares for me, notwithstanding her escape to Christianity.

But how can I stay with this sister whose Polish-Christian world has no room for my Judaism, no room for my need to continue the traditions of my decimated people and no need for me to belie Hitler's Final Solution by raising a Jewish family of my own? How can I stay here? I must leave Poland and go where I can be true to myself.

I spend time with my sister and her family and friends, even though I have to dull my senses with vodka to weather my loss of pride in hiding my Jewish identity and to swallow the anti-Semitic jokes of her friends. I share with my sister and her family their holidays and their way of life, even though I sometimes have to lie that the reason I don't go to church and don't know much about Christian holidays is that I am a "nonbeliever." Along with my sister, I revisit the shadows of our childhood and have to duck the questions of onlookers who want to know what brings me to the long forgotten "Jewish places." On buses and trains, my sister and I encounter "sniffers" of Jews who ask about my religion. I lie by saying I am part of an esoteric American denomination.

The worst part of my stay is my sister's lack of awareness as to how much pain she has exacted from me all these years. She asks, "Why do you need to identify yourself as a Jew? Why can't you be just an American?"

Yet, my sister often recalls minute details about the Passover Seder at our parents home, she asks about our grandsons' Bar Mitzvah rituals, and she asks me to sing for her the songs of the extinct Polish-Jewish community. And finally, she secretly joins Warsaw's organization of the Children of the Holocaust where she uses her real first name and maiden name and wistfully says to me: "It feels good to be myself again." And I feel good about having found and having maintained my Polish sister connection, despite all its drawbacks.

THE LONG WAY TO THE STATUE OF LIBERTY

On the night of November 5, 1950, as I was sleeping off the travails of the childbirth of my daughter at the Lebanon Hospital in the Bronx, I was awakened by a flashlight shining in my face and a voice from my past that said in Polish: "You quit Heidelberg for that?" The mocking voice and the smiling face belonged to Maciek, my colleague from the Heidelberg Medical School and now a resident at Lebanon Hospital. It was hard to believe that only four years had passed since I quit my studies in Europe and came to New York. And it was a little painful to see that Maciek, and most of the other Jewish students, did finish their studies at Heidelberg and had become physicians in Israel or here in the United States. But then, I came my own long way home and my home now included a sweet little girl, my own daughter.

Many a time I relived the voyage on the SS Marine Perch. It was a voyage that started in Bremen-Hafen in Germany and brought the first 2000 displaced persons (including me) to the Port of New York. But my long way home had started in Poland months before I enrolled at Heidelberg, and months before I boarded this venerable Victory Ship that steered me in the direction of life that I so badly needed. I needed a family life with a loving husband and children, and a profession that enhanced my enjoyment of that life.

On the night of the birth of my daughter, I knew that the long way to America had brought me to a home that was right for me.

It is the fall of 1945. A day after I finish packing my valise and my knapsack, Aunt Giza and my sister take me to the train that goes into the border town of Zgorzelec. Zgorzelec lies across the river Odra from Goerlitz, its East German equivalent. Most of the train's passengers are the former German inhabitants of this area who have been coaxed to emigrate into East Germany. I board the train and allow a friendly Polish officer to carry my valise into my compartment, an officer who simply disappears with my valise. All I can do is think sadly that this theft is Poland's appropriate send-off for the likes of me. Now, all my possessions amount to what I have in my backpack. My aunts have given me quite a bit of German money so I can eventually refurbish my wardrobe, or so I hope. We arrive at the train station of Zgorzelec at night. There are men at the station who, for a price, offer lodging in their homes. A young woman and I make sure that the man who invites us to his home has a wife, so that if we must share a bed with someone, it will be with his wife and not with him.

But what we do not know is that the two of us will share a bed with his wife and with him. We sleep with our clothing on and I promptly snuggle up to his wife. The other young woman gets to sleep next to her husband and ends up battling his unwanted advances all through the night. Obviously, these doings keep us all awake until the wife finally chases her husband into another room.

Early in the morning, we walk to the guard house on the Polish side of the bridge. One by one, the train passengers from last night pass the interrogation and inspection of the Polish border police. When my turn comes, I take out my British documents and perform the "show" I have rehearsed for days. I treat the guards to my British cigarettes and chocolates and in broken Czech, tell them about my wandering through Czechoslovakia and southwestern Poland until I arrived in Zgorzelec. The guards don't know any English so I read my documents for them and embellish my recital, in pantomime and in broken Czech, to convey the message that I am a British subject by birth and an employee of the British Army. Lo and behold, they believe me! They call out to the Soviet border guards at the opposite end of the bridge that I am "an Ally girl and not a German Fraulein, so please guys, no monkey business with this girl!" In a properly dignified manner, I cross the bridge and receive a salute from the Soviet guards who direct me to the railway station of the East German Goerlitz.

Two Soviet KGB servicemen intercept me at the entry to the Goerlitz railway station and scrutinize my British documents. I retell my story, this time in English, and request help in getting to the nearest British authority. One of the KGB officers who hardly understands a word of what I say points to the train platform and tells me to go to Berlin and find there the British Occupation Office. I pretend that I do not understand his Russian too well so he simply walks me over to the train and points to the Berlin sign, to which I nod my head to show I understand him. My scanty German proves to be good enough at the ticket window where I not only buy my ticket and get the train schedule, but also learn about the location of the British Occupation Zone in relation to the East Berlin Train Station (*Ost Bahnhoff*) where I will arrive.

Within a few hours, I find myself in East Berlin. Men equivalent to the German KGB grill me about my reasons for wanting to leave the East. Fortunately, my British documents impress the German Secret Service and the lengthy story about my British citizenship appears genuine. Before I am allowed to go on, however, some of the documents and the letter of recommendation from my British supervisor, are confiscated "for future verification"!

I have been given directions to the camp for British Subjects, a camp located on the boundary of the West (Allied) Zone and East (Soviet) Zone of Berlin. I get there by metro, and now I become frightened. Surely the British will not buy my story about being a "British subject by birth." But if I tell the truth, they will surely send me back East! I decide to modify my story, saying that I came from Poland rather than Czechoslovakia. If they indeed send me back, it will be to Poland rather than to Czechoslovakia. But, come hell or high water, I stick to the British part of my story. Officers of AK—the right-wing Armja Krajowa (the National Army) of General Anders who fled Poland a month or two ago—are my welcoming committee here, and I stick to my story in their presence as well.

When I get to the camp, it does not resemble the Displaced Persons' Camps at all. Here, families are housed in suites of rooms and singles share small double or triple bedrooms that, by my standards, are quite comfortable. I am assigned to share a room with a Canadian mother and daughter, both of whom were stranded during the war in Germany. The girl teaches me my first "non-military" English song, a Canadian folk song that sounds so much softer than the "I've Got Six Pence" or "It's a Long Way to Tipperary" that I've learned from the Allied servicemen. The words of the Canadian folk song, "Come sit by my side, little darling, come, lay your cold hand on my brow, and promise me that you won't ever be nobody's darling, but mine..." tell me that there are sensitive and loving men in that distant rough and tough North America. I am so taken by the Canadian girl's songs that I ask her to sing them with me nightly and I reciprocate by singing some equally melodious Polish folk songs.

The rest of the British people in this camp are mostly older women and men, but there are also a few couples with children, and we all meet during mealtimes. I have a feeling that my mannerisms and speech betray the fact that I don't belong amidst these "stiff upper lip" British. So, to allow for the loss of my British manners and of my fluency in English, I keep lengthening (in my story) the time that I had spent in Poland with my mother.

It is more difficult to sound convincing when, a few days after my arrival, a British Intelligence official interrogates me in his office. I conceal my legitimate Displaced Persons' ID card from Kaunitz and, using modified names for both of my parents, I fill out a new Displaced Persons ID card. My "cock'n bull" story is meticulously recorded. When I am finished with it, the officer tells me that an inquiry will be made with the officials of the town in England which I claim to be my birthplace, to see if perhaps there are, in Great Britain, some relatives of John Adam Hass (who, in the early 1930s, disappeared into an unknown location). I am promised that, as soon as pertinent information arrives, I will be considered for repatriation to Great Britain.

I spend most of my time in this British camp not with the British, but rather with the officers of General Anders' Armja Krajowa or AK (National Army). General Anders formed the Polish National Army in Great Britain soon after Poland's downfall; his men had fought alongside the British Army in Africa and in Italy, where they had famed themselves by their heroic stand at Monte Casino. General Anders had also sent his men to

German-Occupied Poland where they had organized the very chauvinistic, anti-Semitic and anti-Communist partisan units of the Armja Krajowa. The AK forces were later outmaneuvered by the communist Polish Peoples' Army, formed immediately after the Warsaw Uprising in 1944. The Soviet forces had chosen to procrastinate in the environs of Warsaw and had allowed the Germans to quash the uprising. After that, however, the Soviets had allowed their refugee Polish Communists to infiltrate Poland and to organize Polish Peoples' Army units sympathetic to the Soviet regime. The AK stayed underground in Socialist Poland until they could escape into the Allied Occupation Zones of Germany, as did the AK officers whom I have befriended here in Berlin.

The metro is running, so it's quite easy to go sightseeing in what is left of bombed-out Berlin, which I enjoy doing in the company of the Polish officers. We visit the famous Berlin Zoo and cross into the Soviet Zone to see the Reichstag Building with the bunker where Hitler and his mistress Ewa Braun committed suicide. We view the scanty remains of the pyre where their bodies were cremated. We also attend evening concerts and other performances. I find a seamstress who makes me a dress from Aunt Rachela's remnant of black lace. I wear the dress to a dance with my Polish companions and pose for a photograph for my sister..

Since I am well aware of the AK's anti-Semitism and since I would have to have been a Christian during my supposed wartime stay in Poland, I hide my Jewish identity both from the Polish officers and the British Intelligence official. My childhood experience of church-going with my nanny helps me get through one Sunday mass, and I claim to have a toothache to excuse myself from another Sunday mass.

The very next day after my interrogation, the Polish AK captain advises me that it is best to tell the British the truth about my Polish nationality because the British would never consider sending me back to Communist Poland. Obviously, the British Intelligence officer spoke to the Polish captain about my story and the two of them decided that I had lied about myself because of my fear of being sent back to Poland. I assure the captain that my story is true and I decide to sweat it out here in Berlin until I can think of a way out of my precarious situation.

The way out suggests itself when I decide to attend classes at Berlin

University. The roof and top floor of the building had been demolished during the severe bombing of Berlin so that the rain constantly comes down on our heads. I wish I could study medicine in a better place. Suddenly I recall my original resolve to study medicine at Heidelberg Medical School. The fact that Heidelberg is in the American Zone of Occupation promises to offer an escape not only from the rain, but also from the British.

The Intelligence official is quite pleased to send me off to the intact University of Heidelberg and promises to notify me if the results of his inquiries in Great Britain are positive. In fact, I learn that the Americans maintain a direct weekly bus from Berlin to their headquarters in Heidelberg and, on December 18, 1945, I get a ride on that bus.

After a long walk from the United States Army's Headquarters to Heidelberg's *Hauptstrasse* (Main Street), I arrive at the UNRRA Student Hostel of Heidelberg University. Although it is quite late in the evening, Mr. William Sudduth, the director of the UNRRA Student Hostel, is still working at his office. I briefly introduce myself, this time disclosing my real identity and the truthful story of my life and survival. As soon as I get into the bedroom assigned to me, I go through the obligatory introductions to my roommates of being Irene Hass, a young woman looking for a place to stay and study medicine; Irene Hass, a young woman looking for those who would befriend a Polish Jewish survivor of concentration camps. I don't quite trust the friendliness of the Ukrainian, Lithuanian, and Estonian students in my room, but I know that I will surely gain the friendship of the fourth girl, the red-haired Jewish girl, Simona, and that is enough for me.

Next morning, I register with Sofia Lasmane, the secretary of Ms. Ruth Prager, our Student Supervisor. I surrender my Kaunitz Displaced Persons' ID card, get instead a UNRRA Student ID card and get instructions about meal times at the UNRRA Student Cafeteria. Since I am quite late for this term's lectures, I hurry off to register at the University's Main Hall this very morning.

I encounter two obstacles. First, I have no school documents to prove what I've studied thus far. Second, I am too late to register for Medical School this term. The registrar directs me to see the Dean of Students anyway, because he is the one that must vouch for my graduation from a secondary school. As best as I can, I describe to the dean the curriculum of the 9th and 10th years of the Soviet high school, showing off my knowledge of Latin, French, mathematics, physics and other subjects. The dean allows me to register at the University with the stipulation that, during this fall term, I take the required preclinical subjects at the Department of Natural Sciences. I can then transfer to the Medical School in February of next year for my second semester. In that way, I could finish the first Physicum (preclinical, comparable to the United States premed) year by May of 1946. I can start the second preclinical year soon after that time.

The registrar affixes my photo to my new green University Student Passport and registers me in this term's classes in genetics, chemistry, physics, and human anatomy, some of which I may start attending this afternoon. But first, I find my way to the UNRRA Student cafeteria and join Simona for lunch at what proves to be the exclusively Jewish students' table.

There are ten to twelve Jewish students seated at our table. Only one man is a German Jew, two girls are Hungarian Jews and the rest are all Polish Jews. Simona is the only chemistry student. The German Jew studies philosophy, and Heniek, whose brother is an assistant professor here, is a first-year medical student. The rest of the men are in their second year of medicine. The two Hungarian girls attend various humanity lectures, as does Hermina who, to my delight, comes from Brzezany and joins us a bit later that term.

Maciek is the funniest of all the men. There is no end to his jokes and he plays a rather nasty one on me. He tells me to hang my coat in one of the front rooms at the entry hall of the Anatomy and Physiology Building. Rather than a coat room, it turns out to be the dissection room full of preserved human cadavers. As I leave the room, Maciek stands there with his cronies. I do my best to conceal my shock and to maintain a nonchalant posture, but it takes me some time before I graciously accept Maciek's apologies and friendly gestures. Maciek is engaged to one of the Hungarian girls, and I wonder how benign his attitude is toward that girl.

I don't particularly like any of these guys; in fact, I find that they are rather obnoxious in snubbing the students of other nationalities. Several of the Polish students attempt to join us, but give up when they get a cold shoulder from Maciek, the self-professed leader of our group. Of course, I remain loyal to my Jewish brethren and sit at their table most of the time.

But occasionally, I do sit at the table of the Polish students and try to make up for the snobbery of the others. Yes, I do understand the underlying reasons for the lack of friendliness of the Jewish students towards their quite likely anti-Semitic Polish classmates. But then I prefer to establish my friendships on a person-to-person basis, preferring to give each Polish student the chance to reach out to me and show me that he or she harbors no anti-Semitic prejudice. And that is how it happens with my very best friend Poldek.

On the first day of my preclinical lectures at the Natural Sciences Building on the other side of the Neckar River, I have a quick breakfast at the UNRRA cafeteria. I follow the students heading for the Neckar River and cross the bridge with them. A tall Polish student whose name is Poldek (Leopold) joins me at the bridge and we attend the chemistry lecture together. Poldek is a first year medical student who also came too late to register for lectures at the Medical School, so he will attend the preclinical science lectures in the Department of Natural Sciences with me.

We soon become friends. Poldek stays with a German family and we do much of our studying together, either at his home or else at the University Library. Since German had been Poldek's foreign language at high school, he volunteers to help me with my textbook readings and we help each other tackling the subject matter itself. We take walks after our studies and learn a bit about each other's lives, although Poldek remains rather secretive about his past. But he does tell me that he comes from Lwow and that he had been engaged to a Jewish girl who broke off their engagement and joined a clandestine emigration trek to Palestine. The two of us defy the taboos of the two separate Polish and Jewish tables, often sitting together at either table. Nevertheless, I refuse to join Poldek in registering for the supplies of soap, toothpaste and other toiletries that are distributed to students of Polish nationality by the Polish Red Cross.

There is an agreement between the Jewish students that when we need to specify our nationality, we will all claim that we are "stateless." There is an ongoing dispute between the Polish and Jewish tables about our obstinate refusal to claim the country of our centuries-old Polish-Jewish heritage. We say the Polish people who silently stood by the slaughter of its three-and-a-half million Jewish countrymen, and who even after that slaughter remained rooted in their vicious anti-Semitism, are not our people. The Polish side argues that many, many Polish people sheltered Jews and risked their own and their family's lives in doing so. Maciek replies, "The Jewish Nation will always remember and take care of the righteous among the Poles and will always be ready to welcome those who prove their friendship to the Jewish people."

After this heated dispute, neither side makes an overture to the other side in public. But Poldek continues to be graciously accepted at our table while I am met with lukewarm friendliness, both at the Polish table and by the Polish students at my hostel. In fact, one day one of my classmates from the Grudziadz Gimnazjum shows up at my hostel and her rapport with me clearly tells me that "I am not one of them." Poldek obviously remains the exception to the rule and I will enjoy my friendship with him till the end of my stay at Heidelberg. But, I apparently must pay a price for fraternizing with a Gentile Pole.

Around the same time the Polish Red Cross dispensed toiletries to the Polish students, a Jewish organization, the Jewish Welfare Board (JWB), began handing out gift bags of toiletries to us. Soon after I receive my gift I also receive an invitation to one of the JWB official's hotel room. I meet a uniformed middle-aged Canadian there who is accompanied by his young, uniformed German-Jewish secretary. The Canadian is seated behind a desk, the secretary stands at the side of the desk and, since they don't ask me to sit down, I begin to feel that something is in the air. The Canadian looks at me sternly and informs me that there have been reports that, unlike what I claim, I am not Jewish. Since the Christian Welfare Organizations have been helping the university students of their own denominations, the Jewish Welfare Board has extended help only to the Jewish students. But now, the JWB is beginning to question helping me because I may not be Jewish.

For a while, I feel at a loss as to what to say and what to do. I just roll up my sleeve and show my tattoo. But the secretary promptly dismisses my proof by saying that non-Jews can also bear concentration camp numbers, and that former Nazi-underlings are also known to tattoo their arms to escape imprisonment.

Now that they have me totally intimidated, I rally all my resources for my self-defense. "Not only am I surely Jewish, I begin, "I am the daughter

298 | REVISITING THE SHADOWS

of a well-known Jewish violinist, I took part in the uprising of the Ghetto of Bialystok, and I have relatives in America and in Palestine!" I give the names of my aunts and cousins in New York, but the Canadian does not appear satisfied.

"Why don't you speak Yiddish, the language of the Jewish immigrants from Eastern Europe to America?" he asks.

"Because I grew up in the formerly German Graudenz (now Polish Grudziadz), where non-Yiddish speaking middle class Jewish families lived. Our parents made us study Hebrew, not Yiddish."

Now, at last, the German Jew is on my wavelength. He approvingly nods his head to the Canadian. I become emboldened by that nod and challenge him: "Let us see if you really are a Jew, if you can understand my Hebrew!" I recite Chaim Nachman Bialik's poem "*Khaia ish, ur'u, einenu od* (there was a man but look, he is no longer here)," I sing one Hebrew song and then another one. I finish my performance with my Yiddish "*Eli, Eli* (My God, my God)" after which the secretary gives me a hug and the unsmiling Canadian concedes his defeat with a loud "OK, OK!"

As I exit the hotel room, I finally let my anger out, saying, "It is too bad I can't just unzip my fly and show my circumcised penis to prove that I deserve the *dreck* (crap) of your welfare packages!" Later on, Miss Prager becomes enraged by the story of the JWB inquisition and promises to pass my story on to the UNRRA Headquarters in Munich. Apparently, however, the Canadian JWB official remains in good standing because later on, he will actually add my name to the list of those entering the United States on the collective visa issued by President Truman in May 1946.

A new girl, Hermina, joins our Jewish group. I am overjoyed to learn that she comes from Brzezany, that she is my cousin Bela's friend, and that both Bela and her mother survived the pogroms of Brzezany and are now living in Munich.

I immediately get in touch with Bela and visit her in Munich. This is a glorious reunion since we have not seen each other since 1938. Both Bela and my Aunt Rose survived, hidden on the farm of the former caretaker of their country estate. Aunt Rose relates to me the horrid details of the Ukrainian pogroms in Brzezany, the merciless clubbing to death of my grandmother and the deportation of the rest of my relatives to Sobibor's or

Belzec's gas chambers. Here in Munich, Bela is studying dentistry, her boyfriend Natek is studying engineering, and both of them are quite impressed with Munich University. I also have a chance to experience the culture of Munich. I am awed by the Munich Opera's performances of "The Marriage of Figaro" and of its "Rigoletto," but my side trip to Garmisch-Partenkirchen tops all that Munich has to offer.

Bela in Munich 1946, my dearest cousin who committed suicide in New york in 1967

The ride up the Alpine slope in the mountain cable-train is exhilarating and the view from the peak of the mountain is unbelievable. I share my impressions with two Jewish GI's whom I meet on the cable-train. The next experience I share with the two GI's on the mountaintop, however, is not enjoyable at all. As we ride the cable car between two mountaintops, there is an electrical failure and the cable car gets stuck in the middle of the ride, suspending us over an abyss for more than an hour. When I look out of the windows of the car, I have a sensation of plunging into the bottomless void. I grab and hold onto the arm of one of the GI's, who lets me bury my face in his uniform jacket. Every so often, I force myself to overcome my fear and peak into the void, but the results are always the same—I have a sensation of falling into that void. When the electricity is finally restored, we complete the trip between the two mountains. During the return trip, I close my eyes and squeeze one of the soldier's arms for safety.

On our way back from Garmisch-Partenkirchen, the two GI's tell me about their family in New York, about their intentions to go to college, and much about the life in their great metropolis. There is something warm and informal about these two American guys, a carefree attitude that I have not experienced in the relationships with my traumatized European co-survivors of the war. It was, perhaps, too early for me to appreciate the simplicity and openness of the Americans I had met right after my liberation. Now I want to meet more Americans to see what they are like and to see how they compare with the Europeans of my environment.

Poldek isn't the only non-Jewish friend whose company I enjoy in Heidelberg. I meet an Estonian girl at our hostel who is very eager, just as I am, to do the fun things available in Heidelberg. On one occasion, the two of us join other university students and climb one of Heidelberg's hills to see the famous giant barrel perched at the top. One of the old-timers there tells us about the old tradition of initiating freshmen students—they would slash the freshmen's student caps and then roll the students down the hill.

On a Saturday evening we venture into the famous *Unter die Laterne* cafe where we find graffiti signed by famous German, French, and English writers and poets, including Goethe and Shelley. We sip soda pop and listen to the singers' rendition of the old Heidelberg street songs. On our way back home, we amuse the passing GI's with our own rendition of these songs. To show their appreciation for our singing, the Americans release a white balloon in our direction, which I innocently pick up and pin above my bed. The next morning there is a rude awakening in store for me. My roommates surround my bed and their roaring laughter shatters my innocence–the balloon over my bed is an inflated condom!

My Estonian friend again coaxes me to have some fun outside the confines of my academic life. We park ourselves at the United States Army's Social Center where there is dancing to live music. I hesitate entering the hall uninvited, but my friend goes in and, after a while, comes out with two GI's who appear to be very eager to dance with us. The hall is crowded and we can't get a table, so we join a GI who is sitting at a table by himself. This is my first opportunity to sample the strangely mobile American mode of dancing—the European fox-trot and the absolutely crazy gyrations of the latest, strictly American dance called "jitterbug." I am shuffled from side to side and forced to turn around my partner, all to the skip-beat staccato of what I am told is the Bronx variety of jitterbugging. I can't help reminiscing about the dignified dancing of my school years. As I am brusquely bent down and rushed across the dancing platform, I long for the suggestive tête-à-tête proximity with the European partners of my past. The two GI's dancing with us invite us to join them for a drink at the bar, but I feel uneasy about leaving the third GI alone. I stay at the table and chat with him while the others disappear at the bar.

The lonely young man, Warren, sounds like a very nice, intelligent guy. He comes from Kansas and sustained a leg injury in battle, which is why he finds it awkward to dance. Before our friends return, Warren and I make a date to meet in a few days at the Social Hall—just to sit, listen to music, watch the dancers, and talk. We meet several times more and I begin to truly enjoy the company of an earthy American country boy. I would be quite happy to go on socializing with Warren, with my Estonian girlfriend, and with the American GI's I met at the dance, but an enticing invitation comes my way from Simona.

None of the Jewish students have ever expressed an interest in the Synagogue Center maintained in Heidelberg by the Jewish Welfare Board, perhaps because they assume the Synagogue Center primarily serves Jewish GI's. But Simona informs us one day at the cafeteria that the Sabbath services are open to everyone and that in the evenings, we are all most welcome to join the Jewish GI's at the center's bar for a coke and a salami sandwich. Maciek and the other guys mock Simona's invitation, but I volunteer to join her Friday evening.

I come out of the Synagogue Center with a warm sense of belonging. The men I meet there tell me about Jewish life in America, a life similar to what I would want for myself, a life closer to my needs than the life that Poldek might one day want me to share with him, a life closer to my dreams than what Warren's life in the Midwestern United States might offer. I keep up the relationships with my Gentile friends but now I begin to enjoy my evenings at the Jewish Center more and more.

In the beginning of February, I reregister as a bona fide medical student for the second semester of preclinical medical studies. I join the human anatomy classes taught by the popular Professor Hoepke, an interesting lecturer who is also greatly respected by the Jewish students. Because Heidelberg University tenaciously held on to its medieval Charters of Autonomy, it was allowed to remain off limits to Nazi encroachment. Professor Hoepke's Jewish wife was sheltered at a campus building throughout the Nazi period. I am particularly glad that Professor Hoepke has a good sense of humor when my dissection of ovaries turns out to be a goof-up because the cadaver I'm working with happens to be male. The good professor assures my giggling classmates that, with proper experience, I will be able to tell the difference between males and females.

About this time, a photographer of the *Philadelphia Inquirer* appears in my dissection class and requests permission to photograph me. I consent and pose for photographs in the various lecture halls, laboratories, and different areas of the campus. I pose with my supervisors, with my friends at the hostel and also with my Jewish friends. The young Philadelphia woman-photographer intends to use those photographs in the Inquirer's story about the survivors of Nazi concentration camps who have managed to overcome the trauma of their past and who brave studying at German universities.

Anatomy: the mandible of the great ape

Heidelberg is a beautiful old town. The sights above the Neckar River are really charming during the snowy winter. The campus buildings lie on both sides of the river, so we must do quite a lot of walking from one lecture hall or laboratory to another. In addition, it is a long walk from our UNRRA Hostel both to the cafeteria and to the campus. To add to this inconvenience, the Hostel does not really offer much in terms of a study room. Most of the time I either study at Poldek's place or at the University library. For these reasons, I follow Poldek's lead and get a private room for myself at the home of Poldek's landlady's friends, Frau Seebacher and her two daughters. Their home is very well kept and conveniently located, close both to the main building of the University and to the student cafeteria. *Mutti* (Mom) Seebacher is a widowed housewife, her two daughters work during the day, and the family relinquishes their sitting room to me.

It is in this sitting room that Warren and I have our heart-to-heart talk during our last day together. I learn at that time that it is very hard to remain casual friends with men. Warren asks me to "go steady" with him, whatever "go steady" means to an army man. Since I always take pride in my willingness to form friendships without regard to race, nationality, or religion, my excuse for breaking up with Warren does not measure up to my standards. Yet I feel compelled to tell Warren that this time I wish to spend more time at the Synagogue Center and perhaps develop closer relationships with the Jewish GI's there, rather than become his girlfriend. Warren cites valid enough reasons why my relationship with him could become just as serious and just as rewarding as a relationship with a Jewish American, but I know that, because of what the Germans have done to my people, I need to seek a serious relationship with someone from my own people.

Oddly enough, I decide to tell the Seebacher ladies why I broke up with Warren. I almost believe they can understand me, but perhaps it is just wishful thinking on my part since I've discovered that *Mutti* (Mom) Seebacher belonged to the Nazi Party. I have been surprised to know, however, that not only does she refuse to take the UNRRA rent money for my lodging, but that she has also developed a concern for my welfare. Yet I am not sure what to make of the Seebacher family's manifested liking of a Jewish girl and I can't accept their sympathy with an open heart. One day, a United States Army Intelligence officer requests Frau Seebacher to come, along with other former Nazi members and sympathizers, to view a film taken during the Allies' liberation of the concentration camps. Mrs. Seebacher comes home from the movies in tears and visibly shaken and swears she had never known about the Nazi atrocities. I find it hard to believe and I will continue to disbelieve it!

There are Oneg Shabbat evenings at the JWB Synagogue Center and I attend them quite often, now that I've become good friends with Abe, the

Jewish students at Heidelberg. From bottom left to right: Heniek, Irene Gluck, Irene Hass, Simona. Mr. Sudduth is in the back in uniform.

rabbi's assistant. Abe comes from the East Bronx and my ears perk up when he tells me he happens to live next door to a grocery store owned by a Mr. Landman. I have told Abe about Sima Landman, my mother's American sister, and Abe volunteers to investigate if his neighbor Landman knows of a Sima Landman. Sure enough, the storeowner proves to be my uncle Srulek Landman, whose wife is my mother's sister, Sima, and whose two daughters Gertrude and Vivian are my cousins.

Other news soon comes from the United States. After my discovery of the Landmans, a letter from the Philadelphia Inquirer's photographer comes to me at the UNRRA Student Hostel. I learn in the letter that my Philadelphia cousin, Bill (Izio), is making inquiries about getting a visa for my immigration into the United States. Now I know that, thanks to the Philadelphia Inquirer's article and photos, the family of my mother's sister Regina has also discovered that I am in Heidelberg, and that I may have the option of going to America. Although Bill Sudduth, the director of the UNRRA Student Hostel, had suggested to me in the past that I may do very well at the Sorbonne School of Medicine (where they are now offering scholarships for women), I am warming up to the idea of going to America and of entering a medical school there.

Early in April 1946, I attend a Passover *Seder* with several other Jewish girls at the JWB synagogue. I quickly accept the American version of *Seder* rituals and chants as substitutes for those of the Polish-Jewish "Galitzianer" (southern Polish) *Seders* at my home. At the JWB *Seder* I meet the Polish-Jewish secretary of the Heidelberg Jewish Community who is engaged to Marvin, one of the GI's at our table. Marvin tells me that he expects to get his fiancée to America just as soon as her visa comes through, and assures me that my cousins will get a visa for me as well. He entices me to give up the idea of the Sorbonne School of Medicine and to come, instead, to the United States. As a student of the Heidelberg Medical School, I will be able to transfer to one of the medical schools in the United States wherever quotas for women and Jews have not been exhausted. This is the first time I hear about quotas at American medical schools, and I wonder how that could be allowed to exist in a democracy. But I decide that, just the same, I would want to go to America.

I learn soon after Passover that I indeed may be a candidate for emigration to the USA. None other than the Canadian "sourpuss" at the JWB office sends for me to receive a telegram from New York in which my uncle Marcus informs me that I am registered with the American Consul in Germany for emigration to the United States and that my visa is in the making. At the same time, the now very friendly official lets me know that another visa, a collective visa for 2,000 professionals and university students, will be issued by President Truman within the next few weeks. The JWB will recommend me as candidate for that visa, if it precedes the arrival of my personal visa.

The JWB keeps their promise and I am included among the first World War II refugees allowed to enter the United States. My personal visa, when it arrives, will be used for someone else later on. In the meantime, I finish my assigned dissections and readings. I also secure a letter of recommendation from one of my Jewish fellow student's brother, who happens to be an Associate Professor of Medicine. I hope to use this recommendation when applying for medical schools in the States.

It is hard for me to part with Poldek. He also has a hard time letting me go and promises to correspond with me, which he will indeed do for quite some time. But I have no difficulty bidding goodbye to the other fellow students with whom I have not bonded too firmly, nor to the Seebacher family about whom I have ambiguous feelings.

Since my sister has never answered the many letters of invitation I sent her from Heidelberg, I no longer have a valid reason to hang around in Europe waiting for her to join me. I know that my cousin Bela will complete her study of dentistry in Munich and will probably marry Natek, perhaps joining her brother Nusiek in Palestine later on. When all is said and done, I begin to feel truly footloose and fancy-free, and I am ready for America.

Our ship is the *SS Marine Perch* and I meet the rest of the refugee elite in Bremen-Hafen, the port from which our converted Victory Ship leaves on May 12, 1946, for New York. The five-day journey is uneventful and quite pleasant, except that I must continuously cure my seasickness by eating mustard. Also, the ship's soap doesn't quite produce suds in the shower's seawater. I kill time by either socializing with the "sparks"(the radio operator) at his radio room, by memorizing bones and muscles in *Grey's Anatomy*

Atlas, or by getting to know some of the passengers. One of these is a flirtatious blonde that hangs around members of the crew.

Late in the afternoon of May 16th, we stop for an overnight stay on the Brooklyn side of New York Harbor. Glued to the ship's railing, we keep watching the never-ceasing flow of the many cars on Brooklyn's elevated highway. I have never seen so many cars speeding along one road, and I keep wondering if perhaps the governor of New York or another official died and everybody is rushing to his funeral.

This evening, the crew is giving us a farewell dinner and we toast our arrival with a glass of wine each. But in the morning, we discover that there is trouble aboard the ship: the sexy blonde is in tears and publicly claims that an African American steward raped her last night. She demands the man be put under house arrest until she can bring formal charges against him after we dock.

Members of the crew get together and their spokesman announces over the loudspeaker that, unless the girl's accusations are withdrawn, the crew will not unload the ship, nor will they let us disembark at the assigned pier. The European passengers are baffled by these strange happenings. Some attempt to appease the crying young woman and others plead with the crew to rescind their work stoppage. Even the captain gets involved and negotiates with the crew to allow the passengers to disembark but to keep the young woman aboard until there can be an official inquiry into the matter. The crew, however, does not relent.

Finally, the radio operator approaches me and explains that it is an extremely serious matter when a black man is accused of raping a white woman—the unfortunate man faces a life-long prison term or possibly death. This arouses my old left-wing sensitivities and I take the aggrieved girl aside and talk to her about the issue of racism which takes on, here in the United States, the same dimensions as fascism did in Germany. The black man will surely die if she does not withdraw her accusations. To make sure that I win my case, I tell the girl that I supposedly learned from a "reliable source" that if she persists in making trouble, she may not be granted citizenship papers because the authorities might think that she is an anti-American subversive, perhaps a Communist or a Nazi passing for a Jew. That does the trick—the girl relents and the crew prepares to move the ship into our assigned dock. (Because of my anti-feminist stance that day, I will be dumping a load of guilt on my raised feminist conscience in the years to come!)

In a daze, I go through the routines of the customs controls, the signing of documents and the answering of embarrassing political and personal questions. Finally I am on the other side of the swinging door where I am greeted by my cousins Rose and Bernard (formerly Bunio), along with a half dozen or so reporters who want to know how I feel about coming here. When we are on our way to Bernard's car, my cousin Rose wants to know if the Statue of Liberty greeted us when we entered the port, and I look out towards the port to see what she is talking about. And there she stands, the greenish lady who, with a torch in her outstretched arm, indeed is there to greet all those who for years may have been running from poverty and persecution, seeking to become new Americans.

Hiding my emotions, I accept the welcome from the Statue of Liberty and without words, I say to myself that I am happy to have come to make my home in this land of the Statue of Liberty, in these United States of America.

Although I come to America not as an immigrant but as a deeply scarred refugee—part of whose innards will always remain with the shadows left behind—I soon become completely Americanized. I soon lose most of the traces of my foreign accent and pass for an ordinary New Yorker—just an ordinary American wife, mom, grandmother and committed American teacher of gifted American youngsters.

But I tenuously hold on to my native language. I hold monologues with myself in Polish, scold my children and count in Polish, curse in Polish, and even scream in Polish during the births of my children. And through more than half a century of my life in the United States, I repeatedly go on European pilgrimages and revisit places from which fate has pulled me away, and look for the shadows I left there.

When I revisit my shadows in Poland for the first time, I drown my soul in vodka and cry out, "Oh, where is my whole self? And where does my whole self belong? Does it perhaps belong with the perished world of Polish Jewry?"

No, I do not hold for long the sense of belonging within the shadows of my childhood. Nature will take its course and, in the fertile soil of the Land of the Free, my transplanted self is regenerated into a whole new self. I look into the eyes of my American daughter, my sons and grandsons, and see in these eyes a confirmation of my belonging with them here.

Now I am able to answer my daughter-in-law's question about why I wasn't motivated to use my old name Rena. I know now that my old name remained with the shards of my old self within the perished Polish Jewry. My new name Irene belongs with the new nurtured self I have here in America, here in the Land of the Statue of Liberty...

AFTERWORDS

I believe…

I believe that no nation could be peopled solely by murderers. My belief that there had been righteous men and women among the Germans of my day made it easier for me to face humanity when my martyrdom was over.

The Germans of my revisited shadows committed genocide of dimensions heretofore unknown to humanity. They set out to annihilate the entire Jewish people and succeeded in murdering nearly one third of them. Purely by a bit of luck, I and a counted few family members were spared from the Holocaust inflicted by the Germans. There is no doubt that during this time the German nation spawned millions of "Hitler's willing executioners." But I have chosen to believe that there also were a multitude of Germans who abhorred the murders committed in their name. I met some of these Germans in the extermination camp of Auschwitz. Some were imprisoned for their anti-fascist political beliefs, others for their deep religious commitment. And there were some Germans who had extended a helpful hand to their Jewish compatriots.

There were also righteous Germans in our ghetto of Bialystok, Germans who offered all possible help both to our armed resistance in the ghetto itself and to our fighters (guerillas) outside the ghetto. Without doubt, the careers of these Germans and often their very lives were at risk. And without doubt, these Germans believed they acted in justice and in good faith. They must have known that their brethren's genocidal schemes would forever remain a blemish on the collective German conscience. And that is why they couldn't come to terms with that vile scheme.

The help given by the Germans to Bialystok's Jews included passing on to them weapons, falsified *kenkarten* (ID's) and other documents. It also included sheltering them from the roundups for deportation to extermination camps. Last but not least was the illicit help of these Germans given to the partisans—without this help the partisans would never have survived.

GLOSSARY

Aktion (German). Roundup of Jews for extermination.

Arbeit Ausweis or *Bescheiniging* (German). A work pass.

Arbeitstaechtig (German). An able-bodied person.

Aryan. A gentile; non-Jewish person.

Aufseherin. (German). An SS woman in charge of inmates of a concentration camp.

Auschwitz. A German extermination camp in southern Poland in which millions of Jews, Gypsies and other "undesirables" were gassed.

Aussen Commando (German). A work detail that worked outside a concentration camp or ghetto.

Belorussia. The Soviet Republic into which Soviet-occupied northeastern territories of Poland were incorporated.

Bergen-Belsen. A German death camp in which survivors of all other concentration camps were annihilated by the denial of food, water and shelter.

Bialy. A flattened onion roll.

Bialystok. A northeastern Polish industrial textile city of 150,000 inhabitants of whom a few thousand were Belorussian and 60,000 were Jewish.

Blizyn. A labor concentration camp located near and much like Plaszow, portrayed in the film "Schindler's List."

Block. Barrack.

Block *Aelteste* (German). An inmate in charge of the barrack.

Bourgeois. Here, a possession- and wealth-oriented middle-class person.

Boryslaw. Located in the Carpathian Highlands, the one and only Polish oil town with refineries in the nearby town of Drohobycz. Both cities were ceded to the Soviet Ukraine after World War II.

Comrade. A titular address that replaced the title "sir" in countries with communist regimes.

Corridor. A pre-Baltic Polish land that separated German East and West Prussian territories. Granted to Poland by the Traty of Versailles after World War I.

Corso (Italian). A promenade. Many small towns in Poland maintained such promenades around their market places.

Diesiatiletka (Russian). A 10-year school. After 1939, these schools replaced

the Polish 12-year elementary and secondary schools in all Soviet-occupied territories.

Druskin Gimnazjum (Polish). An exclusive private secondary school for
Jewish youngsters of Bialystok.

Dzikie. A summer resort near Bialystok.

Endeks (Polish). The right-wing antisemitic National Democratic party of
pre-World War II Poland. Popular among university students.

Felcher (Polish). A medic.

Folksdeutch (German). A German national living outside Germany.

Galicja. An Austrian name for southern Polish lands annexed by Austria
after the infamous partition of the Polish Republic by the emperors of Germany, Russia and Austria in the 18th century.

Gauleiter. A governor of a German province.

Gestapo (German). Nazi Secret Service.

Ghetto (Jewish). A walled-in and heavily-guarded area of a city portioned
off to warehouse the Jews before they were deported to extermination camps.

Gimnazjum (Polish). School consisting of the "Male Gimnazjum"(Junior
High School) and the "Lyceum" (Senior High School).

Grudziadz. A medieval, pre-Baltic Vistula town lying near the Polish-Ger-
man East Prussian border.

High Holidays. The Jewish New Year (*Rosh Hashana*), and eight days
later, Day of Atonement (*Yom Kipur*).

Irena (Irene). Usually used in its diminutive forms of Irka, or Irenka

Jaremcze. A well-known summer and ski resort of the East Carpathian
mountains.

Koenigsberg. The capital of former German East Prussia (now Polish
Mazuryland).

Kosciuszko (Street, and other references). Tadeusz Kosciuszko inspired
and led the 1774 uprising of Poles against the Austrian usurpers of their
lands. He then distiguished himself in the American revolutionary war
against the British.

Lazarets (German). Infirmaries and field hospitals in the concentration
camps whose patients were periodically killed off by lethal injections or
gassing.

Lwow. A major sub-Carpatian university city. Prior to World War I it was known as Austrian's Eastern Galicja's Lemberg; from 1918-1939 it was Poland's Podole's Lwow; currently it is known as Lveev in the Ukraine.

Maccabi (Hebrew). A clan of heroic fighters of ancient Israel.

Mach schnell! (German). Means "Hurry it up!" A customary German order directed towards the inmates of the concentration camps.

Mama se tante felice (Italian). A popular Italian pop song of the 1940s.

Marxism. The Socialist-Communist ideology consecutively formulated and reinterpreted by Marx, Engels, Lenin and Stalin

Mazury. Poland's pre-Baltic lake lands that include the former Polish Corridor (the later Pomorze) and East Prussia. A "clipped" Polish-Mazurian dialect is quite characteristic of the area.

Mikveh (Yiddish). A bathouse of Orthodox Jews that includes a ritual bath for the women.

Molotov. Prime Minister of the USSR before and during World War II.

NKVD (KGB). Soviet Secret Service.

Ogrodniczki. A summer resort of the Bialystok region.

Otlichnik-otlichnitsa (Russian). An all-A student who may enter college without taking an entrance exam.

Purim (Hebrew). A holiday celebrating the rescinding of a verdict of death against the Jewish exiles in the ancient Babylon.

Podworko (Polish). A backyard, but more specifically in this story, the backyard behind the Jewish Community House in Grudziadz which was a "hangout" of Jewish youths.

Pomorze (Polish). The former Polish Corridor.

Parisian Commune. An 1860 revolutionary uprising in Paris.

Partisans (guerillas). Irregular troops engaging in harassing the enemy.

Podole (Polish). Former Eastern Galicja.

Politburo (Russian). Former USSR's body of highest ranking communist leaders.

Pricha (Polish). Bunk bed.

BIBLIOGRAPHY

The references for "Holocaust: Bialystok, 1939-1945" (see Acknowledgements), are listed below.

Ajzensztajn, Betti. Ruch Podziemny w Getach i Obozach. Krakow: Centr. Zyd. Komisja Hist., 1946. (In Polish.)

Datner, Szymon. Walka i Zaglada Bialostockiego Geta. Lodz: Centr. Zyd. Komisja Hist., 1946. (In Polish.)

Krausnick, Helmut et al. Anatomy of the SS State. New York: Walker & Company, 1968. (Translated into English by Wm. Collins & Son).

Mark, B. Ruch Oporu w Getcie Bialostockim. Warszawa : Zyd. Inst. Hist., 1952. (In Polish.)

Raisner, Raphael. The Destruction of the Bialystok Jews 1939-1945. Melbourne: Bialystok Centre, 1946. (In Yiddish.)

Reitlinger, G. The Final Solution. Great Britain: Sphere Books Limited, 1953.

Other books of interest

Gilbert, Martin. The Holocaust: The History of the Jews of Europe During the Second World War. New York: Henry Holt and Company, 1985.

Lace, William W. The Holocaust Library: The Nazis. San Diego: Lucent Books, Inc., 1998.

Rogasky, Barbara. Smoke and Ashes. New York: Holiday House, 1988.

Saunders, Alan. Turning Points of World War II: The Invasion of Poland. New York: Franklin Watts, 1984.

ABOUT THE AUTHOR

Irene Shapiro is a native of Poland. She is the daughter of a virtuoso violinist who was forced to perform, before his own execution, with the orchestra of the extermination camp of Majdanek in Poland. Her mother was a schoolteacher who suffered with Irene the horrors of the concentration camps, until she died just before the end of the war at the Bergen-Belsen camp in Germany. Her younger sister witnessed the bestial pogroms of Jews from behind the windows of her hideout but then was lucky enough to find shelter in a Christian home where she survived the war.

Ms. Shapiro's identity was shaped by a lonely Jewish childhood in the Christian Polish environment of northwestern Poland, as well as through assimilation into the Jewish community of Bialystok in eastern Poland. It was with that Jewish community that she experienced the various phases of the war: the Soviet occupation of Bialystok, the life and the uprising in the city's Jewish ghetto, and the subhuman conditions in concentration camps. The author's postwar journey toward the Statue of Liberty was a long one. She worked in Germany for the American and British armed forces, she traveled into and out of Poland in search of her family, and she returned to Germany where she briefly studied premed courses at the University of Heidelberg. Ms. Shapiro's professional background in the biomedical sciences and technology include nearly forty years of teaching, curriculum writing, and laboratory research.

In 1946, Irene Shapiro was among the first few hundred displaced persons granted a collective visa for immigration into the United States. Years later, she felt an urgent need to tell the stories that germinated within her life experiences. Her attempts at art and music did not prove adequate to communicate the truths about her life prior to, or during, the Holocaust. She therefore began writing about it.

Revisiting the Shadows is unique in several ways. To begin with, Ms. Shapiro is one of the very few surviving participants of the uprising of the ghetto of Bialystok, rated by historians as second only to the uprising of the Warsaw Ghetto in terms of historic significance. She is also one of the few descendants of the now extinct Jewish intellectuals and artists of prewar Poland, and as such, she tells a story of Jewish life quite different from that of the many other immigrants that came to America with a predominantly Jewish *shtetl* (Jewish enclave) background. Being a scientist and educator has also allowed Ms. Shapiro to discern truths and relationships in and about her past that are socio-politically insightful. And finally, there is an uniquely tragic resolution of the saga of Ms. Shapiro's survival of the Jewish Holocaust: her only sister survived it as a Catholic who renounced her Judaism and who has chosen to keep her children and grandchildren unaware and ignorant of their Jewish roots.

ORDER FORM

Please fill out this form (or copy this page), add the necessary information, and mail it to:

DeForest Press
P.O. Box 154
Elk River, MN 55330

Please enclose personal check or money order, payable to: DeForest Press.

Revisiting the Shadows by Irene Shapiro $19.95 each
ISBN 1-930374-06-2

Qty. _____   Total: _____

MN residents add 6.5% sales tax ($1.30 / book)   _____

Shipping & Handling: Add $2.00 for first book
$1.00 for each additional book   _____

Total enclosed   _____

Name: _____

Address: _____

City: _____ State: _____ Zip: _____

Phone: (_____) _____

Email: _____

_____ Yes, please send me information about your other books, greeting cards, and posters.

You can also order this book and others from our secure web site at:
www.DeForestPress.com for immediate delivery